THE EXECUTION PREMIUM

THE
EXECUTION
PREMIUM

LINKING STRATEGY TO OPERATIONS
FOR COMPETITIVE ADVANTAGE

Robert S. Kaplan
David P. Norton

HARVARD BUSINESS PRESS

BOSTON, MASSACHUSETTS

No part of this publication may be reproduced, stored in or introduced into a retrieval system, or transmitted, in any form, or by any means (electronic, mechanical, photocopying, recording, or otherwise), without the prior permission of the publisher. Requests for permission should be directed to permissions@hbsp.harvard.edu, or mailed to Permissions, Harvard Business School Publishing, 60 Harvard Way, Boston, Massachusetts 02163.

Library of Congress Cataloging-in-Publication Data
Kaplan, Robert S.
   The execution premium: linking strategy to operations for competitive advantage/Robert S. Kaplan, David P. Norton.
      p.   cm.
   Includes bibliographical references and index.
   ISBN-13: 978-1-4221-2116-0
   1. Strategic planning. 2. Business planning. 3. Organizational effectiveness.
   I. Norton, David P., 1941– II. Title.
   HD30.28.K35434   2008
   658.4'012—dc22

                                                                    2008004645

The paper used in this publication meets the requirements of the American National Standard for Permanence of Paper for Publications and Documents in Libraries and Archives Z39.48-1992.

CONTENTS

PREFACE

IN 1992, WE INTRODUCED the Balanced Scorecard as a performance measurement system.[1] We helped several companies implement this approach and learned how they used this performance measurement tool as the cornerstone of a new management system that would drive the implementation of their strategies.[2] We spent the next several years refining the strategy management system and published our updated framework in our second book, *The Strategy-Focused Organization.* The framework was built around five management principles:

1. *Mobilize* change through executive leadership
2. *Translate* strategy into operational terms
3. *Align* the organization to the strategy
4. *Motivate* to make strategy everyone's job
5. *Govern* to make strategy a continual process

Our third book, *Strategy Maps*, expanded on Principle 2 by introducing a general framework for translating a strategy into objectives that are linked, in cause-and-effect relationships, across the four Balanced Scorecard perspectives: financial, customer, internal process, and learning and growth. The framework aligned processes, people, technology, and culture to the customer value proposition and shareholder objectives.

Our fourth book, *Alignment*, expanded on Principle 3 and showed how to use strategy maps and scorecards to align organizational units, both line business units and corporate staff ones, to a comprehensive corporate strategy. The organizational alignment enabled the enterprise to capture the synergies from operating multiple units within the same corporate entity. The last chapter in *Alignment* described the application of Principle 4, communicating the strategy and aligning individuals' goals and incentives to business unit and corporate objectives.

Most companies, in implementing the strategy management system based on the Balanced Scorecard, followed a sequence that generally began with Principle 1 (mobilize the executive team), followed quickly by Principle 2 (translate the strategy into a strategy map of linked strategic objectives with an accompanying Balanced Scorecard of measures and targets) and Principle 3 (align the various parts of the business through linked scorecards). Principle 4 required redesign of some key Human Resource systems (goal-setting, incentives), while Principle 5 required the redesign of various planning, budgeting, and control systems. Typically, the implementation of Principles 4 and 5 did not start until the program was one or more years down the road. In fact, we found that companies were able to get breakthrough results just by implementing Principles 1, 2, and 3 in their entirety and performing a few basic activities in Principle 4, such as a program to communicate strategy to employees, and, following one practice in Principle 5, instituting a new management meeting to review strategy. This limited approach produced results until the leader who had introduced the program departed. The message was clear; a strong leader using the tools of Principles 1, 2, and 3 could mobilize, focus, and align the organization to achieve excellent performance. However, because the new approaches had not been embedded in the ongoing management systems of the organization (Principle 5), the performance was often not sustained. We had not yet found a way to embed the ongoing management of strategy into the organization's way of doing business.

In 2004, we and our colleagues at the Balanced Scorecard Collaborative convened an Action Working Group (AWG) of about twelve companies to address how to sustain a focus on strategy implementation. Our group included several Balanced Scorecard Hall of Fame companies, including Hilton Hotels, Motorola, Ricoh, Serono, KeyCorp, Canon, and the U.S. Army. Among their most important innovations was to introduce a small but dedicated group of managers to oversee the various processes required for strategy execution. We described this group as an office of strategy management (OSM) and published this finding in a 2005 *Harvard Business Review* article.[3]

Through continued engagement with this working group, both in North America and Europe, we eventually identified all the key processes required to implement Principle 5, "Make strategy a continual process."

The current book, *The Execution Premium*, reports on these findings. In the book, we describe how companies can establish strong linkages from strategy to operations so that employees' everyday operational activities will support strategic objectives. We introduce a new framework for management review meetings that clearly separates the operational review meetings, which solve short-term problems and monitor the improvement of key operational processes, from the meetings that review and improve strategy execution.

While we set out, in writing this book, to document the best practices for SFO Principle 5, we ended up with a self-contained and comprehensive management system that links strategy and operations. The system integrates the contributions from our four earlier books, and those of many other recent management innovations, including strategy development, operational management and improvement, activity-based costing, business intelligence, and analytics. The closed-loop management system described in this book represents the "end-state" that enterprises can aspire to reach for connecting excellence in operational execution to strategic priorities and vision.

Since the strategy execution closed-loop management system is a recent development, we would like to encourage a dialogue between us and our readers. We have established a Web site, executionpremium.org, where we will post links to surveys, assessment tools, and references to assist managers in applying the ideas in the book. Further, we hope to use the site as a bulletin board or to host blogs that facilitate an exchange of views and best practices.

NOTES

1. R. S. Kaplan and D. P. Norton, "The Balanced Scorecard: Measures that Drive Performance," *Harvard Business Review* (January–February 1992): 71–79.
2. R. S. Kaplan and D. P. Norton, "Using the Balanced Scorecard as a Strategic Management System," *Harvard Business Review* (January–February 1996):75–85; Part Two, "Managing Business Strategy," in R. S. Kaplan and D. P. Norton, *The Balanced Scorecard: Translating Strategy into Action* (Boston: Harvard Business School Press, 1996).
3. R. S. Kaplan and D. P. Norton, "The Office of Strategy Management," *Harvard Business Review* (October 2005): 72–80.

ACKNOWLEDGMENTS

WE HAVE BENEFITED GREATLY from the experiences of the organizations that we cite in this book. Their ability to extend our ideas with sophisticated applications is a true source of managerial innovation and progress. In particular, our thanks go to the following contributors:

Bank of Tokyo-Mitsubishi	Takehiko Nagumo
Borealis	Thomas Boesen
Brazilian National Confederation of Industry (CNI)	José Augusto Coelho Fernandes
Canadian Blood Services	Graham Sher, Sophie de Villers, Andy Shaw
Federal Bureau of Investigation	
Hillside Family of Agencies	Dennis Richardson, Maria Cristalli
HSBC Rail	Peter Aldridge
KeyCorp	Michele Seyranian, Lesa Evans
Lockheed Martin	Ed Meehan, Pamela Santiago, Richard Dinnan, Lance Freedman, Jeff DeLeon, Maria Rasmy, Josh Stalher
LG Philips LCD	Ron Wirahadiraksa
Luxfer Gas Cylinders	John Rhodes, David Rix
Marriott Vacation Club International	Karl Sweeney

Motorola GEMS	Mark Hurlbert
Nemours	David Bailey
Nordea	Sven Edvinsson
Oracle/Latin America	Cheryl McDowell
Ricoh Corporation	Sam Ichioka, Brad Nelson, Marilyn Michaels
SAS International	David Schwerbrock
Merck Serono	Roland Baumann, Lawrence Ganti
Statoil	Bjarte Bogsnes
State Street Corporation	Jack Klinck
Thai Carbon Black	S. Srinivasan
University of Leeds	Michael Arthur, Simon Donoghue

We are indebted to the professional staff of the Balanced Scorecard Collaborative and the Palladium Group who, using these approaches, help their clients create *execution premiums*. In particular, we recognize Kit Jackson, who taught us how to use strategic themes for multiple strategy execution processes and provided invaluable feedback on an early draft of the book; Ed Barrows for his work on the strategy development process; Anne Nevius for her contributions to health care management; and Laura Downing for her contributions to the management of public sector organizations and her constructive feedback as a reviewer of an earlier version of the book. Additional thanks go to Peter LaCasse, Michael Contrada, and Mathias Mangels for their work on initiative management; Cary Greene, Philip Peck, and Duane Punnewaert for their work on dashboards, driver-based planning, and rolling forecasts; to our colleagues in Symnetics, Brazil—Reinaldo Manzini and Fanny Schwarz—for providing examples of how to link strategy to operational process improvements; and to André Coutinho for his facilitation of strategy maps, scorecards, and strategic initiatives for Brazil and its provinces, such as Rio Grande du Sol. We would also like to acknowledge Randy Russell, who managed our group research programs; and Rob Howie and Linda Chow for their management of our Balanced Scorecard Hall of Fame program.

Dennis Campbell, of Harvard Business School, showed us how to use analytics to design operational dashboards (the TD Canada Trust example in Chapter 6) and to test the causal linkages in a strategy (the Store 24 example in Chapter 9).

The staff of HBS Press provided their usual excellent encouragement and support from the original conception of the book through its production and delivery. We especially thank Hollis Heimbouch, who has been the editor for all five of our Balanced Scorecard books, Brian Surette, who took over the editorial role during the production process, production editor Jen Waring, and copy editor Betsy Hardinger.

Finally, we are indebted to Steve Fortini, who prepared many of the complex graphics, and to our assistants—Rose LaPiana and David Porter—who managed the logistics of the writing, graphics, and production processes, and our wives, Ellen and Melissa, who tolerate our continued passion for writing at a time of life when many of our contemporaries are lowering their golf handicaps.

CHAPTER ONE

INTRODUCTION

"Strategy without tactics is the slowest route to victory. Tactics without strategy is the noise before defeat."[1]

MANAGING STRATEGY DIFFERS from managing operations. But both are vital, and need to be integrated. As strategy authority Michael Porter has noted, "Operational effectiveness and strategy are both essential to superior performance . . . but they work in very different ways."[2]

A visionary strategy that is not linked to excellent operational and governance processes cannot be implemented. Conversely, operational excellence may lower costs, improve quality, and reduce process and lead times; but without a strategy's vision and guidance, a company is not likely to enjoy sustainable success from its operational improvements alone.

Michael Hammer, a visionary leader of reengineering and process management, concurs: "High performance operating processes are necessary but not sufficient for enterprise success."[3] A senior strategic planner at a *Fortune* 20 company reinforced Hammer's view: "You can have the best processes in the world, but if your governance processes don't provide the direction and course correction required to achieve your goals, success is a matter of luck."

Companies generally fail at implementing a strategy or managing operations because they lack an overarching management system to integrate and align these two vital processes. Consider the experience of Marriott Vacation Club International (MVCI), a wholly owned subsidiary of Marriott International, Inc.[4] MVCI develops, sells, and manages time-share, fractional ownership, and wholly owned five-star resort properties under four leading brands: Marriott Vacation Club, Grand Residences by Marriott, Horizons by Marriott Vacation Club, and The Ritz-Carlton Club.

During the late 1990s, MVCI's executive team transformed the high-growth company into a process-based organization that used multiple metrics—process time, cost, and quality—to manage each brand and property. But with more high growth projected in the years ahead, executives wanted to create more focus and alignment with MVCI's strategy. The company had hundreds of simultaneous unrelated initiatives under way, and efficiency gains in a given process generated only limited benefits because the gains were not leveraged or integrated with the efforts of other groups.

In 2002, MVCI's senior vice president of strategic planning asked two associates to join him as a strategy management team to craft a new strategy and an enterprise-level strategy map and Balanced Scorecard (BSC). The proposed strategy emphasized offering complete customer solutions to resort property owners, including dedicated vacation planning assistance and 24/7 access to information. The strategy would require complete integration of the company's operating and support processes.[5] The twelve-member MVCI Executive Council discussed, debated, and ultimately approved a strategy map and BSC to implement the new strategy.

The strategy management team then cascaded the scorecard to the operating processes. The team implemented a "kill the initiatives" campaign to streamline MVCI's portfolio of initiatives, many of which were not strategically essential. By 2004, MVCI had further cascaded BSCs down to its individual property levels both for on-site resort operations and for each site's sales and marketing team, eventually deploying 120 scorecards. Over time, process owners embedded their most important process measures into the BSC system and discontinued the remaining metrics that did not help them execute and monitor their strategies. MVCI's project team also led the communication of the strategy to all employees and worked with the human resource department to ensure that each employee's personal objectives were linked to one or more of MVCI's strategic objectives.

MVCI enjoyed rapid and substantial gains—what we refer to as the *execution premium*—by linking the planning of strategy to its operational execution. MVCI's execution premium is summarized in the insert.

MVCI CEO Stephen Weisz remarked on the benefits of implementing the new management system at MVCI's brands and properties: "The Balanced Scorecard [has worked] hand-in-glove with process reengineering [to focus] MVCI on measurable improvements to all areas of our business."[6]

MARRIOTT VACATION CLUB INTERNATIONAL'S EXECUTION PREMIUM

- Operating profit rose from $149.3 million in 2003 to $306 million in 2007, a 20 percent annual increase.
- The number of customers rating MVCI as being "easy to do business with" rose 70 percent from the 2003 level.
- Organizational alignment improved; the percentage of MVCI employees who reported that they understood the company's strategy and how their role contributed to it increased from 74 percent to 90 percent in 2007.

The success that MVCI enjoyed by linking strategy and operations is replicable. Later in this chapter we present several case studies of other companies that earned an execution premium after implementing a new management system that aligned their strategic priorities with operational execution and feedback. We describe, in this book, the design and use of this new management system for strategy execution.

STRATEGY EXECUTION

In a 2006 global survey, The Monitor Group asked senior executives about their priorities. Number 1, by a clear margin, was strategy execution. The Conference Board in its 2007 survey reported that executives' number 1 priority was "excellence in execution." After the number 2 priority, "sustained and steady top-line growth," strategy execution again appeared as priority number 3, "consistent execution of strategy by top management." Placing a high priority on effective strategy execution can be traced to the considerable and well-documented problems most companies have experienced when attempting to execute their strategies. Various surveys over the past two decades indicate that 60 to 80 percent of companies fall far short of the targets expressed in their strategic plans. In October 2007, Tony Hayward, new CEO of BP, stated, "Our problem is not about the strategy itself, but about our execution of it."[7]

We conducted a survey in 1996 about the state of strategy execution. We learned that most organizations did not have formal systems to help them execute their strategies. Only 40 percent of organizations linked their budgets to their strategies, and only 30 percent linked incentive compensation to strategy. In the great majority of surveyed companies, fewer than 10 percent of employees reported that they understood their company's strategy. Clearly, employees who do not understand the strategy cannot link their daily activities to its successful execution.

Moreover, 85 percent of executive teams spent less than one hour per month discussing strategy, with 50 percent reporting that they spent virtually no time on strategy discussions. Executives relied on local, tactical operating systems (such as budgets) for managing finances, management-by-objectives (MBO) systems for motivating employees' performance, and decentralized IT, marketing, and sales plans. Companies had no system explicitly designed to manage the implementation of strategy.

We conducted a follow-up survey in 2006, receiving responses from 143 performance management professionals about the systems their organizations used to manage strategy execution. The survey results, summarized in Figure 1-1, had some similarities with the 1996 survey but also significant differences. The similarities occurred among the 46 percent of respondents who reported that they still did not have a formal strategy execution system; 73 percent of these reported average to below-average performance of their strategies, a percentage consistent with those reported in prior strategy execution surveys. But 54 percent of respondents now reported that they had a formal process to manage strategy execu-

FIGURE 1-1

Organizations with a formal strategy execution process outperform organizations without one

Do you have a formal strategy execution process in place?	Yes (54%)	No (46%)	
Describe your organization's current performance.			
• We have *breakthrough* results	12%	7%	
• We are performing *better* than our peer group	58%	20%	**Winners**
Subtotal	70%	27%	
• Performing at the *same* level as our peer group	18%	30%	
• Performing at a *lower* level than our peer group	9%	27%	**Losers**
• *Not performing* at a sustainable level	3%	16%	
Subtotal	30%	73%	

Source: BSCol Research (survey of 143 performance management professionals, drawn from BSCol Online Community, March 2006).

tion.[8] Of these, 70 percent reported that they were outperforming their peer group of companies, a reversal of the odds for success. Having a formal strategy execution system made success two to three times as likely as did not having such a system.

Figure 1-2, drawn from that survey, illustrates the differences in the use of six strategy execution processes between companies with and without a formal strategy execution system:[9]

- Translate the strategy.
- Manage strategic initiatives.
- Align organizational units with the strategy.
- Communicate the strategy.
- Review the strategy.
- Update the strategy.

FIGURE 1-2

Strategy management: State-of-the-art practices

Do you have a formal management process in place?

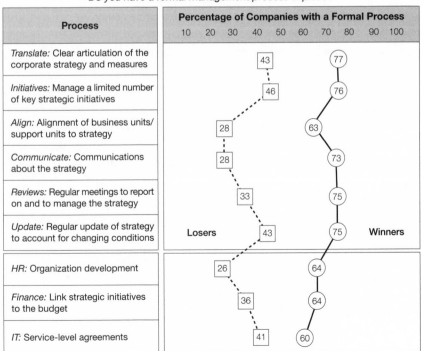

Process	Percentage of Companies with a Formal Process
Translate: Clear articulation of the corporate strategy and measures	43 ... 77
Initiatives: Manage a limited number of key strategic initiatives	46 ... 76
Align: Alignment of business units/support units to strategy	28 ... 63
Communicate: Communications about the strategy	28 ... 73
Reviews: Regular meetings to report on and to manage the strategy	33 ... 75
Update: Regular update of strategy to account for changing conditions	Losers 43 ... 75 Winners
HR: Organization development	26 ... 64
Finance: Link strategic initiatives to the budget	36 ... 64
IT: Service-level agreements	41 ... 60

Source: Survey of 143 performance management professionals, BSC Research, 2006.

For example, 73 percent of companies achieving outstanding performance clearly communicate their strategy and strategic measures, whereas only 28 percent of the underperformers take such an action. A survey conducted by Cranfield University in 2003 found that 46 percent of organizations use a formal process of performance management.[10] Of those organizations, 25 percent use some form of total quality management (TQM) as their principal performance management system, whereas 75 percent use a management system based on the Balanced Scorecard. A study sponsored by the U.S.-based Institute of Management Accountants reported that the Balanced Scorecard had become, by far, the leading system for managing company performance, outdistancing systems based on quality management (Baldrige Criteria, European Foundation for Quality Management [EFQM], and six sigma) or financial management (economic value added).[11]

THE PROLIFERATION OF STRATEGY AND OPERATIONAL MANAGEMENT TOOLS

Even with the increased adoption of strategy execution systems based on the Balanced Scorecard, we have learned that gaps still exist between the formulation of high-level strategic plans and their execution by frontline departments, process teams, and employees. In part, this gap between strategy and operations stems from the large number of diverse tools for strategy formulation and operational improvement that have been introduced during the past thirty years. Strategy development starts with tools such as mission, values, and vision (MVV) statements, along with external competitive, economic, and environmental analyses, which are summarized into statements of company strengths, weaknesses, opportunities, and threats (abbreviated as SWOT). Strategy formulation methodologies include Michael Porter's five forces and competitive positioning framework, the resource-based view of strategy, core competencies, disruptive strategies, and blue ocean strategies. Companies also use scenario planning, dynamic simulations, and war-gaming to test the robustness of their strategies.

Strategy maps and Balanced Scorecards help companies translate, communicate, and measure their strategies. Some companies use the "catchball" component of the Japanese *hoshin kanri* policy-deployment process to cascade high-level strategic objectives to specific goals and targets for operating departments, followed by MBO systems to set goals for individual employees. Companies also employ TQM methodologies—six sigma, kaizen, and assessment methodologies from the Malcolm Baldrige and

EFQM award programs—to promote continuous improvements in the efficiency and responsiveness of their operating processes. For radical process improvements, they deploy reengineering approaches.

Business intelligence software offers a myriad of tools to support strategy planning and the design of customized dashboards to facilitate operational improvement programs. Companies use sophisticated analytic tools to review the performance of their strategies, including customer relationship management software and analytic modeling to capture and profile customer behavior. Activity-based costing is used to assess product and customer profitability, key indicators of strategy success.

It is good that companies now have a large number of strategic and operational tools to choose from, but they still lack a theory or framework to guide the successful integration of the many tools. Companies struggle with the question of how to make these various strategy planning and operational improvement tools work together in a coherent system. The implementation of the tools is ad hoc, with little interchange and coordination.

The only common or standard feature in most companies' management systems is the financial budget, which is still being used as the primary tool for coordination, forecasting, and performance evaluation. Yet even this practice has been questioned. Our initial motivation for introducing the Balanced Scorecard in 1990 was to challenge the exclusive use of financial measures for motivating and evaluating performance. More recently, a "beyond budgeting" movement, starting in Europe and migrating to the United States, has severely criticized the use of budgets both to plan for the future and to evaluate past performance.[12]

In summary, strategy development and the links between strategy and operations remain ad hoc, varied, and fragmented. Given the myriad strategy and operational management tools now available, we believe that companies can benefit from taking a systems approach to link strategy with operations. Having a comprehensive and integrated management system can help companies overcome the difficulties and frustration that most of them experience when attempting to implement their strategies—particularly new, transformational strategies.

A MANAGEMENT SYSTEM FOR INTEGRATING STRATEGY PLANNING AND OPERATIONAL EXECUTION

We have formulated the architecture, shown in Figure 1-3, for a comprehensive and integrated management system that links strategy

FIGURE 1-3

The management system: Linking strategy to operations

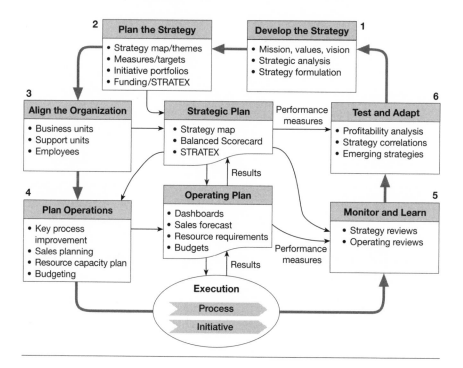

formulation and planning with operational execution. The system has six major stages.

Stage 1: Managers *develop the strategy* using the strategy tools described in the preceding section.

Stage 2: The organization *plans the strategy* using tools such as strategy maps and Balanced Scorecards.

Stage 3: Once the high-level strategy map and Balanced Scorecard have been articulated, managers *align* the organization with the strategy by cascading linked strategy maps and Balanced Scorecards to all organizational units. They align employees through a formal communication process and link employees' personal objectives and incentives to strategic objectives.

Stage 4: With all organizational units and employees aligned with the strategy, managers can now *plan operations* using tools such as quality and process management, reengineering, process dashboards, rolling forecasts, activity-based costing, resource capacity planning, and dynamic budgeting.

Stage 5: As the strategy and operational plans are executed, the enterprise *monitors and learns* about problems, barriers, and challenges. This process integrates information about operations and strategy in a carefully designed structure of management review meetings.

Stage 6: Managers use internal operational data and new external environmental and competitive data to *test and adapt the strategy*, launching another loop around the integrated strategy planning and operational execution system.

We briefly describe each of the six stages in the integrated management system next, and explicate them fully in separate chapters in the remainder of the book.

Stage 1: Develop the Strategy

The integrated management system begins with managers developing the strategy. During this process, companies address three questions:

1. *What business are we in, and why? (Clarify your mission, values, and vision):* Executives begin strategy development with an affirmation of the organization's purpose (mission), the internal compass that guides its actions (values), and its aspiration for future results (vision). The MVV statements establish guidelines for formulating and executing the strategy.
2. *What are the key issues? (Conduct strategic analysis):* Managers review the situation in their competitive and operating environments, especially major changes that have occurred since they last crafted their strategy. Three sources provide input into this update: the *external environment* (PESTEL: political, economic, social, technological, environmental, and legal); the *internal environment* (key processes, such as the state of human capital, operations, innovation, and technology deployment); and the progress of the *existing strategy*. The environmental assessment is summarized in

a SWOT table of strengths, opportunities, weaknesses, and threats, which identifies a set of strategic issues that must be addressed by the strategy.

The executive team develops and communicates a set of guidelines, called a *strategic change agenda,* that explains the need for the changes in the strategy.

3. *How can we best compete? (Formulate the strategy):* In the final step, executives create a strategy by addressing these issues:
   - In what *niches* will we compete?
   - What *customer value proposition* will differentiate us in those niches?
   - What *key processes* create the differentiation in the strategy?
   - What are the *human capital* capabilities required by the strategy?
   - What are the *technology enablers* of the strategy?

Chapter 2 contains a detailed description of the three strategy development processes: clarify mission, values, and vision; conduct strategic analyses; and formulate the strategy.

Stage 2: Plan the Strategy

In this stage, managers plan the strategy by developing strategic objectives, measures, targets, initiatives, and budgets that guide action and resource allocation. Companies typically address five questions in this stage:

1. *How do we describe our strategy? (Create strategy maps):* A *strategy* encompasses various dimensions of organization change, from short-term productivity improvements to long-term innovation. A *strategy map* provides a one-page visual representation of all the strategic dimensions, which we now call *strategic themes*. Companies have found it difficult to manage the simultaneous performance of the fifteen to twenty-five objectives on a typical strategy map. They now cluster related objectives into four to six strategic themes that represent the major components of the strategy. By building a strategy map around a collection of strategic themes, executives can separately plan and manage each of the key components of the strategy but still have them operate coherently. The themes, which operate across functions and across business units, also support the boundaryless approach necessary for successful strategy execution.

2. *How do we measure our plan? (Select measures and targets):* In this step, managers convert the objectives defined in the strategy

maps and strategic themes into a Balanced Scorecard of measures, targets, and gaps. The overall value gap, typically defined by the ambitious vision statement articulated during strategy development, is split into gaps that each strategic theme must close over three to five years.

3. *What action programs does our strategy need? (Choose strategic initiatives):* Strategic initiatives are action programs aimed at achieving targeted performance for the strategy map objectives. Initiatives cannot be looked at in isolation; they must be viewed as a portfolio of complementary actions, each of which must be successfully implemented if the company is to achieve its theme targets and overall strategy target.

4. *How do we fund our initiatives? (Establish STRATEX):* Executing strategy requires that the portfolios of initiatives be executed simultaneously in a coordinated manner. This requires explicit funding for the portfolios of strategic initiatives. The traditional budgeting system focuses on the resources provided to existing organizational functions and business units, and the accountability and performance of these units. The strategic investments, for initiatives that cross functions and business units, must be removed from operational budgets and managed separately by the executive team. The creation of a special budget category called *STRATEX* (strategic expenditures) facilitates this process.

5. *Who will lead the execution of the strategy? (Create theme teams):* Companies are introducing a new accountability structure for executing strategy through strategic themes. They assign executives to become *theme owners*, fund them with STRATEX, and support them with *theme teams* drawn from across the organization. The theme owners and teams provide accountability for and feedback on the execution of the strategy within each theme.

Chapter 3 describes the first two strategy planning processes: creating the theme-based strategy map and selecting measures and targets for the strategy map objectives. Chapter 4 describes the three initiative management processes: selecting, funding, and establishing accountability for theme-based portfolios of strategic initiatives.

Stage 3: Align the Organization with the Strategy

To capture the full benefits of operating a multibusiness, multifunction organization, the executives must link the company strategy to the strategies of its individual business and functional units. All employees must understand the strategy, and they must be motivated to help the company succeed with the strategy. Companies address three questions during the alignment process:

1. *How do we ensure that all organizational units are on the same page? (Align business units):* Strategy is usually defined at the individual business unit level. But companies typically consist of multiple business or operating units. Corporate-level strategy defines how the strategies of individual business units can be integrated to create synergies not available to business units that operate independently from each other. Corporate strategy is described by a strategy map that identifies the specific sources of synergies. Managers then cascade this map vertically to business units, whose own strategies can then reflect (1) objectives related to their local strategies and (2) objectives that integrate with the corporate strategy and the strategies of other business units.

2. *How do we align support units with business unit and corporate strategies? (Align support units):* Executives often treat support units and corporate staff functions as discretionary expense centers, that is as overhead departments whose goals are to minimize their operating expenses. As a result, the strategies and operations of support units do not align well with those of the company and business units they are supposed to support. Successful strategy execution requires that support units align their strategies to the value-creating strategies of the company and its business units. Support units should negotiate service-level agreements with business units to define the set of services they will provide. Creating support unit strategy maps and scorecards, based on the service-level agreements, enables each unit to define and execute a strategy that enhances the strategies being implemented by business units.

3. *How do we motivate employees to help us execute the strategy? (Align employees):* Ultimately, employees are the ones who improve the processes and run the projects, programs, and initiatives required by the strategy. They must understand the strategy if they are to successfully link their day-to-day operations with the strategy. Employees cannot help implement a strategy that they are not aware of or do not understand. Companies use formal communication programs ("communicate seven times seven dif-

ferent ways") to help employees understand the strategy and motivate them to achieve it. Managers reinforce the communication program by aligning employees' personal objectives and incentives with business unit and company strategic objectives. Also, training and career development programs help employees gain the competencies they need for successful strategy execution.

Chapter 5 describes the best practices companies use to align organizational units and employees to the strategy.

Stage 4: Plan Operations

A distinguishing feature of the comprehensive management system articulated in this book is its explicit link between long-term strategy and daily operations. Companies need to align their process improvement activities with strategic priorities. Also, funding for resources to operate the business must be consistent with the strategic plan. During the operational planning process, managers address the following two key questions:

1. *Which business process improvements are most critical for executing the strategy? (Improve key processes):* The objectives in a strategy map's process perspective represent how strategy gets executed. The map's strategic themes originate in the key processes defined on the map.[13] For example, a strategic theme to "grow through innovation" requires outstanding performance from the new product development process; a theme to "create heightened loyalty with targeted customers" requires greatly improved customer management processes. Some process improvements are designed to deliver the financial perspective's cost reduction and productivity objectives, whereas others focus on excelling at regulatory and social objectives. Companies need to focus their total quality management, six sigma, and reengineering programs on enhancing the performance of those processes identified as critical for delivering the desired improvements in the strategy's customer and financial objectives.

   After identifying their critical processes for improvement, companies support their process management teams by creating customized dashboards consisting of key indicators of local process performance. The dashboards provide focus and feedback to employees' process improvement efforts. Chapter 6 explains how to align process improvements with the strategic plan and how to design process dashboards.

2. *How do we link strategy with operating plans and budgets? (Develop the resource capacity plan):* The process improvement plans and the high-level strategic measures and targets on the Balanced Scorecard must be converted into an operating plan for the year. The operating plan has three components: a detailed sales forecast, a resource capacity plan, and budgets for operating expenses and capital expenditures.

- *Sales forecast:* Companies need to translate their strategic plan's revenue targets into a sales forecast. The beyond budgeting movement, mentioned earlier, advocates that companies continually respond to their dynamic environments by reforecasting quarterly sales for five to six quarters into the future. Whether done annually or quarterly, any operating plan is launched from a sales forecast, a task facilitated by analytic approaches such as driver-based planning. Anticipating the need to derive a detailed operating plan, the sales forecast should incorporate the expected quantity, mix, and nature of individual sales orders, production runs, and transactions.

- *Resource capacity plan:* Companies can use a time-driven activity-based costing (TDABC) model to translate detailed sales forecasts into estimates of the resource capacity required for the forecast periods.[14] Activity-based costing has been widely promoted as a tool to measure the cost and profitability of processes, products, customers, channels, regions, and business units. But its "killer app" is for resource planning and budgeting. Because a TDABC model uses capacity drivers, typically time, to map resource expenses to the transactions, products, and customers handled by each process, such a model can easily map the forecasts of sales and process improvements to the quantity of resources—people, equipment, and facilities—required to fulfill the plan.

- *Operating and capital budgets:* Once managers have agreed on the quantity and mix of resources for a future period, they can easily calculate the financial implications (summarized in a financial profit plan) and operating and capital budgets. The company knows the cost of supplying each unit of resource. It multiplies the cost of each resource type by the quantity of resources it has authorized and thereby obtains the budgeted cost of supplying the resource capacity for the sales and operating plan. Most of the resource capacity represents personnel costs and would be included in the operating expense (OPEX) budget. Increases in equipment resource capacity would be reflected in the capital budget (CAPEX). The outputs from this process are operating and capital budgets that have been derived quickly and analytically from the sales and operating plan.

Because the company starts with detailed revenue forecasts and now has the resource costs associated with delivering these forecasts, simple subtraction yields a forecast and detailed profit-and-loss statement for each product, customer, channel, and region.

Chapter 7 describes how to convert a strategic plan into plans for resource capacity and for operating and capital expenses.

Stage 5: Monitor and Learn

Once the strategy has been determined, planned, and linked to a comprehensive operational plan, the company begins to execute its strategic and operational plans, monitor the performance results, and act to improve operations and strategy based on new information and learning.

Companies use *operational review meetings* to examine departmental and functional performance and to address problems that have arisen or persist. They conduct *strategy review meetings* to discuss the indicators and initiatives from the unit's Balanced Scorecard and assess the progress of and barriers to strategy execution. By separating the operational and strategy review meetings, companies avoid the pitfall of having short-term operational and tactical issues drive out discussions of strategy implementation and adaptation. The two meetings address different questions:

1. *Are our operations under control? (Hold operational review meetings):* Companies conduct *operational review meetings* to review short-term performance and respond to recently identified problems that need immediate attention. Operational review meetings correspond to the frequency with which data are generated on operations and the speed at which management wants to respond to sales and operating data as well as to the myriad of other tactical issues that continually emerge. Many companies have weekly, twice-weekly, or even daily meetings to review operating dashboards of sales, bookings, and shipments and to solve short-term

issues that have just arisen: complaints from important customers, late deliveries, defective production, a machine breakdown, a near-term cash shortfall, the extended absence of a key employee, or a newly identified sales opportunity. Operational review meetings are typically departmental and functional, bringing together the expertise and experience of employees to solve the issues of the day in departments such as sales, purchasing, logistics, finance, and operations. These meetings should be short, highly focused, data driven, and action oriented.

2. *Are we executing our strategy well? (Hold strategy review meetings):* Typically, companies schedule *strategy review meetings* monthly to bring together the leadership team to review the progress of the strategy. The leadership team discusses whether strategy execution is on track, detects where problems are occurring in the implementation, attempts to determine why the problems are occurring, recommends actions to correct the cause, and assigns responsibility for achieving the targeted performance. If one thinks of strategy and problem solving through the lens of the plan-do-check-act (PDCA) cycle, strategy review meetings are the check and act portions of strategy execution.

Theme owners distribute data on the Balanced Scorecard's measures and initiatives in advance of the meeting. The meeting time focuses on discussion and selection of action plans for the issues that have emerged since the last strategy review meeting. Because in-depth discussion of every BSC objective, measure, and initiative would require too much time at each monthly meeting, companies now organize their strategy review meetings by strategic themes, covering one or two in depth at each meeting. In this way, they enable each theme and objective to be examined and discussed carefully at least once per quarter.

Chapter 8 presents the structure, frequency, participants, agenda, and actions for operational and strategy review meetings.

Stage 6: Test and Adapt the Strategy

In addition to frequent operational and strategy review meetings, the company needs to conduct a separate meeting that tests whether its fundamental strategic assumptions remain valid. Since the last major review and update of the strategy, the company has access to additional data from its operational dashboards and monthly Balanced Scorecard metrics, new information on changes in the competitive and regulatory environment, and new ideas and opportunities that employees may have contributed. The *strategy testing and adapting meeting* addresses the following fundamental question:

1. *Is our strategy working? (Hold a strategy testing and adapting meeting):* Periodically, the executive team meets to question and challenge the strategy and, if necessary, adapt it. We believe that every company should conduct a strategy testing and adapting meeting at least annually, and perhaps as often as quarterly (depending on the speed of competitive, technological, and consumer dynamics in the industry). In this meeting, the executive team assesses the performance of its strategy and considers the consequences of recent changes in the external environment. In fact, testing and adapting the existing strategy should be part of the strategic analysis done as part of the first management system process. We treat and list it separately because this process is for modifying an existing strategy rather than for introducing a new, transformational strategy, as discussed in Chapter 2. The meeting to test and adapt an existing strategy closes the loop on the integrated system of strategy planning and operational execution.

   This meeting should be informed by current external conditions (via PESTEL analysis) and the competitive environment, as previously described. But the company now has, in addition, multiple inputs that describe the successes and failures of the existing strategy. Activity-based profitability reports summarize profit-and-loss data by product line, customer, market segment, channel, and region. Executives see where the existing strategy has been successful and where it is failing. They can formulate new approaches to transform losses into profits and expand the scope and scale of existing profitable operations. A second set of reports shows statistical summaries of the links among strategic metrics. The associations validate and quantify the hypothesized links on the company's strategy map and strategic themes. Occasionally, when the correlations are zero or opposite in sign to the strategy's expectations, the executive team questions or rejects components of the existing strategy.

As the executive team updates its strategy, it also modifies the organization's strategy map and Balanced Scorecard and starts another cycle of strategy planning and operational execution: new targets, new initiatives, next period's sales and operating plan, process improvement priorities, resource capacity requirements, and an updated financial plan. The strategic and operational plans set the stage and establish the information requirements for next period's schedule of operational review, strategy review, and strategy testing and adapting meetings. Chapter 9 provides the details and several case examples of these testing and adapting meetings.

THE OFFICE OF STRATEGY MANAGEMENT

The six management processes provide an integrated and comprehensive closed-loop system that links strategic planning with operational planning, execution, feedback, and learning. The system has many moving parts and interrelationships, and it requires simultaneous coordination among all line and staff units.

Existing processes that are run by different parts of the organization—such as budgeting by finance, personal goals and communication by human resources, and process management by operations—must be modified and coordinated to create strategic alignment. They must work as a system instead of as a set of uncoordinated processes. In addition, we have proposed some new processes, such as creating strategy maps and Balanced Scorecards that align organizational units and employees with the strategy. Because these processes are new to most organizations, they have no natural home within the existing structure. Clearly, organizations face a complex task to implement such a complex, interrelated system of mature and newly introduced management processes.

Most organizational processes are assigned to owners who run them and are accountable for their performance. The chief financial officer is the owner of the budgeting process; the vice president of human resources runs the employee performance management process; the vice president of quality facilitates total quality management and six sigma improvement processes. But few organizations identify an individual or department to run the multiple linked processes of the strategy execution system. We have identified the need for a new organizational function, which we call the *office of strategy management* (OSM), to be the process owner of the strategy execution system.[15]

In high-performing companies, the OSM integrates and coordinates activities that align strategy and operations across functions and business units. The OSM synchronizes the various planning and control processes, which operate at different frequencies. Dashboards and operational control meetings operate daily and weekly, information on strategic measures and initiatives is collected monthly to inform the strategy review meetings, and the organizational scan of the external environment and analytic studies are done quarterly or annually for strategy testing and adapting meetings. All these cycles must be compatible with and integrated with one another.

The new office of strategy management plays three generic roles (summarized in Figure 1-4). First, the OSM, as *architect*, designs the new strategy and operational management processes. The OSM ensures that all the planning, execution, and feedback components are in place and that they are linked in a closed-loop system.

The OSM is the *owner* of many of the key processes in the management system. The OSM facilitates the execution of processes that cross business and functional lines, including processes to develop the strategy, plan the strategy, align organizational units with the strategy, review the strategy, and test and adapt the strategy.

FIGURE 1-4

Office of strategy management plays three important roles

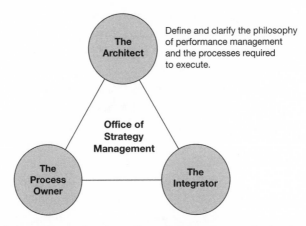

The Architect
Define and clarify the philosophy of performance management and the processes required to execute.

Office of Strategy Management

The Process Owner

The Integrator

Define, develop, and oversee the execution of processes required to manage the strategy.

- Develop the strategy.
- Plan the strategy.
- Align the organization.
- Plan operations.
- Review the strategy.
- Test and adapt the strategy.

Ensure that processes owned and run by other functional executives are linked to the strategy.

- Human resource management
- Strategy communications
- Initiative management
- Financial resource management
- Key process management
- IT management

Finally, the OSM must ensure that strategy guides a diverse range of existing processes, including financial management, strategy communication, human resource planning, performance management, IT planning, initiative management, and best-practice sharing. In most organizations, these processes already exist and have owners. But they operate independently and may not be aligned with the strategy. The OSM serves as an *integrator* to align all these diverse processes with the strategy.

Chapter 10 closes the book by describing the roles and responsibilities of the new office of strategy management as the architect, process owner, and integrator of the processes embedded within the strategic planning and operational execution management system.

THE ROLE FOR LEADERSHIP:
NECESSARY AND SUFFICIENT

While not an explicit part of any of the six strategy management stages, executive leadership pervades every stage of the management system. Throughout the book, we describe organizations—located in different regions and countries, including North and South America, Europe, India and Japan—that have successfully implemented their strategies. They operate in varied industries, such as manufacturing, financial services, consumer services, nonprofit, educational, and public sector. Their strategies differ; some produce low-cost commodity products and services, others deliver complete solutions to their customer, and still others innovate with high-technology products. About the only common element all these diverse successful strategy implementers have in common is exceptional and visionary leadership. In every example, the unit's CEO led the case for change and understood the importance of communicating the vision and strategy to every employee. Without such strong leadership at the top, even the comprehensive management system we introduce in this book cannot deliver breakthrough performance.

In fact, leadership is so important to the strategy management system we believe it to be both *necessary* and *sufficient*. The necessary condition comes from our experience with the more than one hundred enterprises around the world who have become members of the Balanced Scorecard Hall of Fame. In every instance, the CEO of the organizational unit implementing the new strategy management system led the processes to develop the strategy and oversee its implementation. No organization reporting success with the strategy management system had an unengaged or passive leader.

In Stage 1, the CEO leads the change agenda and drives it from the top to reinforce the mission, values, and vision.

In Stage 2, the executive leader validates the strategy map as an expression of the strategy articulated in Stage 1 and challenges the organization with stretch targets that take all employees outside their comfort zones.

In Stage 3, leadership drives alignment of organizational units and is essential for communicating vision, values, and strategy to all employees.

In Stage 4, leadership supports the cross-organizational unit process improvements.

In Stage 5, the leader's openness and skill in running the strategy management review meeting determines its effectiveness for fine-tuning the strategy throughout the year.

In Stage 6, the leader must allow even a well-formulated and executed strategy to be challenged in light of new external circumstances, data collected about the performance of the existing strategy, and new suggestions from employees throughout the organization. Being willing to welcome and subject existing business strategies to fact-based challenges is one of the hallmarks of effective leadership.

Our *sufficiency* claim, however, is even bolder. The management processes we describe in this book give an effective leader a framework for effective strategy execution. None of the six stages in the management system is simple or brief. But collectively, the management processes in the six stages provide leaders with a comprehensive, proven system for managing the development, planning, implementation, review, and adaptation of their strategies. While we report, at the beginning of this chapter, the discouraging statistics on the frequent failures of strategy execution, we believe that our eighteen years of observation and work with enterprises in all sectors and regions of the world has led to an emerging science of strategy execution. Each of the six stages in the strategy management system is doable, especially when guided by a senior strategy management office. The one component we cannot provide a blueprint for is visionary and effective leadership. That is why we have come to believe that executive leadership is now both necessary and sufficient for successful strategy implementation.

THE EXECUTION PREMIUM

In 2000, eight years after the introduction of the BSC, we and our colleagues at the Balanced Scorecard Collaborative founded the Balanced Scorecard Hall of Fame. We wished to publicly recognize organizations around the world that had used the BSC in an exemplary manner to successfully execute their strategies and achieve breakthrough performance results. We also sought to identify and learn the best practices from the successful organizations. We used two criteria to select organizations for this award:

1. Do they use strategy maps and Balanced Scorecards within a formal strategy execution system?[16]
2. Have they successfully executed their strategies, as evidenced by significant quantified and validated results?

Since the program was introduced, approximately one hundred organizations have received the award.[17] Although the organizations come from every sector and every part of the world, their approach for describing and executing their strategies follows similar principles and yields a significant execution premium. This chapter started by describing the experiences of Marriott Vacation Club International, a 2006 inductee into the BSC Hall of Fame. Several other Hall of Fame companies also stand out in having developed and implemented the high-level processes in the new management system. We close the chapter with short case studies of the experiences at Ricoh, Luxfer Gas Cylinders, and Nordea.

Ricoh

After a spate of acquisitions begun some ten years ago, Ricoh needed an overarching strategy around which to unify four business units: Ricoh U.S., Lanier, Ricoh Canada, and Ricoh Latin America.[18] With significant changes in market demand for the company's office automation equipment and electronics products, executives at the New Jersey–based subsidiary of Japan's Ricoh Company Ltd. knew they needed to act decisively.

In 2001, then CEO Katsumi "Kirk" Yoshida concluded that growth in demand for the company's traditional products—black-and-white digital copiers, fax machines, and laser printers—was slowing, while the market for color products, multifunction copiers, and printers was growing rapidly. In addition, he knew that Ricoh could no longer depend on product excellence and innovation alone to drive sustainable value creation. Customer intimacy would be critical to Ricoh's future success, and that meant introducing a solutions approach to its offerings. Ricoh's many units, Yoshida realized, would have to be more fully integrated to deliver comprehensive, customized solutions. That year, the company launched discussions about its new market focus and began to introduce the Balanced Scorecard as the framework for the required strategic transformation.

The timing was fortuitous: Ricoh's cross-organizational executive team had recently convened to begin developing the company's fourteenth three-year strategic plan (the Mid-Term Plan, or MTP). The team crafted a corporate strategy map and BSC and then built strategy maps and scorecards for all four units. In Latin America, the company cascaded strategy maps and BSCs to its twelve country-based subsidiaries. Yoshida established ten key universal BSC measures that put all units on the same page, and a consulting team trained executives in BSC development and implementation. To foster employee alignment, the team measured every employee on three to five goals that were aligned with corporate objectives and measures, as well as with those on the employee's unit's BSC. It also tied employee compensation and performance bonuses to achieving the employees' personal objectives.

Ricoh further refined its BSC program in 2005, when it crafted its fifteenth MTP. Yoshida's successor, Susumu "Sam" Ichioka, set an ambitious growth strategy: to turn the $2.9 billion company into a $3.85 billion enterprise by 2007. Although the refined strategy was based on the same mission, vision, and core values that had been established in 1999—"to become the Americas' number-one document solutions company"—Ricoh updated these elements to reflect the company's changed focus on the customer. Its vision, for example, grew more far-reaching: "to become a *Fortune* 500-level company providing the most effective return on customers' document investments." Strategic themes now put even greater emphasis on customer needs.

The company also refined its strategy formulation process and developed new strategy maps and BSCs. Over a six-month period in 2004 and 2005, executives from four companywide strategic planning teams held regular strategy formulation meetings in which they also identified strategic initiatives. The Strategy and Planning Office (SPO), established in 2004 to orchestrate strategic planning, led a series of meetings for the four key cross-functional teams charged with overseeing strategy execution throughout the organization. Sam Hosoe, SPO head and vice president, and other executives developed new strategy maps and BSCs to reflect the revised

---

RICOH'S EXECUTION PREMIUM

- Ricoh sales in the Americas rose 6.8 percent in FY 2004 over the preceding year. In 2004, for the first time, Ricoh Latin America achieved profitability in every country of operation.
- Market share for color and black-and-white digital copiers increased to 24.1 percent in 2004 from 17.6 percent in 2001.
- The Alliance Program, a strategic initiative launched in 2003 to enhance customer relationships, boosted revenues 42 percent in its first full year (FY 2004), and by late FY 2005 had already achieved a 172 percent revenue increase over the preceding year.
- Brand awareness rose significantly from 2003 to 2004, as measured by Consensus Research, an independent survey company.
- Ricoh boosted total recyclable outgoing waste from 19.1 percent in 2001 to 25.2 percent in 2004. Its manufacturing facilities in the Americas achieved zero waste to landfill, or 100 percent resource recovery.

---

strategy. Ricoh instituted a program of quarterly and monthly strategy review meetings at both the corporate level and the business unit level.

The company introduced a unique approach for defining, aligning, and prioritizing projects beyond the normal operating budget. Each year, business units proposed initiatives that competed for incremental investment funds for strategic projects. The CEO and members of the SPO selected the winning initiatives and allocated money according to the initiatives' strategic importance.

As a result of these actions, Ricoh showed improved results. Vice President and CFO Kuni Minakawa concluded, "Our strategy maps and Balanced Scorecards represent a revolutionary way to manage the business, a way that enables every person to understand his contribution to achieving our strategies. Through this approach, we are transforming Ricoh into a strategy-focused organization." See the insert for a snapshot of Ricoh's execution premium.

Luxfer Gas Cylinders

Luxfer Gas Cylinders (LGC) was founded in the United Kingdom in 1958 and began operations in the United States in 1972.[19] LGC is the world leader in developing, producing, and distributing seamless extruded aluminum and composite high-pressure cylinders for storage of gases. LGC's product markets include medical gases; life support gases for firefighters and rescuers; gases for beverages, fire extinguishers, and scuba diving; automotive, industrial, and specialty gases; aviation and shipboard inflation; and gases for alternative-fuel vehicles. Luxfer, headquartered in Nottingham, England, and Riverside, California, posted revenues of £120.4 million in fiscal 2006. It had four manufacturing facilities in the United States and one each in England, France, and China, along with sales, refurbishment, and distribution centers throughout the world.

Between 1996 and 2000, LGC pursued an operational excellence strategy to integrate the performance of new business units acquired in a buyout. Each unit was successful, earning a dominant position in all the major markets LGC served.

In late 2001, as executives looked outward, they discovered a threatening marketplace. Market share in high-volume commoditized products was being eroded by increased competition, technological advances were threatening the core business, and the company had an inadequate presence in emerging markets and new technologies. LGC President John Rhodes realized that a continued focus on operational excellence for high-volume products was not likely to maintain LGC's current position, much less provide a platform for growth: "I felt strongly that we needed to redirect where we were going, and to get everyone on the same page—because I already suspected that a few of our managers would strongly resist some of the changes that I had in mind."

New developments, including heightened competition and a price war in the U.S. medical market (LGC's largest), pointed to the need for a fresh strategy. Furthermore, the "us-versus-them" attitude among managers in LGC's European business units had intensified. "LGC wasn't really [acting as] one company," said Rhodes. "It was a group of decentralized, regional businesses."

Rhodes convened a global management off-site meeting in the second quarter of 2002 to develop a new strategic approach for the future. The meeting engaged a broad cross section of managers from around the world, who participated actively in a lively and often contentious discussion. The participants coalesced around a new strategy to help shift LGC from its short-term focus on selling commodity products to a longer-term, customer-oriented one that emphasized innovative high-value, high-margin offerings, such as lightweight composites instead of aluminum. According to Rhodes, the new strategy would enable LGC to "maintain its solid market leadership based on value, instead of simply reacting to the market instability brought on by competitors' short-term tactics."

The management team translated the new strategy into the company's first strategy map and Balanced Scorecard, as well as scorecards for the company's three regions. Although the regional maps contained some elements identical to the corporate map, they also reflected local markets and strategic thrusts. The Asia-Pacific and Europe regions' maps, for example, emphasized expanding sales of composites, because sales were weaker there than elsewhere.

In addition, the executive team introduced key strategic themes on the map (described in more detail in Chapter 3) and assigned an owner to each theme. Each theme also had a steering committee composed of representatives from around the world. With the new structure, LGC was no longer a collection of autonomous regional units.

Recognizing that strategy is a living thing, Rhodes and his team in 2005 reviewed and refined the LGC strategy map to reflect changes in the global marketplace (e.g., shortages and rising prices of crucial materials) and lessons learned from three years of BSC experience. The new map focused even more sharply on customers and on market-driven innovation. LGC stepped up its investments in training—to bolster employees' marketing skills—and product development.

The company embedded the BSC throughout its culture. The BSC is now, as Rhodes put it, in LGC's "DNA." Managers respond to new ideas by asking, "Is it on the map?"—meaning, "Is it strategic?" If the answer is no, people don't "waste their time" investigating the idea. The execution premium developed by LGC is summarized in the insert.

LGC'S EXECUTION PREMIUM

- Sales grew (in Europe, by 22.4 percent) and profits doubled, even as one of LGC's foreign rivals went bankrupt and its major domestic competitor verged on the same.
- LGC slashed fixed costs as a percentage of sales from 31.9 percent to 26.5 percent, yielding £6.9 million ($12.8 million) in savings.
- LGC's product portfolio is now dominated by higher-technology, higher-margin products (composites versus aluminum). Sales of composites more than doubled and now constitute 43.5 percent of total revenues (versus 24.5 percent in 2001).

• LGC's sharper focus on customer service enabled the company to win back a former major customer that had gone to a lower-priced rival. This same customer now prominently features the LGC brand in its advertising—as do several others.

(All figures are from 2001 to 2006.)

Nordea

Nordea was formed in the 1990s through the merger of four national banks—from Denmark, Norway, Sweden, and Finland—into a single financial institution.[20] By 2000, Nordea had become the leading financial services group in the Nordic and Baltic Sea region, and a world leader in Internet banking. Its stock was listed on the Stockholm, Helsinki, and Copenhagen exchanges. It had 31,000 employees, 11 million customers, and a 45 percent market share in Nordic countries. A retail banking operation, with 1,225 bank branches, was its largest business area, but it also had major operations in corporate and institutional banking and in asset management.

Nordea senior managers had become disenchanted with the traditional profit-and-loss budgeting used at their former companies. They felt that the budget focused management attention too much on past rather than future performance. Also, the annual budget process required a great deal of work. Changes in interest rates and equity markets that occurred after the budget had been approved often made the budget obsolete before the start of the budget year. The budget process was inflexible, did not accommodate post-approval changes, and led to frustration among managers. Apart from its operational rigidity and high cost to prepare, approve, and operate, the budget had little connection to the bank's strategic issues. Management lacked a framework for monitoring the progress of its strategy after the budget had become obsolete due to changing market conditions.

Nordea executives decided to introduce a new management system that would focus on shareholder value creation and would link strategy to operations. They wanted the system to be future and action oriented and to provide a continually updated view of current and future performance. The system would contribute to a culture of "One Bank—the Nordea way" that would engage all employees throughout the corporation in contributing to strategy execution.

The new system, called the Planning and Performance Management Model (PPMM), consisted of three new components. First, PPMM developed a Balanced Scorecard to convert business plans into operational metrics, targets, and action plans. Second, PPMM replaced the annual, inflexible budget with quarterly *rolling financial forecasts* (RFFs) for the next five quarters. Third, PPMM required service-level agreements between internal service providers and business units to ensure a cost-efficient supply of services demanded by the units to execute their strategies.

Nordea Balanced Scorecard. Nordea's corporate Balanced Scorecard described strategy through the use of four strategic themes:

- Ensure capital efficiency and high credit portfolio quality.
- Ensure operational excellence, strict cost management, and reduced complexity.
- Ensure stable and profitable growth of income.
- Attract, develop, and retain highly motivated, competent, and performance-oriented employees (the learning and growth perspective).

Nordea cascaded the corporate scorecard out to business and support units throughout the company, where business-area heads used the group map-development experience to clarify their own divisions' strategies. Each business-area map contained all four strategic themes from the high-level strategy map, with some customization to reflect different areas' specific strategic challenges. For example, effective risk management within Nordea's corporate and institutional banking area supported the group map objective "Ensure capital efficiency and high credit portfolio quality."

By mid-2004, Nordea had one thousand scorecards in its retail operations, as well as scorecards for each major corporate and institutional banking and asset management business unit and all major support functions, including information technology, finance, legal, and human resources.

Nordea communicated its strategy extensively and systematically throughout the company. The company's intranet gave all employees access to instructions, training modules, and presentations about the BSC. Employees in each of Nordea's core countries of operation could find local pages in their language as well as in English (the group language). Interest in this vehicle proved high; the home page received more than six thousand hits per month during the first quarter of 2004. *Nordic Ideas*, the company's quarterly internal magazine (published in Danish, Finnish, Norwegian, Swedish, and English), featured interviews with internal BSC users and instructional articles about the BSC.

To further bolster alignment, Nordea tied senior managers' (and some middle managers') goals and incentives to their BSCs. Five hundred individuals had personal Balanced Scorecards. The company evaluated managerial performance against such measures as the number of service-level agreements in operation and establishment of personal development plans for all full-time employees.

The extensive deployment of scorecards across the more than one thousand branches in the retail network enabled internal benchmarking of key performance metrics and led to considerable competition among the branches. Senior managers reviewed the strategy map each quarter and updated targets based on actual and forecast operating conditions.

Rolling Financial Forecasts. Nordea replaced its annual bottom-up budget process with quarterly forecasts of key financial metrics for the next five quarters. It based the forecasts on recent business performance—as reported by the various Balanced Scorecards in the company—and current and forecast conditions in the external business environment. The heads and controllers of the major business-area and support functions led the forecasting process. The forecasts reflected managers' best possible estimates of future financial performance. Executives did not use the forecasts to set targets or evaluate performance.

In contrast to the detailed line-item format of the now-abandoned budget, the quarterly forecast encompassed only high-level financial numbers corresponding to the financial metrics on each unit's Balanced Scorecard. The quarterly report showed, on a single page, actual results for the prior year, current year, and a portion of the subsequent year.

All managers felt that implementing the new high-level forecasting process was much easier, less costly, and more flexible than using the budget method. Accompanying each forecast, business unit heads provided commentary on central assumptions, critical drivers of trends in revenues, costs, and volumes, and the impact of the forecast on the unit's Balanced Scorecard.

By mid-2004, the rolling quarterly forecasting process had been implemented in all four country units in retail banking, the four business units in corporate and institutional banking, the five business units in asset management and life, and the four IT and operations units. The remaining support units made annual forecasts, because changes in short-term business conditions did not greatly influence the demand for their services.

Calendar of Meetings. Nordea launched the annual strategic planning process in the second quarter, culminating in the forecasts prepared in the fourth quarter of each year. The fourth-quarter forecasts incorporated group and business unit strategic directions and target setting and service-level agreements for the following year. The rolling forecasts for the four quarters in the following year became the financial performance targets in the Balanced Scorecards for that year, the only time when BSC targets and the RFFs were aligned.

During the following year, management compared actual to targeted BSC performance while controlling for changes in BSC performance due to changes in the financial forecasts. The flow of information from BSC to RFF reflected the impact of new strategic initiatives decided on during the quarterly review of Balanced Scorecard performance. During the time between the quarterly BSC reviews and RFF updates, management monitored operational key performance indicators monthly and sales data weekly, taking short-term, tactical actions to deal with any problems or opportunities revealed.

At the quarterly strategy review meetings, managers reviewed market conditions and competition and overall performance, as displayed on the quarterly Balanced Scorecard report. Each strategy map contained managers' comments on reasons for underperformance and updates on the status of strategic initiatives. To understand root causes of performance gaps and suggest corrective actions, managers analyzed underperforming (red) objectives or strategic themes in depth.

In addition to responding to the red zones, management teams examined one of the four strategic themes in depth during each quarterly meeting. Managers discussed whether the theme had the right performance metrics, targets, and initiatives, and whether changes in the strategy should be contemplated. After the strategy review meeting, and with knowledge of any corrective actions and changes in strategic initiatives, managers updated their rolling financial forecasts.

The Execution Premium. Sven Edvinsson, senior vice president and head of group planning, commented on the impact of the new management systems: "The Balanced Scorecard has changed the agenda and mind-set at Nordea. Previously, management discussions were about budget deviations and their causes. Now, we talk about what to do to close performance gaps. We have created a team-based management culture that is more future and action oriented, and with increased focus on strategic direction and execution. Meetings use the BSC to communicate priorities and report on performance, including the status of strategic initiatives."

Arne Liljedahl, Nordea CFO, stated, "The BSC has increased the accountability of executives, managers, and employees with clearly defined targets, based on the BSC, which has strongly influenced their behavior."

NORDEA'S EXECUTION PREMIUM

- Total shareholder return reached 47.9 percent in 2003, making Nordea the number 3 bank among twenty of its peers.
- In 2003, Nordea's operating profit increased 17 percent.
- Its market cap ranking went from fifteenth to eighth place from 2003 to 2004.
- Senior managers can more easily prioritize their activities and focus on the most strategic efforts.

And Edvinsson concluded, "The BSC has made strategy a continual process and speeded up the process to create Nordea as One Bank." See the insert for a summary of Nordea's execution premium.

SUMMARY

Many of the building blocks of effective strategy execution already exist. Strategic visioning and strategy formulation tools have been developed. Strategy planning tools, including strategy maps and Balanced Scorecards, have been available for use by companies for more than ten years. And almost all companies use operational tools for quality management, process improvement, dashboards, and activity-based costing. Lacking, however, is a comprehensive framework to integrate all these tools so that they are properly aligned and synchronized.

We present in this book a six-stage comprehensive, closed-loop management system that integrates management tools to help companies to the following strategy execution processes:

- Develop the strategy
- Plan the strategy
- Align organizational units and employees with the strategy
- Plan operations by setting priorities for process management and allocating resources that will deliver the strategy
- Monitor and learn from operations and strategy
- Test and adapt the strategy

Companies need a formal structure for these components. In addition, they need a new organizational unit that helps design the integrated system, performs key processes in it, and coordinates the remainder with other organizational functions—a unit we call the office of strategy management.

The strategy execution processes and the organizational infrastructure represent a new way of managing. They create a systems approach to the planning of strategy and its link to operations. The case studies in the chapter illustrate the execution premiums—the rewards from successful strategy implementation—being realized by early adopters that have embraced this approach. Through a combination of concepts, cases, and methodologies, this book describes the foundations of a system for managing strategy and operations with the Balanced Scorecard at its core.

NOTES

1. Anonymous; the quote is widely attributed to Sun Tsu, *The Art of War*, though a careful reading of several translations does not identify the actual use of this quote.
2. M. Porter, "What Is Strategy?" *Harvard Business Review* (November–December 1996).
3. M. Hammer, "Redesigning the Practice of Management," presentation at *Management: The Last Process Frontier*, Hammer & Company Conference, Cambridge, MA, December 4, 2006.
4. *Balanced Scorecard Hall of Fame 2007* (Boston: Harvard Business School Publishing, 2007).
5. The eight key processes were customer relationship management, product supply management, new product to market, finance and accounting, human resources, information resources, law, and resort services.
6. "Marriott Vacation Club International," *Balanced Scorecard Hall of Fame Report: 2007* (Boston: Harvard Business School Publishing, 2007): 28.
7. S. Hawkes, "Thousands of Jobs to Go at BP as Chief Acts to Cut Overheads" *The Times (London)*, Business Section, October 12, 2007.
8. We surveyed members of our online community, www.bscol.com. The members self-select and join the community because of their interest in using the Balanced Scorecard for strategy execution, so the 54 percent figure is almost surely higher than the underlying rate of strategy execution management systems among all private- and public-sector enterprises.
9. These processes are drawn from our survey. They should not be confused with our six-stage system for integrating strategy planning and operational execution, which we introduce later in this chapter and elaborate throughout the rest of the book.
10. B. Marr, *Business Performance Management: Current State of the Art*, survey report, Cranfield School of Management and Hyperion, 2004.
11. R. Lawson, D. Desroches, and T. Hatch, *Scorecard Best Practices: Design, Implementation, and Evaluation* (Hoboken, NJ: John Wiley, 2008), 59–60.
12. J. Hope and R. Fraser, "Who Needs Budgets?" *Harvard Business Review* (February 2003): 108–115; T. Hope and J. Hope, *Beyond Budgeting: How Managers Can Break Free from the Annual Performance Trap* (Boston: Harvard Business School Press, 2003).

13. Horizontal strategic themes, such as for a collection of learning and growth or finance objectives, are exceptions and may not have originated within the process perspective.
14. R. S. Kaplan and S. R. Anderson, "Time-Driven Activity-Based Costing," *Harvard Business Review* (November 2004): 131–138; and Kaplan and Anderson, *Time-Driven Activity-Based Costing* (Boston: Harvard Business School Press, 2007).
15. R. S. Kaplan and D. P. Norton, "The Office of Strategy Management," *Harvard Business Review*, October 2005, 72–80.
16. We articulated the five principles for successful strategy execution in R. S. Kaplan and D. P. Norton, *The Strategy-Focused Organization* (Boston: Harvard Business School Press, 2000).
17. Information about the Balanced Scorecard Hall of Fame, including membership by region, industry, and year, can be found at http://www.thepalladiumgroup.com/about/hof/Pages/Welcome.aspx.
18. *Balanced Scorecard Report Hall of Fame 2006* (Boston: Harvard Business School Publishing, 2006).
19. *Balanced Scorecard Hall of Fame 2007.*
20. *Balanced Scorecard Hall of Fame 2005* (Boston: Harvard Business School Publishing, 2005).

CHAPTER TWO

DEVELOP THE STRATEGY

STRATEGY MANAGEMENT is a closed-loop process, as shown in Figure 2-1, with each part of the system influencing every other part. The system starts with a process to develop the strategy. Our prior work on translating strategy into strategy maps and Balanced Scorecards has helped organizations put their strategies into action but has generally accepted the enterprise's strategy as given. During the past fifteen years, our work with companies has enabled us to observe the practices they followed to develop their strategies. We have also seen new practices introduced into the process that develops the strategy, such as quantifying the vision and describing an explicit change agenda.

Figure 2-2 shows a structured strategy development and translation process that represents a synthesis of the best practices. The approach starts by defining a high-level vision of the organization's destination and finishes with executive leaders and teams launching the organization into action by implementing portfolios of aligned strategic initiatives.

In this chapter, we discuss a comprehensive process for clarifying the vision and developing the strategy, which encompasses the first two steps in Figure 2-2. We discuss the remaining steps, in which managers translate and plan the execution of the strategy, in Chapters 3 and 4.

Corporate-level strategic planning has received much criticism as bureaucratic, command-and-control, inflexible, and hierarchical or even authoritarian. Despite the many criticisms and complaints levied against it, strategic planning remains senior executives' favorite management tool. The Bain & Company *2007 Survey of Management Tools* showed that

FIGURE 2-1

The management system: Develop the strategy

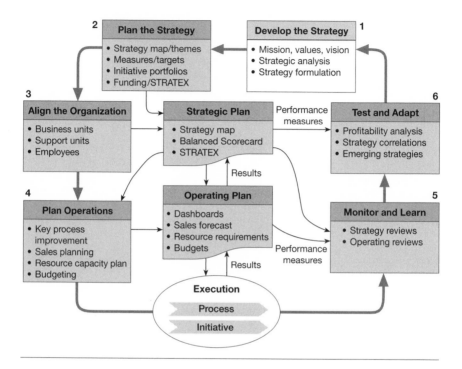

strategic planning was the most widely used; 88 percent of organizations reported using formal strategic planning.[1] Strategic planning also had the highest user satisfaction ranking—3.93 on a scale of 1 to 5—among the twenty-five management tools featured. A recent McKinsey survey confirmed the Bain & Company findings, with 79 percent of the eight hundred polled companies reporting the use of a formal strategic planning process.[2] Among these companies, more than half reported that it played a significant role in helping develop corporate strategy. That number goes up for organizations that are satisfied with their planning process.

As summarized in Figure 2-3, companies start by developing or reaffirming their mission, values, and vision. They then consider the external and internal forces impinging on the company's strategy. This step flows naturally into the identification and analysis of key issues, followed by formulation of the new strategy itself and—especially for new, transformational strategies—creating the case for change throughout the organization. We discuss each in turn.

FIGURE 2-2

Building the strategic plan

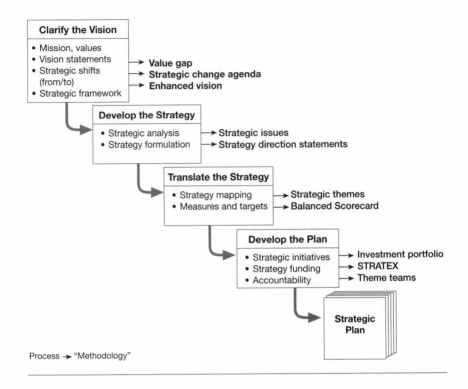

Process →► "Methodology"

CLARIFY MISSION, VALUES, AND VISION STATEMENTS

Before formulating a strategy, managers need to agree on the company's purpose (mission), the internal compass that will guide its actions (values), and its aspiration for future results (vision). The organization's mission and values typically remain stable over time. The vision, although not as stable as the mission and values, is often constant during an organization's three- to five-year strategic plan. Despite their stability, most organizations still begin their annual strategy development process by reviewing and reaffirming their mission, values, and vision statements. One chief executive officer stated, "The executive team must constantly remind itself of the foundations for what we are doing."

FIGURE 2-3

The strategy development process model

Strategy Development Process	Objective	Barriers	Representative Tools
1. Clarify Mission, Values, and Vision *Why are we in business?*	Affirm high-level guide-lines about organizational purpose and conduct.	The vision is frequently described in terms not conducive to execution.	• Clear mission • Core values • Quantified vision (BHAG) • Strategic change agenda • Enhanced vision
2. Conduct Strategic Analysis *What key issues affect our strategy?*	Identify, through struc-tured analysis, the events, forces, and experiences that impact and modify the strategy.	Analysis is frequently focused on outcomes and not on the drivers of strategy.	• Environmental scan (PESTEL) • Competitive scan (SWOT) • "Strategy of record" analysis • Strategic issues
3. Formulate the Strategy *How can we best compete?*	Define where and how the organization will compete.	There is a myriad of possible methodologies. There is no consensus on which approaches to use in which circumstances.	• Key issue analysis • Strategy methodologies • Strategy direction statements • Do-wells

The Mission Statement

A *mission statement* is a brief statement (typically one or two sentences) that defines why the organization exists. The mission should describe the fundamental purpose of the entity, especially what it provides to customers and clients (or, for public-sector and nonprofit entities, citizens and beneficiaries). The mission statement should inform executives and employees about the overall goal they have come together to pursue.

Here are examples of excellent mission statements:

- "We want to discover, develop and successfully market innovative products to prevent and cure diseases, to ease suffering and to enhance the quality of life. We also want to provide a shareholder return that reflects outstanding performance and to adequately reward those who invest ideas and work in our company" (Novartis).[3]
- "Organize the world's information and make it universally accessible and useful" (Google).[4]

The Values Statement

The *values* (often called *core values*) of a company prescribe its attitude, behavior, and character. Whole Foods, on its corporate Web page, describes the importance of its core values better than we can express:

> *The . . . core values reflect what is truly important to us as an organization. These are not values that change from time to time, situation to situation, or person to person, but rather they are the underpinning of our company culture. Many people feel Whole Foods is an exciting company of which to be a part and a very special place to work. These core values are the primary reasons for this feeling, and they transcend our size and our growth rate. By maintaining these core values, regardless of how large a company Whole Foods becomes, we can preserve what has always been special about our company. These core values are the soul of our company.*[5]

Indigo, Canada's number 1 book retailer, declares the following values:

- "We exist to add joy to customers' lives. We anticipate their needs and exceed their expectations.
- "Excellence matters in everything we do.
- "Success is only attainable through outstanding people working together in an open environment that promotes knowledge and growth.
- "Books, reading, and storytelling are an integral part of advancing society.
- "Innovation is the key to growth and can come from anyone, anytime.
- "We have a responsibility to give back to the communities in which we operate."[6]

Earthlink, an Internet service provider, has an extensive values statement that includes the following statements:

- "We respect the individual, and believe that individuals who are treated with respect and given responsibility respond by giving their best.
- "We are frugal. We guard and conserve the company's resources with at least the same vigilance that we would use to guard and conserve our own personal resources.
- "In all our dealings we will strive to be friendly and courteous, as well as fair and compassionate.

- "We feel a sense of urgency on any matters related to our customers. We own problems and we are always responsive. We are customer-driven."[7]

The Vision Statement

A *vision statement* defines the mid- to long-term (three- to ten-year) goals of the organization. It should be market oriented and should express—often in visionary terms—how the enterprise wants to be perceived by the world. A statement such as, "We will be among the top three transporters of goods and people in North America by 2012" provides a clear, specific aspiration.

The vision of Cigna Property and Casualty, an insurance company we worked with in the 1990s, was "to be a top-quartile specialist within five years."[8] Though short, this vision statement contains three vital components:

- *Stretch goal:* To be in the top quartile in profitability (at the time, Cigna P&C was at the bottom of the fourth quartile)
- *Definition of niche:* To be a specialist, and not a general-purpose, underwriter, as it had been
- *Time horizon:* Five years

Consider also the vision statement issued in 1997 by the Internet banking division of Wells Fargo bank: "To have one-million on-line customers by the end of the decade."[9] This short statement contains the same three critical elements:

- *Stretch goal:* Number of customers (1 million)
- *Definition of niche:* The online banking customer
- *Time horizon:* By the end of the decade (2000)

The vision statement for a nonprofit or government organization should define a stretch goal that relates to its mission. In 1961, U.S. President John F. Kennedy offered one of the most famous and effective public-sector vision statements when he declared that the U.S. space program would "land a man on the moon and return him safely to earth before the end of the decade." In addition to the vision's inspirational power, it described a clear measure of success and a specific time horizon.

The University of Leeds (United Kingdom) provides an excellent example of a well-crafted vision statement for a nonprofit enterprise: "By 2015, our distinctive ability to integrate world class research, scholarship, and education will have secured us a place among the top 50 universities in the world."[10] The statement contains each of the three critical components:

- *Stretch goal:* To be ranked among the top fifty universities
- *Definition of niche:* To integrate world-class research, scholarship, and education
- *Time horizon:* By 2015

The stretch goal in the vision statement should be different from the company's current position. It's important to be ambitious in setting the company's goals, and the CEO must take the lead. Indeed, one of the principal roles of an effective leader is to create a sense of urgency and formulate a target that challenges all employees, even in a well-performing organization, to become much better. Without strong leadership, an organization becomes complacent and, at best, achieves incremental improvement from the status quo.

Great leaders understand that complacency is the enemy. A classic example is Jack Welch's challenge, upon becoming CEO, for every GE business unit to either become the number 1 or 2 in its industry or else depart from the corporation. Collins and Porras note, "Visionary companies may appear straitlaced and conservative to outsiders, but they're not afraid to make bold commitments to BHAGs, 'Big Hairy Audacious Goals.'"[11] Setting a stretch target and a specific time frame for achieving it is one of the most important roles of leadership.

Companies that have used the Balanced Scorecard to achieve success consistently have had inspirational leadership. In taking over the troubled Cigna Property and Casualty insurance division, Gerry Isom started by declaring his stretch goal: for the division to move from the bottom of the fourth profitability quartile to the top quartile in five years. Dudley Nigg, CEO of the online banking unit of Wells Fargo in 1997, understood that even though the division was the leading online bank in the United States, it had to get dramatically better if it was to retain its first-mover advantages. And Michael Arthur, upon becoming vice-chancellor of the University of Leeds in 2004, challenged the deans, the faculty, and the administrative staff to help the university become one of the world's greatest research and teaching institutions.

Great leaders set ambitious targets for their organizations. The vision statement should declare, at the highest organization level, ambitious targets for the strategy, including a clear measure of success and a specific time horizon for achievement.

The Strategic Change Agenda

The vision statement provides a target and a high-level description of how the organization intends to create value in the future. But people in the organization may not understand why it needs a new strategy and why they need to change in order to achieve the stretch target. Creating a sense of urgency and communicating the need for change are critical roles for leadership.[12] Leaders can use a management tool that we call the *strategic change agenda* to provide the motivation for why transformational change is necessary. The strategic change agenda compares the current status of several organizational structures, capabilities, and processes with what they need to become over the next three to five years.

Consider the situation faced by Graham Sher when he became CEO of Canadian Blood Services (CBS). CBS was created during a corporate crisis in the 1990s as the successor organization to the Canadian Red Cross after an infamous scandal. In this scandal, multiple failures in governance, management, and decision making resulted in thousands of Canadians becoming infected from contaminated blood. The scandal led to an irreparable loss of trust in the system as a whole. In its initial years, CBS focused on operational issues to fix the system. After about four years of intensive work, CBS was able to report that the blood supply system in Canada was secure, with adequate amounts of safe, high-quality blood products meeting clinical needs when and as required.

At this point, the founding CEO resigned, and Sher became head of CBS. He noted that the enterprise had launched a great many independent initiatives, each often competing with the others for the same limited resources and without coherent management. Having fixed and stabilized CBS's operational issues, Sher saw the opportunity for CBS to create a modern and robust blood system, as good as any worldwide, and leverage CBS's unique operating model to help solve other health-care delivery challenges in Canada. But doing so would require a clear strategy, a new strategy execution process, and far greater alignment throughout the organization.

Before embarking on this difficult journey, Sher and his senior management team created an explicit agenda for change, as shown in Figure 2-4, to articulate the need for change and explain it to all CBS employees. Employees are often resistant to change, not the least because they are skeptical of the CEO's commitment to sustain the change process. Having the CEO clearly express dissatisfaction with the status quo—and, at the same time, articulate a clear, detailed, and compelling case for change—helps immensely to overcome such resistance.

FIGURE 2-4

The strategic change agenda defined the journey from where CBS was to what it could become

Canadian Blood Services Change Agenda

from ...		... to
Blood products	Mission	Expanded products and services
Tactical, operational, crisis	Executive team focus	Longer-term strategic dialogue
Resisted and not understood	Implementation of quality systems	Championed and owned
Short-term, single-source funding	Funding	Multisource funding, strategic investments
Inherited, ineffective	Infrastructure	Refurbished, modern, purpose-built
Responsive and limited visibility	Medical R&D	Targeted, strong, and visible thought leadership
Manual	Core processes	Standardized and automated
Top-down	Leadership	Identify, develop, empower
Unclear benchmark	Unit cost	Well defined, near benchmark
Focused on local jobs and tasks; unaware of strategy	People	Connected to the strategy

As another example, consider the challenges faced by the U.S. Federal Bureau of Investigation (FBI), in the aftermath of the 9/11 terrorist attacks. To respond to its new challenges and competitive threats, the FBI needed a completely new strategy and major changes in the organizational culture. FBI Director Robert Mueller recognized the need to prepare and educate all the employees about the massive changes ahead. He prepared the strategic change agenda shown in Figure 2-5 to describe the scale and scope of the transformation.

The change agenda indicates that the FBI would have to undergo a major shift from being a case-driven organization (reacting to crimes already committed) to becoming a threat-driven organization (attempting to prevent a terrorist incident from occurring). Instead of being secretive, agents had to work outside traditional operational silos and become contributors

FIGURE 2-5

FBI senior leadership created a strategic change agenda to sharpen the vision and to make the case for change

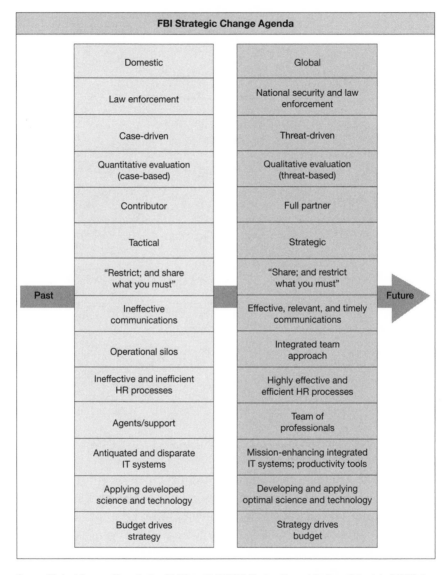

FBI Strategic Change Agenda	
Domestic	Global
Law enforcement	National security and law enforcement
Case-driven	Threat-driven
Quantitative evaluation (case-based)	Qualitative evaluation (threat-based)
Contributor	Full partner
Tactical	Strategic
"Restrict; and share what you must"	"Share; and restrict what you must"
Ineffective communications	Effective, relevant, and timely communications
Operational silos	Integrated team approach
Ineffective and inefficient HR processes	Highly effective and efficient HR processes
Agents/support	Team of professionals
Antiquated and disparate IT systems	Mission-enhancing integrated IT systems; productivity tools
Applying developed science and technology	Developing and applying optimal science and technology
Budget drives strategy	Strategy drives budget

Past → Future

Source: "Federal Bureau of Investigation (B)," Case #9-707-553 (Boston: Harvard Business School, April 2007): 8.

to integrated teams. In even more of a discontinuity, the FBI had to learn to share information and work collaboratively with other federal and local agencies to prevent incidents that could harm U.S. citizens.

These guidelines, which emerged from extensive dialogue throughout the organization, engaged all levels of the FBI to participate in setting the goals for the new strategic direction and contributed to widespread understanding and support for the new strategy that subsequently was crafted. Director Mueller carried the laminated FBI strategic change agenda chart (Figure 2-5) with him whenever he visited a field office. If agents expressed skepticism about or resistance to the new initiatives and structures, he reminded them, using the single-page summary, why change was necessary.

In summary, the start of the strategy development process requires the leadership team to reaffirm the enterprise's mission, values, and vision, perhaps updating the targets in the vision statement as needed. If the enterprise is about to embark on a major new strategy and organizational transformation, the leadership team should articulate and communicate a strategic change agenda to describe the necessary cultural, structural, and operating transitions from the past to the future.

Defining the Enhanced Vision

Strategy execution requires an architecture that integrates the strategies and operations of diverse units scattered throughout an enterprise. Research shows, however, that more than 60 percent of organizations currently lack an integrated strategy perspective, with functional units such as human resources, information technology, and finance not linked to business unit and corporate strategy.[13]

The strategy map, as we have described in our earlier books, provides a framework for an integrated view of strategy.[14] While the detailed design of the strategy map will occur at a later stage, executive teams can introduce the basic architecture of the map during the strategy development process. The executive team can use a strategy map's four-perspective framework to define an *enhanced vision*, as shown in Figure 2-6. The enhanced vision statement provides a comprehensive picture of the enabling factors to achieve the vision, including the customer value proposition, key processes, and the intangible assets of people and technology.

Consider the approach taken by Nemours, a health-care organization focused on the well-being and treatment of children. Its vision statement—"Freedom from disabling conditions"—was a simple and succinct way to describe its aspirational destination, but it provided little guidance for shaping

FIGURE 2-6

Enhancing the vision to promote depth of thought and strategy alignment

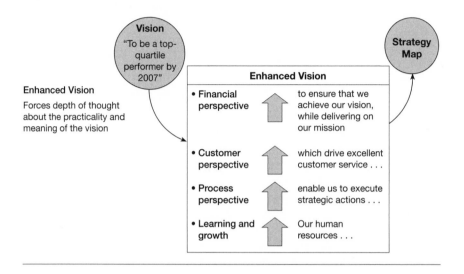

the strategy. Nemours developed an enhanced vision to guide the development of its strategy map (see Figure 2-7). Nemours placed its vision and mission at the top because they represented the enterprise's ultimate objectives and accountability. Nemours placed its core values at the bottom of the map, recognizing that they were foundational for everything it did. The enhanced vision, running along the left side of the strategy map, described the transition from vision to strategy. You can also see that within the strategy map, Nemours defined several strategic priorities that would help it achieve its enhanced vision and mission.

The enhanced vision divided the strategy into four substrategies:

- *Impact and community:* Be a leader in improving children's health through our integrated health system; becoming a preeminent voice for children.
- *Service and quality:* Care for each and every child as if they were our own.
- *Efficiency and environment:* Be effective stewards of all of our assets, continually improving them to advance our mission.
- *People and learning:* Be a great place to work.

These substrategies led naturally to the representation of the complete strategy, as we illustrate in Chapter 3.

FIGURE 2-7

Nemours strategy map architecture

That supports
our mission

Ensuring
stewardship
of the trust
and assured
financial
strength

That provide
a uniquely
satisfying
customer
experience

To deliver
the strategic
processes

We will
enable our
people

Vision: Freedom from disabling conditions

Mission: To provide leadership, institutions, and services to restore and improve the health of children through care and programs not readily available, with one high standard of quality and distinction regardless of the recipient's financial status

Stewardship
Financial strength into perpetuity

Customers
A uniquely satisfying experience

Processes

Impact and Community	**Service and Quality**	**Efficiency and Environment**
Be a leader in improving children's health through our integrated health system; becoming a pre-eminent voice for children.	Care for each child as if he or she were our own.	Be effective stewards of all of our assets, continually improving them to advance our mission.

People and Learning
Be a great place to work.

Core values: • Excel • Respect • Serve • Honor • Learn

Commitment: I will do whatever it takes to make every contact with Nemours a uniquely satisfying experience . . . for our patients, parents, visitors, colleagues, and business partners

CONDUCT STRATEGIC ANALYSIS

Once the vision has been clarified and enhanced, the company has a clear picture of what it needs to achieve. Now it performs an external and internal analysis that includes a comprehensive assessment of its own capabilities and performance relative to those of competitors, as well as its positioning relative to industry trends.

External Analysis

The executive team needs to understand the impact of macro- and industry-level trends on the company's strategy and operations. The external analysis assesses the macroeconomic environment of economic growth, interest rates, currency movements, input factor prices, regulations, and general expectations of the corporation's role in society. Often this is called a PESTEL analysis, reflecting political, economic, social, technological, environmental, and legal components (see Figure 2-8). The external analysis also includes an industry-level examination of industry economics using frameworks such as Michael Porter's five forces: bargaining power of buyers, bargaining power of suppliers, availability of substitutes, threat of new entrants, and industry rivalry.[15] The five forces model calibrates the attractiveness of an industry and aids in identifying specific forces that are shaping the industry, either favorably or unfavorably. The industry analysis should also include a summary of the company's performance on multiple financial ratios compared to its industry competitors.

Finally, the external analysis includes competitor assessments. Some companies summarize their competitive situation by positioning all their competitors in the industry on a 2×2 table, with the axes representing key

FIGURE 2-8

External analysis can be organized by the PESTEL framework

Political Analysis

- Risk of military invasion
- Legal framework for contract enforcement
- Intellectual property protection
- Trade regulations and tariffs
- Favored trading partners

Social Analysis

- Demographics
- Class structure
- Education
- Culture (gender roles, etc.)
- Entrepreneurial spirit
- Attitudes (health, environmental consciousness, nutrition)
- Leisure interests

Environmental Analysis

- Greenhouse gas emissions
- Solid waste produced
- Liquid waste discharged
- Energy consumption
- Recyclability
- Clean water consumption
- Overall environmental footprint

Economic Analysis

- Type of economic system in countries of operation
- Government intervention in the free market
- Comparative advantages of host country
- Exchange rates and stability of host country currency
- Efficiency of financial markets
- Infrastructure quality
- Skill level of workforce
- Labor costs
- Business cycle stage (e.g., prosperity, recession, recovery)
- Economic growth rate
- Discretionary income
- Unemployment rate
- Inflation rate
- Interest rates

Technological Analysis

- Recent technological development
- Technology's impact on product offering
- Impact on cost structure
- Impact on value chain structure
- Rate of technological diffusion

Legal Analysis

- Antitrust laws
- Pricing regulations
- Taxation—tax rates and incentives
- Wage legislation—minimum wage and overtime
- Workweek
- Mandatory employee benefits
- Industrial safety regulations
- Product labeling requirements

competitive dimensions such as product scope, technological capabilities, and geographical reach. Dimensions can be changed to provide various screens of performance. They superimpose a third dimension—performance—on the table by identifying each competitor with a circle whose size is proportional to a key performance indicator such as sales, assets, market share, or profitability.

Internal Analysis

The internal analysis examines an organization's own performance and capabilities. Companies that have not yet developed a Balanced Scorecard of performance measures will rely heavily on financial information to assess recent performance.

A widely used analytic tool is *value chain analysis*, also introduced by Michael Porter.[16] The *value chain* identifies the sequence of processes necessary to deliver a company's products and services to customers. In addition to the primary activities of creating a market, producing and delivering products and services, and selling to customers, the value chain can encompass secondary, or support, activities—such as research and development, human resource management, and technology development—that facilitate the primary value-creating processes. The value chain model helps a firm identify those activities that it intends to perform differently or better than competitors to establish a sustainable competitive advantage.

Companies can also estimate activity-based cost models for each process in the value chain, a practice that helps them identify processes they perform at lower cost than competitors (a source of competitive advantage), as well as processes in which they currently have a cost disadvantage relative to competitors. For companies implementing a differentiating strategy, the costing model provides feedback about whether the increased value from the differentiation in a given process exceeds the higher costs to produce and deliver the differentiating features and services.

Identifying Strengths, Weaknesses, Opportunities, and Threats (SWOT)

Once the external and internal analyses have been performed, the strategic planning participants conduct a SWOT analysis. Perhaps the earliest and most fundamental of all strategy analysis tools, the SWOT analysis identifies the company's existing strengths and weaknesses, its emerging opportunities, and the worrisome threats facing the organization, as summarized in the following matrix.[17]

	Helpful for achieving the organization's vision	Harmful for achieving the organization's vision
Internal attributes	Strengths	Weaknesses
External attributes	Opportunities	Threats

The external attributes are classified as either opportunities or threats, and the internal attributes are classified as either strengths or weaknesses. The attributes selected for classification and evaluation are determined during the strategic planning process.

A well-conducted external and internal analysis generates a host of information for a management team, much of which can be confusing when examined in totality. A SWOT table summarizes these conditions into a succinct list that helps the executive team understand the key issues that the organization must address when formulating its strategy. For example, strengths can be leveraged to pursue opportunities and to avoid threats, and managers can be alerted to internal weaknesses and external threats that need to be overcome by the strategy. Infosys, an India-based IT consulting and services provider, considers alternative scenarios that illustrate best- and worst-case situations. The best-case scenario leads to the articulation of organizational aspirations, and the worst-case scenarios help identify key business risks that must be mitigated.

Some organizations structure their SWOT analysis using the four BSC perspectives, as shown in Figure 2-9. For example, Nemours presented its SWOT analysis in this manner, as shown in Figure 2-10. Nemours managers now had a single-page summary of the issues that needed to be addressed by their new strategy, organized by shareholders (or stakeholders in the Nemours example), customers, processes, and people.

Each component of the strategic analysis identifies issues that have potential strategic implications. The planners, working with the executive team, should cull the list to identify those of greatest import. Again, the taxonomy of the strategy map helps create continuity and focus. Figure 2-11 shows the strategic issue list developed by a fashion retail company. The strategy map helped identify seven categories that would make up the strategy. The external (PESTEL) and internal (SWOT) analyses identified issues within each of these categories.

FIGURE 2-9

SWOT matrix organized by Balanced Scorecard perspectives

SWOT Guidance			
Strengths	**Weaknesses**	**Opportunities**	**Threats**
Financial Current financial performance strengths and weaknesses		Revenue growth and productivity improvement opportunities that can close the gap between current performance and the overarching financial objective	Threats to sustaining or improving financial performance; competitor threats that will influence our defensive strategy and clarify the extent and velocity of improvement required
Customer Existing strengths and weaknesses of our value proposition as perceived by customers, competitors, and the market		Opportunities to expand the customer base, target new markets, and improve the customer value proposition strategy as perceived by customers and their requirements	Threats from customer and competitors
Process Strengths in our internal processes; where we excel	Weaknesses in our internal processes and value chain	Opportunities for internal process improvement to achieve opportunities	Threats posed by internal process weaknesses
Growth People, culture, core competencies, and strategic capabilities strengths and weaknesses		Opportunities to develop culture, competencies, and capabilities to enable strategic priorities	Threats and risks to delivering on the strategy due to shortfalls in the capabilities of our people, structure, competencies, and culture

In category 1 (growth), the company needed to define its overall growth objectives. In category 5 (shopping experience), it had to translate the growth objectives into specific targets for the number and types of stores. Another category 5 issue looked at how to increase revenue per customer by making the shopping experience more fun.

The strategic issues guide the agenda for the strategy review meetings described in Chapter 8. This list of issues shows the key issues that must be continually discussed and managed if the strategy is to be executed successfully. The strategic issues list also feeds naturally into strategy formulation, the next step in strategy development.

FIGURE 2-10

The SWOT matrix at Nemours

	Strengths	Weaknesses	Opportunities	Threats
Stewardship	• Financial strength • Support from the trust • Debt capacity • Triple A credit rating and low cost of capital	• Slowdown in managed care rate increases • Declining state revenues • Declining revenue sources for community organization partners • Office of Development infancy	• External funding of biomedical research • Charitable giving to Nemours • Approaching 2008 elections to be able to educate candidates	• Cost pressures (labor and professional liability) • Bad debt particularly related to growing uninsured and underinsured population • Medicaid reimbursement • Significant capital needs • Change in Delaware governor in 2008
Customers	• Prevention and advocacy programs unique among providers • Focus on children's health • Respected as an expert in child health and health matters	• Decline in inpatient admissions • Patient and family dissatisfaction as relates to access (i.e., phone, scheduling, Web site navigation)	• Advocate changes in policies, programs, and practices to support child health • Increase market share in Delaware and Florida • Branding Nemours and other social marketing	• Unreimbursed preventive services • Intense competition in Delaware Valley • Declining birth rate and flat demographics in Delaware • Litigious environment
Processes	• Integrated child health system • Robust electronic environment • Commitment to use IS in clinical care • Priority on patient safety and quality • Special programs: Kidshealth, NHPS, and Brightstart • Community and government partnerships to advance policy and practice change in prevention	• Infrastructure needs at AIDHC	• Distinguishing ourselves in clinical quality, patient safety, and child health promotion • Improve service excellence • Address access issues (phone, appointments, bundling) • Integration of clinical treatment and community-based prevention	• Consumer-driven health plans • Pay-for-performance • Price transparency • Inflation on capital projects • Technology obsolescence
People	• Quality health-care professionals and delivery • Low vacancy rates • Below industry turnover rate	• Competitive pay and benefits package, particularly for physicians • Organizational culture • Performance management • Staffing requirements in Orlando	• Culture change initiatives	• Pediatric specialist and nursing shortages • Aging workforce • "Whitewater" change • Erosion of trust

FIGURE 2-11

Strategic analysis results in a set of strategic issues that must be addressed

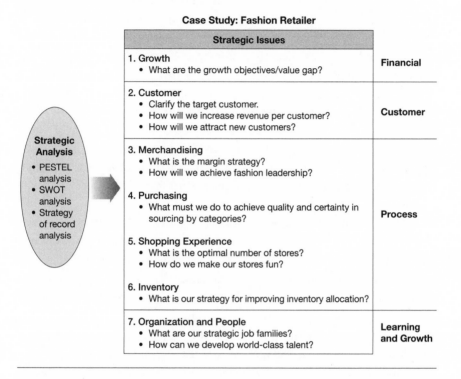

Case Study: Fashion Retailer

FORMULATE THE STRATEGY

We have now reached the point where the formal discipline of the strategy development process intersects with the art of strategy formulation. At this point, executives must decide how they will accomplish the organization's agenda in light of their analyses to date, their objectives, themes, critical issues, opportunities, and threats.

Stimulating Creative Strategies

The literature on strategy formulation and development can be overwhelming, with many approaches and schools of thought. Some prominent strategy approaches include positioning (associated with Michael Porter), the resource-based view, core competencies, value-based management, profit-from-the-core, blue ocean, emergent strategy, experience cocreation, and disruptive innovation.[18] Beyond these strategic approaches is a range of operational improvement philosophies that companies have been urged to follow, including total quality management, six sigma, ISO (International Organization for Standardization), lean manufacturing, and the learning organization. Supplementing both strategic and operational approaches are methodologies designed to minimize risk, including enterprise risk management, internal controls, and COSO (for financial institutions).[19]

Our work on strategy execution is agnostic with respect to these various strategic approaches, operational improvement methods, and risk-management tools. We have seen various companies use each of them effectively to formulate their strategies. Whichever is employed, the formulated strategy can be translated, in the next strategy execution stage, into a strategy map and then made operational through a Balanced Scorecard of objectives, measures, targets, and initiatives.

In fact, Figure 2-12 shows ways that many of the strategic, operational, and risk-management approaches can be visualized on a strategy map. Starting at the top, most organizations use some form of financial portfolio to frame their corporate strategies. The portfolios profile the financial characteristics of each business unit to find the desired balance of growth, cash flow, and risk. Value-based management approaches, such as economic value added, focus on selecting objectives that are consistent with long-term financial perspective objectives. Enterprise risk management, including COSO and internal controls, focuses on reducing the financial, operating, technological, and market risks that can impair a company's ability to execute its strategy. Typically, however, these financial strategy and risk-management approaches do not feature customer value propositions, key business processes, or investment in intangible assets, all of which are critical for sustained value creation.

The most visible strategy formulation approaches focus on customers. Porter's competitive advantage framework emphasizes selecting a focus on market and customer segments and deciding whether to win in that focused segment with either a low-cost or a differentiated strategy. Chris Zook of Bain & Company argues that most successful companies build strategies around core market niches in which they have expertise, credibility, and a deep knowledge of customer preferences. For example, he cites organizations like Gartner Group and Bausch & Lomb, which performed poorly after diluting their focus by entering new niches and subsequently returned to success only after returning to market segments in which they had already experienced success.[20]

FIGURE 2-12

Many different methodologies are available to support the strategy formulation process

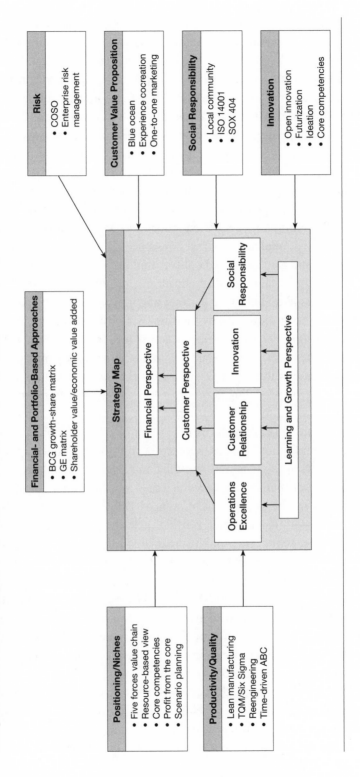

Companies that adopt the blue ocean approach develop creative and sustainable new competitive positioning for a large customer base.[21] For example, Southwest Airlines created a new market segment by combining the speed of air travel with the low prices and frequent on-time departures that led many customers to use buses for intercity travel. Southwest's targeted customer base of price-sensitive travelers tolerate the lack of reserved seating, long queues to board the planes, and absence of first-class options in return for low prices, convenient flights, and on-time arrivals.

As another blue ocean example, Cirque du Soleil found a large market niche for young adults by combining the acrobatics and constant excitement of a circus with the music and dance associated with musical theater. The company generated enormous cost savings by eliminating traditional animal acts—which consumed nearly 50 percent of operating expenses and also generated controversy from animal rights groups—and invested the savings in story lines and original music and dance acts. Companies like Southwest Airlines and Cirque du Soleil changed the dynamics of their industries by their innovative offerings.

Experience cocreation enables companies to develop the value proposition jointly with their customers.[22] With this approach, agricultural equipment manufacturer John Deere makes the farmer's life easier and more productive by providing access to necessary information through a combination of technology and a peer-group network. A real-time system called Deere Trax allows farmers to monitor the operation of their fleets of tractors and other vehicles. Moreover, the system connects farmers who have similar problems and similar demographics with various thematic communities that can share knowledge and draw upon the collective experiences of the group. The design of Deere's products and services is cocreated with its customer, putting farmers at the center of the process.

Another school of thought looks at strategy as an active, competitive process. *Scenario planning* is a widely used approach, first developed at Shell, in which the organization develops responses to competitive and environmental moves. LG Philips LCD uses war game simulations (discussed in Chapter 9) to identify likely competitor reactions to various strategies that it might introduce. Chapter 5 describes how strategies connect to various operational improvement programs, such as TQM, process management, and cost management.

Whatever the methodology used, the outcome from any strategy formulation approach is to develop a direction that differentiates the company's position and offering from those of its competitors so that it can create a sustainable competitive advantage that leads to superior financial performance (or, for nonprofits, demonstrably favorable social effects). The creativity of the strategy becomes an important means to this end. Strategic planning participants can draw upon the toolbox of methodologies illustrated in Figure 2-12 to develop their differentiating strategy. As executives become more knowledgeable about the range of strategy formulation tools, they can use the approach that seems most relevant and helpful for their company's situation, history, culture, and competencies.

Using the Strategy Map to Guide Strategy Selection

The strategy map framework shown in Figure 2-12 may help guide strategy selection. If, for example, the company has poor capital utilization, then some use of a value-based management approach would help define a financial strategy. If the company does not have a distinctive brand or market presence, a focus on identifying an attractive customer segment—perhaps through a positioning framework, a blue ocean approach, or a customer cocreation process—might prove most relevant. If the company has distinctive capabilities in important business processes—operations management, customer data mining, or product features and innovation—that are superior to or not possessed by competitors, then the resource-based view and identification of core competencies are effective frameworks for strategy formulation. If the company has a great human capital base, with skilled, experienced, and highly motivated employees, then striving to create a learning organization and encouraging the proposal of emergent strategies can identify promising new strategic approaches.

As one illustration, consider the case of Bank of Tokyo-Mitsubishi, UFJ, one of the largest banks, measured by assets, in the world. Figure 2-13 shows how the bank has integrated various planning methodologies into its strategy development process. At the center is the high-level architecture for its strategy map, showing the topics, such as operations quality, for which specific strategic objectives have been defined. On either side of the strategy map, the figure identifies the methodologies available for use at the next strategy review and update in four areas: the customer value proposition, employee engagement, corporate social responsibilities, and compliance and risk management.

Because the company updates its strategy incrementally each year, most of the tools are used for data gathering and performance assessment. For example, the customer value proposition methodologies are used to collect customer satisfaction scores from external customers, management, business lines, and branch offices. Other methodologies that support the

FIGURE 2-13

Foundations of business strategy at Bank of Tokyo-Mitsubishi, UFJ

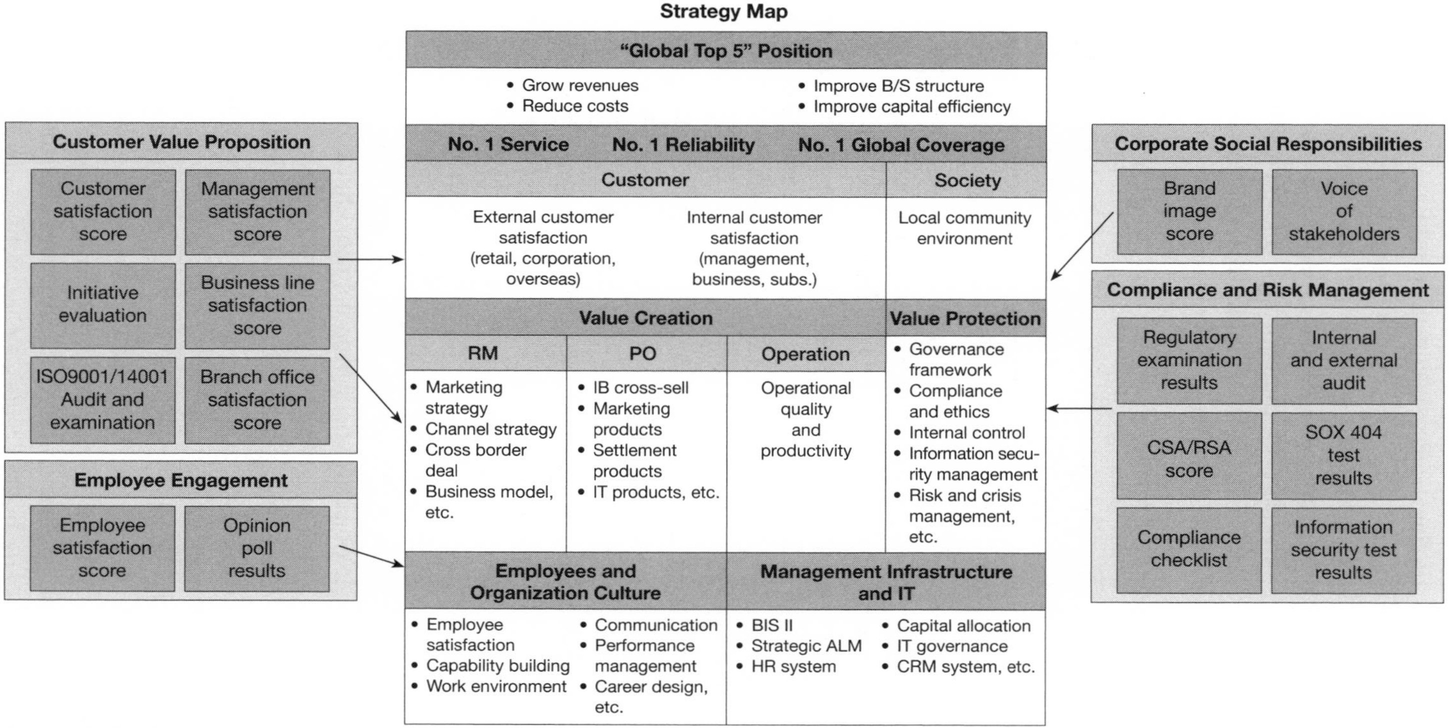

Strategy Map

Source: BSCol Conference, Boston, July 2007.

review of the customer value proposition are used to evaluate strategic initiative performance and ISO 9001 and ISO 14001 audit results. Using these inputs, the bank updates its strategy for the next year. Its execution premium is summarized in the insert.

BANK OF TOKYO-MITSUBISHI, UFJ'S EXECUTION PREMIUM

- BTMU executives successfully completed a historic merger between two megabanks with virtually no significant operational or systems failures, thanks to the strategic alignment already in place between BTM and its divisions.
- BTMU became one of the world's top five financial institutions two years ahead of its original strategic plan.
- By linking the COSO-based control self-assessment methodology to the Balanced Scorecard, BTMU's U.S. operation has achieved high marks in the U.S. regulatory examinations. (By law, details about regulatory examinations cannot be disclosed in the United States.)
- In the two-year period, March 2004 to March 2006, BTMU's net business profit increased by 117.5 percent and its Moody's/S&P credit rating improved from A2/BBB to A1/A.
- BTMU is ranked as the number-one brand among Japanese financial institutions in the Nikkei Corporate Brand Survey.

The OAS Statement

Once the executive team has selected its strategy, it needs to codify it so that it can be communicated to all managers and employees. Recent work at Harvard Business School has concluded that a good statement of the strategy, whatever its source, should contain three fundamental elements:[23]

- *Objective (O):* The ends that the strategy is designed to achieve
- *Advantage (A):* The means by which the enterprise will achieve its objective
- *Scope (S):* The domain—or, as we referred to it earlier, the niche—in which the enterprise intends to operate

The *objective* part of the OAS statement is similar to the vision statement we described earlier: it contains a quantitative goal—typically profitability, size, market share or rank, or total shareholder returns—as well as a time frame, such as three to five years, for reaching it.

Advantage represents what the enterprise will do differently, better, or uniquely compared with competitors. It describes the value proposition the company will offer to attract customers. The value proposition should describe those aspects of the buying experience or relationship that the company intends to offer uniquely or significantly better than competitors. It can be expressed in traditional strategy terms, such as low cost or differentiation through product features, services, or customer relationships.

The *scope* defines the market segment in which the enterprise intends to compete and win. Scope can be a targeted customer segment, the breadth of the product line, the technologies employed, the geographic locations served, or the degree of *vertical integration* (which value chain activities it will perform).

For example, consider how the OAS framework might be used to describe the strategy of Southwest Airlines:[24]

To be the most profitable U.S.-based airline . . . (O)

by offering the speed of airline travel at a price, frequency, and reliability of cars, buses and trains . . . (A)

to travelers who are price sensitive and who value convenient flights (S)

The company's objective is unsurprising, to be the most profitable airline. The time frame is omitted, because it is already number 1 on this metric and it likely wants to retain this position. Its advantage, as previously described, is to offer the speed of airplanes at the price and convenience of cars, buses, and passenger trains. Its scope is to appeal to price-sensitive travelers, who are willing to endure the inconvenience of unreserved seats, a mass boarding process, and no premium classes or airport lounges for the opportunity to travel at low prices between cities at airplane speed and arrive on-time. This example shows how the organization's vision and high-level strategy can be expressed in a crisp and powerful OAS statement of fewer than fifty words.

Strategy Direction Statements

After the strategy has been formulated, the process moves down a level of detail, addressing such things as measures, targets, initiatives, budgets, and accountability, as described in the next two chapters. Before moving to the planning process, the executive team can capture the creativity of the strategy development process and carry it forward using a technique we call *strategy direction statements*, as shown in Figure 2-14. Managers, after conducting their strategic analysis, prepare a direction statement for each of the identified strategic issues. A direction statement is like a vision statement for each strategic issue. The strategy direction statement spawns three components that are critical to the subsequent development of detailed plans:

- *Strategic objectives:* These define the specific goal to be achieved.
- *Do-Wells:* These identify the critical few activities that must be mastered if the objective is to be achieved. Do-wells become critical inputs to the subsequent design of strategy maps and initiatives.
- *Preliminary measures:* These are a first pass at the potential measures to be used on the Balanced Scorecard.

FIGURE 2-14

Strategy formulation resolves the issues and establishes the new directions

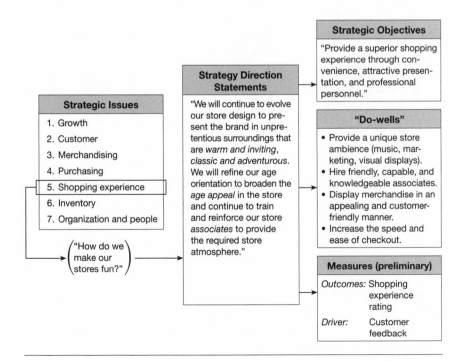

For example, consider the strategic issue: "How do we make our stores fun?" Analysis of this issue might lead to a strategy direction statement that envisions a new store environment, as well as detailed strategic objectives, do-wells, and tentative metrics for this issue, as shown in Figure 2-14. Similar strategy direction statements are prepared for each identified strategic issue, facilitating the translation of the formulated strategy into the next stage: developing the strategic plan of action.

INCREMENTAL VERSUS TRANSFORMATIONAL STRATEGY UPDATE

One of our conference participants, Karl Sweeney, the current strategy management officer at Marriott Vacation Club International (MVCI), responded to a question about the purpose of the annual strategy review meeting at his organization: "If I had been asked that question last year, I would have responded, 'Incremental change.' We were busily and successfully executing our strategy. But this year something changed. We're now in a phase where our existing business model has encountered some new challenges. Our next meeting will require an intensive review of our strategy, likely leading to major new directions."[25]

The experience at MVCI mirrors what happens at most organizations. A strategy, whether good or bad, eventually runs its course. A company's competitors observe successful strategies and eventually adapt to counter the advantages created by the first mover. The competitive moves typically take three years or more to affect a company's performance.

Peter Aldridge, head of HSBC Rail, proactively launched a major strategic review even while the company was delivering excellent financial performance. Aldridge noted that even though HSBC Rail was currently enjoying a patch of good weather, he could see storm clouds approaching from various directions. HSBC, the parent corporation, was asking for major improvements in capital utilization. A key stakeholder, the U.K. Department for Transport, was looking to greatly improve the value for money it received from subsidizing the U.K. rail network. Industry trends such as environmental and climate concerns as well as growth in passenger and freight traffic would put pressures on HSBC Rail's existing strategy.

Rather than wait for the storm to arrive, Aldridge launched a series of ten workshops for senior and middle managers. The initial workshops explored four future scenarios. The managers studied each scenario and identified common priorities and drivers for each one. They mapped these into a change agenda and ensured that they were all addressed when they later built the HSBC Rail strategy map and Balanced Scorecard. The workshops helped people truly understand and accept the purpose (mission), vision, and values of the organization. This agreement set the stage for developing the new strategy and making it actionable through a strategy map and Balanced Scorecard (we will present HSBC's strategy map in Chapter 8).

Our tentative conclusion from surveying clients and conference attendees is that new strategies generally have a three- to five-year useful life. Within this period, the companies make incremental strategy changes each year (assuming that the existing strategy is delivering successful performance). Only when the company sees that the strategy has run its course, experiences a major transformational event, or begins to fail does it decide to consider a new, transformational strategy.

To develop a new, transformational strategy, a company might start by reexamining and changing major components of the existing strategy, including the long-term mission, values, vision, and strategic themes, as well as financial (mission) expectations, customer niche and value proposition, key strategic processes, and enabling human, information, and organizational capital capabilities.

Triggers of a Transformational Strategy

The trigger of a transformational strategy can be negative, such as the *burning platform* of a failed strategy. We observed this in the 1990s when several companies adopted the Balanced Scorecard to help them implement a radically different strategy after experiencing financial distress: Cigna Property and Casualty had the largest losses in the industry, including a combined ratio (expenses to premiums) of 140; Mobil US Marketing and Refining had a negative cash flow year of $500 million and was the most unprofitable company in its industry; and AT&T Canada in 1996 lost Can$350 million. Under pressure from a burning platform, an organization has high motivation to seek a new strategy rather than continue to be immolated by the failed existing strategy.

The appointment of a new leader, especially one from outside the organization, triggers a comprehensive review and a transformational update of the existing strategy. New leaders frequently are summoned to deal with burning platforms, but leadership changes have become the norm in all organizations, including the public sector, where new civilian leaders are appointed after elections, and in the military, where leaders have limited-term tenure.

Technological change can serve as a trigger, as many retail and financial institutions learned in the 1990s when the Internet suddenly emerged as a powerful new channel. In that dot-com boom, many companies talked about being "amazoned." Wells Fargo saw the Internet as the catalyst for it to move its strategy from productivity enhancements and cost reduction in its traditional bricks-and-mortar retail banks to revenue growth and customer relationships through online banking. Clay Christensen, among others, has documented how technological change has disrupted existing strategies in many industries.[26]

The trigger could be macroeconomic, such as a major increase in an input price (such as energy) or a foreign exchange revaluation. It could be a change in the regulatory regime, such as when new competition is allowed to enter an existing market or when companies are allowed to enter new markets and business segments previously proscribed to them.

In summary, companies can introduce a new transformational strategy either on a regularly scheduled basis, as done by organizations like Ricoh every three years, or when the executive team recognizes that its existing strategy has run its course and a new approach is needed. For example, Andy Grove triggered Intel's transformational strategy shift from memory chips to microprocessors in the 1980s when he asked his management team, "If we were starting the company today, would we be building capacity to produce commodity memory chips?"

MVCI had a strategy that had been in place for five years (see Figure 2-15). During the preceding four years, MVCI's annual review made only minor changes in the existing strategy, a practice that seemed to be working fine. But, as noted by Sweeney in the earlier quotation, in the strategy's fifth year, the competitive environment had changed so much that the executive team realized that its existing strategy needed to be redone. In advance of the next annual strategy meeting, the organization made a major investment in management time and analysis to understand its new competitive environment, setting the stage for a new and transformative strategy to be developed at the meeting.

On one level, the annual strategy update process had worked, with a new strategy introduced as business conditions changed. But as one senior officer stated, "I'm not happy with the planning process that we used a year ago. If we had done a better job with our environmental scan and been more disciplined with analysis of the data we had on hand at the prior annual strategy update meeting, we could have seen the problems coming a year earlier and dramatically improved our reaction time. The value of moving a year earlier in our business is enormous!"[27]

FIGURE 2-15

Triggers of strategy change at Marriott Vacation Club International

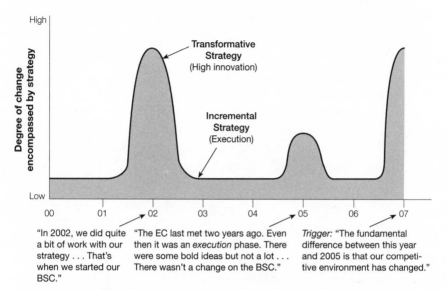

"In 2002, we did quite a bit of work with our strategy . . . That's when we started our BSC."

"The EC last met two years ago. Even then it was an *execution* phase. There were some bold ideas but not a lot . . . There wasn't a change on the BSC."

Trigger: "The fundamental difference between this year and 2005 is that our competitive environment has changed."

The trigger came as a result of the annual strategy review.

We tell a similar story in Chapter 9 about a convenience store chain, Store 24. A special-purpose study—an after-the-fact statistical analysis of the cause-and-effect linkages on the strategy map—revealed that the company could have signaled the failure of its existing strategy one year earlier than it took the management team to recognize the problem. Thus, even when the existing strategy seems to be working and no major changes are apparently indicated, the executive team may still want to perform a careful analysis each year of external changes and internal data to validate that the existing strategy should be continued for another year. In Chapter 9 we return to this use of operational performance data to inform the annual strategy update meeting.

The two extremes of fine-tuning the existing strategy or introducing a transformational strategy are not the only possibilities for implementing strategic change. As we will discuss in Chapter 3, strategy usually consists of several simultaneous strategic themes. One of these themes may require dramatic revision, whereas the remaining ones require little or no change. For example, Chase, while assimilating major mergers in the 1990s, learned that its stated goal of "100% customer retention" was wrong; many existing customers, especially those with low asset balances, were unprofitable. So Chase changed the goal for its customer relationship strategic theme to "retaining assets" rather than "retaining customers," striving to keep only profitable customers. Chase's strategic themes for corporate branding, operations excellence, and developing employee capabilities remained unchanged.

SUMMARY

A company's executive team should meet at least annually to update strategy. At the meeting, the team reviews and reaffirms the company's mission, values, and vision statements. It analyzes external and internal information, and summarizes critical strategic issues in a SWOT analysis. If the executive team sees that major strategic and culture change is required in the years ahead, it clarifies the need for change through a strategic change agenda that it can communicate throughout the organization.

If the existing strategy is still functioning effectively, the team may choose to make only incremental changes to it. But given that all strategies have only a finite effective life—typically five years or less—the executive team periodically draws on a wide range of strategy formulation tools to develop a transformational strategy that will guide the company forward for the next several years.

NOTES

1. D. K. Rigby, *Management Tools 2007: An Executive's Guide* (Boston: Bain & Company, 2007).
2. "Improving Strategic Planning: A McKinsey Survey," *McKinsey Quarterly* (September 2006).
3. See http://www.novartis.co.uk/about/mission.shtml.
4. See http://www.google.com/corporate/.
5. Whole Foods values statements are extensive; see http://www.wholefoodsmarket.com/company/corevalues.html.
6. Indigo 2007 Annual Report.
7. See http://www.earthlink.net/about/cvb/.
8. R. Nolan and D. Stoddard, "Cigna Property and Casualty Reengineering (A)," HBS Case # 9-196-059 (August 1995): 3–4.
9. R. Kaplan and N. Tempest, "Wells Fargo Online Financial Services (A)," HBS Case # 9-198-146 (June 1999): 4.
10. "Our Vision & Purpose," University of Leeds Strategic Plan 2006: 4.
11. J. Collins and J. Porras, *Built to Last: Successful Habits of Visionary Companies* (New York: Harper Collins, 1994), 9.

12. J. Kotter, *Leading Change* (Boston: Harvard Business School Press, 1996), 21–22.
13. SHRM/Balanced Scorecard Collaborative, Aligning HR with Organization Strategy Survey Research Study 62-17052 (Alexandria, VA: Society for Human Resource Management, 2002); "The Alignment Gap," *CIO Insight*, 1 July 2002.
14. R. S. Kaplan and D. P. Norton, *Strategy Maps* (Boston: Harvard Business School Press, 2004); and Kaplan and Norton, *The Strategy-Focused Organization* (Boston: Harvard Business School Press, 2000).
15. Recently, a sixth force, the role of complementors, has been added to the five forces framework. See M. E. Porter, "The Five Competitive Forces That Shape Strategy," *Harvard Business Review* (January 2008) 86–87.
16. M. E. Porter, *Competitive Advantage: Creating and Sustaining Superior Performance* (New York: Macmillan, Free Press, 1985), 33–163.
17. One of the early SWOT references is E. P. Learned, C. R. Christensen, K. Andrews, and W. D. Guth, *Business Policy: Text and Cases* (Homewood, IL: Irwin, 1969).
18. Numerous articles and books have been written on strategy formulation. Here are some of the most important:

Porter, M. E. *The Competitive Advantage: Creating and Sustaining Superior Performance*. New York: Free Press, 1985. (Republished with a new introduction, 1998.)

Porter, M. E. *Competitive Strategy: Techniques for Analyzing Industries and Competitors*. New York: Free Press, 1980. (Republished with a new introduction, 1998.)

Porter, M. E. "What Is Strategy?" *Harvard Business Review* (November–December 1996).

Barney, J. *Gaining and Sustaining Competitive Advantage*. 3rd ed. Saddle River, NJ: Prentice-Hall, 2006.

Barney, J. B., and D. N. Clark. *Resource-Based Theory: Creating and Sustaining Competitive Advantage*. Oxford: Oxford University Press, 2007.

Hamel, G., and C. K. Prahalad. *Competing for the Future*. Boston: Harvard Business School Press, 1996.

Collis, D. J., and C. A. Montgomery. "Competing on Resources: Strategy in the 1990s." *Harvard Business Review* (July–August 1995): 118–128.

Kim, W. C., and R. Mauborgne. *Blue Ocean Strategy*. Boston: Harvard Business School Press, 2005.

Christensen, C. M., and M. E. Raynor, *The Innovator's Solution: Creating and Sustaining Successful Growth*. Boston: Harvard Business School Press, 2003.

Zook, C., and J. Allen, *Profit from the Core: Growth Strategy in the Age of Turbulence*. Boston: Harvard Business School Press, 2001.

Mintzberg, H. "Crafting Strategy." *Harvard Business Review* (July–August 1987).

Hamel, G., "Strategy Innovation and the Quest for Value." *Sloan Management Review* (Winter 1998).
19. COSO is the abbreviation for the Committee of Sponsoring Organizations of the Treadway Commission, a voluntary private-sector organization that sets standards for business ethics, internal controls, and corporate governance.
20. C. Zook and J. Allen, *Profit from the Core*.
21. Kim and Mauborgne, *Blue Ocean Strategy*.
22. C. K. Prahalad and V. Ramaswamy, *The Future of Competition: Cocreating Unique Value with Customers* (Boston: Harvard Business School Press, 2004).

23. This section draws upon material from D. Collis and M. Rukstad, "Can You Say What Your Strategy Is?" *Harvard Business Review* (April 2008) 89–90.
24. The Southwest Airlines OAS statement has been created by the authors for illustrative purposes, based on public information. We do not know whether the company would agree with our representation of its strategy.
25. K. Sweeney, comment at "Achieving and Sustaining Breakthrough Performance: 2007 Leadership Conference," Balanced Scorecard Collaborative, Boston, MA (July 2007).
26. C. M. Christensen, *The Innovator's Dilemma: When New Technologies Cause Great Firms to Fail* (Boston: Harvard Business School Press, 1997).
27. K. Sweeney, comment at "Achieving and Sustaining Breakthrough Performance: 2007 Leadership Conference," Balanced Scorecard Collaborative, Boston, MA (July 2007).

CHAPTER THREE

PLAN THE STRATEGY

THE STRATEGY DEVELOPMENT STEPS described in Chapter 2 are the starting point for strategy execution. Managers performing these steps reaffirm the mission, values, and vision of the organization, assess current strengths, weaknesses, opportunities, and threats, and select a specific course of action to achieve the vision's targets. But these steps end in word statements that are generally too vague to be implemented successfully. The process to *plan the strategy*—stage 2 in Figure 3-1—converts statements of strategic direction into specific objectives, measures, targets, initiatives, and budgets that guide actions and align the organization for effective strategy execution.

In this chapter, we address the translation of the strategy into a strategy map, built around strategic themes, and an associated Balanced Scorecard of measures and targets for each of the map's strategic objectives. (We will discuss the selection, funding, and management of strategic initiatives in Chapter 4.) Developing the strategy map and Balanced Scorecard addresses the questions and issues shown in Figure 3-2.

CREATE THE STRATEGY MAP

The strategy map provides an architecture for integrating the strategies and operations of diverse units scattered throughout the enterprise.[1] (If you are new to strategy maps and the Balanced Scorecard, see the brief overview in the appendix to this chapter.) In our latest best practice, we construct strategy maps upon *strategic themes*—collections of related strategic objectives within the map—as illustrated in Figure 3-3.

FIGURE 3-1

The management system: Plan the strategy

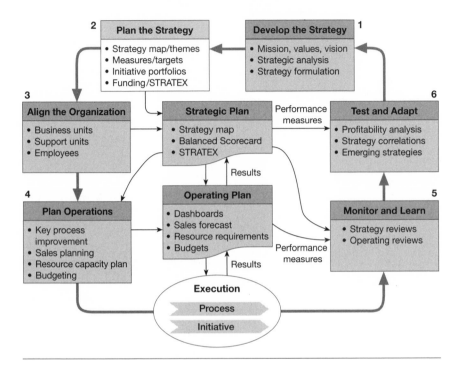

Most strategic themes are vertical combinations of objectives that originate in the process perspective, where the strategy is executed. A process-based strategic theme can connect upward to customer and financial outcomes, as well as downward to the enabling objectives in the learning and growth perspective. Strategic themes, however, can also be defined across a Balanced Scorecard perspective. For example, often companies define a strategic theme that encompasses learning and growth objectives for developing the employee capabilities, culture, and values to drive improvements in customer-focused processes.

Strategic themes split a strategy into several distinct value-creating processes. Each entity, of course, needs to customize its strategic themes to its own customer value proposition—the heart of the strategy—as well as the financial perspective's growth and productivity objectives. For example, one strategic theme in Figure 3-3 focuses on improving productivity and customer loyalty through operational excellence whereas another theme features growth through innovation. Clearly both are important, but each requires a different approach to execution.

FIGURE 3-2

The strategy translation process model

Strategy Translation Process	Objective	Barriers	Enabling Tools
Create the Strategy Map *How do we express our strategy?*	To develop a comprehensive integrated model of the strategy that pulls together the many diverse components of the plan	Typical strategies are built by different groups in different parts of the organization. They are not integrated.	• Strategy map (cause and effect) • Strategic objectives

Select Measures and Targets
 	
How do we measure our strategy?
	To convert strategic direction statements into measures and targets that can be linked to the management system	Lower-level objectives and targets are not aligned with the higher-level goals.	• Balanced Scorecard
			  – Measures
			  – Targets
			  – Gaps

FIGURE 3-3

Strategy consists of several parallel and complementary themes

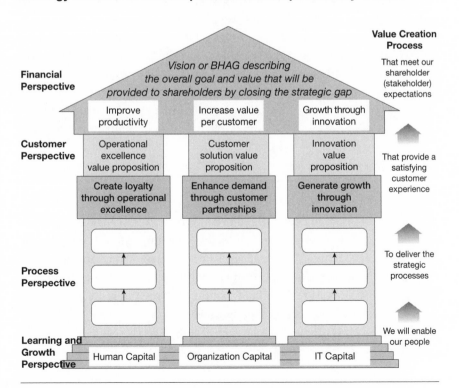

Strategic themes, such as the three shown in Figure 3-3, generally deliver their benefits over different time periods. Cost savings from improvements in operational processes deliver quick benefits (six to twelve months). Changing the customer value proposition and improving customer relationships accrue benefits in the mid-term (one to three years). Innovation processes generally take longer to produce revenue and margin improvements (three to five years). All the themes are critical to the strategy. A strategy that ignores long-term innovation in order to create short-term profitability is not sustainable. A strategy that ignores the customer relationship is not practical. A strategy that ignores short-term operational improvements cannot deliver on product, customer, and financial commitments. A strategy map, organized by several parallel strategic themes, enables companies to simultaneously manage short, intermediate, and long-term value-creating processes. By constructing a strategy map based on a collection of strategic themes, executives can separately plan and manage each of the key elements of the strategy and yet still have them operate coherently. The themes that cross functions and business units also support the boundaryless approach necessary for successful strategy execution.

To examine a strategic theme in more detail, consider Figure 3-4, which shows a theme—revenue growth through innovation—of NeoSystems, a company that competes through product innovation. The company offers state-of-the-art technology embedded in new product releases for its targeted customers. NeoSystems expects to earn high customer loyalty, measured by customer retention and account share, from its innovative offerings.[2] The company's hypothesis embedded in the strategic theme is that it can create sustained customer loyalty by continually improving the product development process so that it can be the first to market with innovative products. The key process for delivering this value to customers is to excel at reducing the product development cycle.

NeoSystems' ability to excel at rapid product development depends on the quality of its technical staff, especially their technological expertise and ability to integrate new technologies from multiple disciplines into final products. The company will implement a new hiring and development program to recruit the requisite talent. But the most important employee qualifications are length of tenure at NeoSystems. Experienced employees understand the company culture and can draw upon their prior product development experience. NeoSystems specifies "key staff retention" as a foundational learning and growth objective for the innovation strategy.

FIGURE 3-4

Innovation strategic theme at NeoSystems

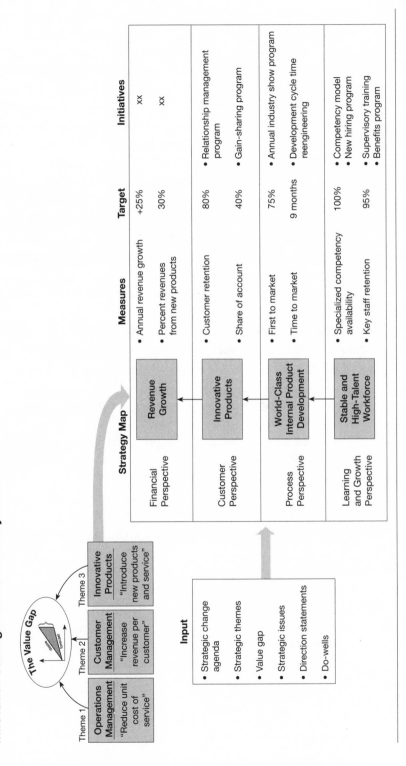

The strategy map of NeoSystems' innovation theme articulates the causal assumptions underlying its strategy. In subsequent steps (also shown in Figure 3-4), NeoSystems will translate the strategic objectives on its strategy map into a Balanced Scorecard of measures that clarify and make operational the meaning of the words used to define each objective. Targets establish clear expectations for each measure's achievement. The strategic initiatives identify the action programs and resource requirements for the company to achieve the targeted performance.

Figure 3-5 shows the strategy map for Nemours, the children's healthcare organization introduced in Chapter 2. The map is displayed as a "strategy house" supported by four strategic themes: impact and community, service and quality, efficiency and environment, and people and learning. The strategy map contains three to four objectives for each of its four strategic themes. The strategic themes provide a structure for easily communicating the strategy within and outside the organization and for developing measures, targets, and initiatives that promote performance and accountability.

The execution premium earned by Nemours' use of the strategy management system, based on the strategy map shown in Figure 3-5, is summarized in the insert.

NEMOURS' EXECUTION PREMIUM

- Total revenues increased 6.4 percent from June 2006 (pre-BSC) to June 2007 (post-BSC), and the percentage of receivables paid within four months increased markedly.
- Patient satisfaction increased by 10 percentage points (measured in a formal survey of all hospital population segments).
- Training to improve staff friendliness, efficiency, and effectiveness led to a 30 percent increase in calls for doctor appointments during the first half of 2007.
- Full implementation of an electronic medical record (EMR) produced a 15 percent increase in on-time patient immunizations (in one year) and a 30 percent reduction in documentation time.
- Standardization of clinical practices increased because of BSC-driven improved cross-functional cooperation and communication.

Case Study on Strategic Themes: Luxfer Gas Cylinders

In Chapter 1 we describe the convening of the Luxfer Gas Cylinders (LGC) management team in 2002 to formulate a new strategy. It translated the

FIGURE 3-5

Nemours' strategy map organized by strategic themes

That support our mission

Vision: Freedom from disabling conditions

Mission: To provide leadership, institutions, and services to restore and improve the health of children through care and programs not readily available, with one high standard of quality and distinction regardless of the recipient's financial status

Ensuring stewardship of the trust and assured financial strength

Stewardship

S1—Create sufficient cash flow and operating margins to achieve our strategic goals

That provide a uniquely satisfying customer experience

S2—Achieve growth through delivery of impactful services in Florida and the Delaware Valley

S3—Manage costs/expenses through process efficiencies and resource decisions

Customers

C1—Children and Families: "Create an environment where each child is treated as if they were your own."

C2—Communities: "Be a catalyst for change, as well as a trusted resource for improving children's health."

Processes

Impact and Community	Service and Quality	Efficiency and Environment
P01—Expand our reach in the Delaware Valley and Florida to ensure vitality and viability	P05—Assure service excellence in order to provide a compassionate, personalized, and informed experience	P09—Create and enhance physical environments that are patient-centered and support excellent care
P02—Create an integrated system of children's health	P06—Achieve exceptional outcomes through coordinated, evidence-based care, health promotion, and improved clinical processes	P10—Assure that operations are efficient and effective
P03—Working with community partners and government, influence issues and drive change relevant to child health and wellness	P07—Leverage technology for process improvement, enhanced quality, safety, and service excellence	P11—Allocate financial and capital resources for efficiency and effectiveness
P04—Improve children's health through research and education	P08—Partner with physicians and other care providers to create an efficient and effective environment for care	

To deliver the strategic processes

People and Learning

L01—Recruit and retain the right people in the right seats	L03—Align, reward, and encourage our associates' passion for excellence
L02—Assure a highly skilled workforce	L04—Value diversity and foster a culture of trust by living our core values

We will enable our people

Core values: • Excel • Respect • Serve • Honor • Learn

Commitment: I will do whatever it takes to make every contact with Nemours a uniquely satisfying experience . . . for our patients, parents, visitors, colleagues, and business partners

strategy into what it called a strategic road map (see Figure 3-6) organized by five strategic themes. LGC's president, John Rhodes, described the rationale for strategic themes: "A theme is a principal melody that recurs throughout a composition. It's an essential series of notes around which other musical embellishment occurs. If it's well composed, the theme is the part that's easy to remember—you can hum or whistle it. And that memorable quality is crucial not only in music, but also in organizational dynamics. You can't whistle a symphony. For that, you need an orchestra. If the orchestra is in tune and the individual players stick to the same theme and work together as a team, the result can be wonderfully melodious and pleasing. Our BSC strategy map is our road map and our sheet music."[3]

LGC's management team recognized that the company needed different value propositions for different product groups in different markets. The map incorporated a customer value proposition based on operational excellence for its traditional high-volume market. The map included other themes to address the opportunities in markets that valued complete solutions and deep supplier relationships, as well as those that valued products incorporating innovative new technologies.

LGC's five strategic themes—customer focus, innovation, image/branding, operational excellence, and learning and growth—are described next.

The "Customer focus" theme highlights creating value by providing complete solutions and superior service. Luxfer wanted customers in this market segment to regard it as the best supplier, not necessarily the low-price supplier. For example, objectives in this theme for alternative fuel vehicle (AFV) products include compressed natural gas vehicles, fuel distribution systems, and hydrogen applications. Luxfer's best-supplier strategy means developing a superior value chain with targeted downstream value-added partners and offering exceptional service in terms of reduced lead times, flexible product development, and competitive pricing.

The Innovation theme encompasses creating value through product innovation. Its goal was to focus the organization on quickly identifying, selecting, and commercializing new products. The objectives in this theme help LGC address questions like the following:

- Have we developed the processes for market sensing, and all the other new product development design processes?
- Are we in tune with our customers and the entire distribution channel? For many of our products, we're two or three layers from the end user.

- Have we learned to ask the right questions so that we can develop new products that the market values? Or should we just tweak last year's model?
- Will we make money at it?

Initially, the marketing department owned the "Image/branding" theme. Over the next five years, however, the theme became more cross-functional and expanded its focus beyond marketing to concentrate on how to change Luxfer from an operationally focused company into a market-led one. The objectives of this theme include building and leveraging the LGC brand, developing new products, and being easy to do business with. These broad objectives span multiple departments and regions.

The "Operational excellence" theme emphasizes cost reductions for high-volume, commoditized products. For these products, competition is not about superior product technology or being the supplier of choice; business is won on price, safety, consistent quality, and reliability. It also requires initiatives to drive world-class manufacturing, quality systems, and supply-chain and cost improvement through new capital expenditures.

LGC realized that it could not deliver an operationally excellent value proposition with processes designed for product leadership and innovation. The company adopted a "focused factory" approach so that each of its worldwide plants would concentrate on one of the value propositions. For example, it moved the production of all the low-margin aluminum cylinders into plants designed and optimized for high-volume production of mature products.

The "Learning and growth" theme includes objectives related to environment, structural alignment, performance management, company values, and pride. It emphasizes how LGC deals with its people and how people deal with each other.

Note that LGC's themes are based on activities and core competencies, not functions. Marketing is not a theme, but "Customer focus" is. Human resources is not a theme, but "Learning and growth" is. Themes do not replace functions.

Candidly, not all managers walked the talk after they returned to their local regional units. Several reverted to their narrow regional or functional focus. As Rhodes anticipated when launching the new strategy in 2003, he had to do some housecleaning and make management changes. The remaining executives clearly understood the global strategic priorities and committed themselves with actions as well as words to the new strategy based on cross-functional themes. Rhodes' willingness to take tough,

FIGURE 3-6

Luxfer Gas Cylinders' strategic road map, organized by strategic themes

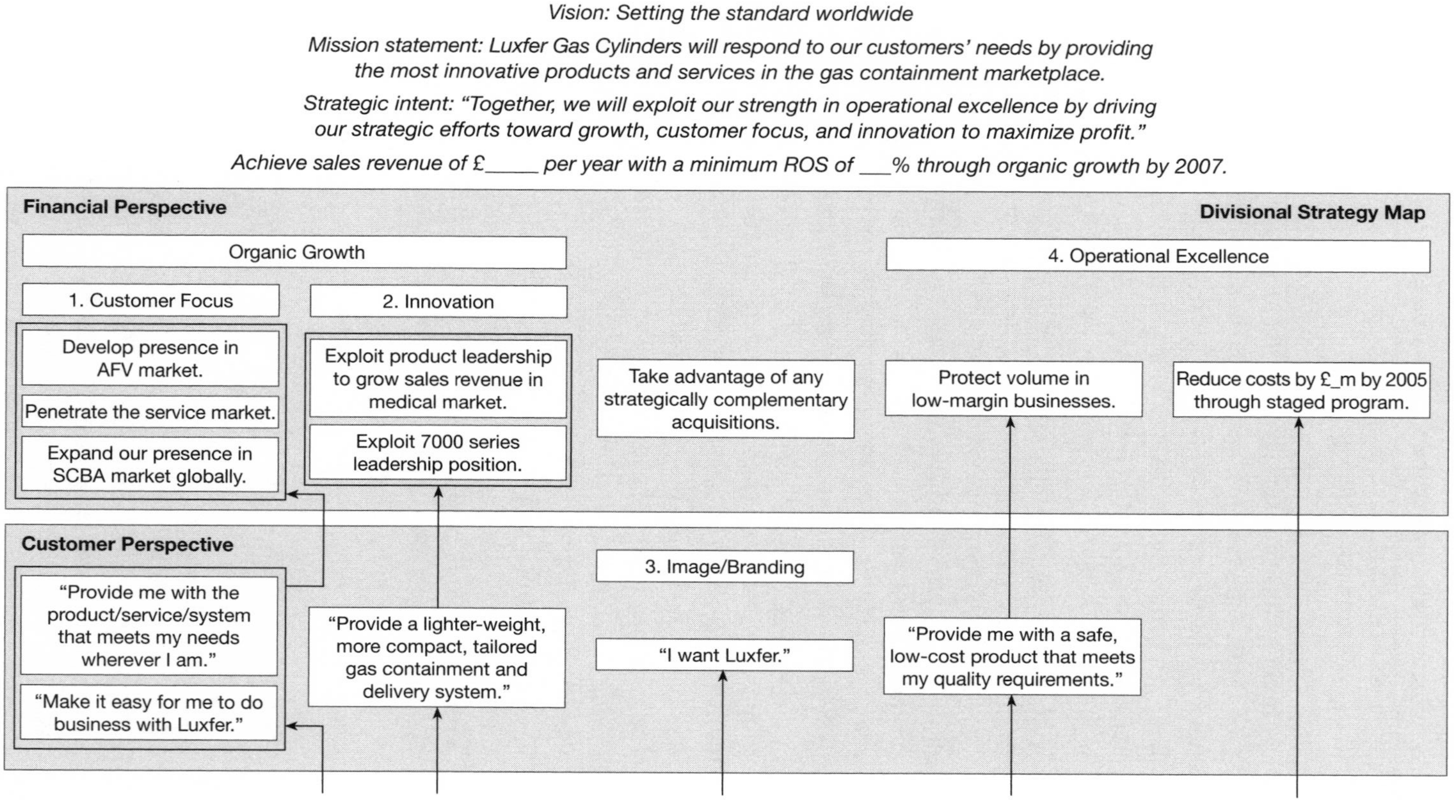

Vision: Setting the standard worldwide

Mission statement: Luxfer Gas Cylinders will respond to our customers' needs by providing the most innovative products and services in the gas containment marketplace.

Strategic intent: "Together, we will exploit our strength in operational excellence by driving our strategic efforts toward growth, customer focus, and innovation to maximize profit."

Achieve sales revenue of £____ per year with a minimum ROS of ___% through organic growth by 2007.

Divisional Strategy Map

Financial Perspective

Organic Growth

1. Customer Focus

Develop presence in AFV market.

Penetrate the service market.

Expand our presence in SCBA market globally.

2. Innovation

Exploit product leadership to grow sales revenue in medical market.

Exploit 7000 series leadership position.

Take advantage of any strategically complementary acquisitions.

4. Operational Excellence

Protect volume in low-margin businesses.

Reduce costs by £_m by 2005 through staged program.

Customer Perspective

3. Image/Branding

"I want Luxfer."

"Provide me with the product/service/system that meets my needs wherever I am."

"Make it easy for me to do business with Luxfer."

"Provide a lighter-weight, more compact, tailored gas containment and delivery system."

"Provide me with a safe, low-cost product that meets my quality requirements."

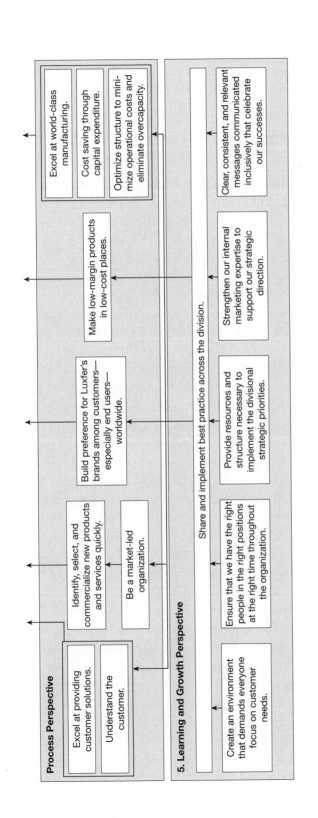

Process Perspective

Excel at providing customer solutions.

Understand the customer.

Identify, select, and commercialize new products and services quickly.

Be a market-led organization.

Build preference for Luxfer's brands among customers—especially end users—worldwide.

Make low-margin products in low-cost places.

Excel at world-class manufacturing.

Cost saving through capital expenditure.

Optimize structure to minimize operational costs and eliminate overcapacity.

5. Learning and Growth Perspective

Share and implement best practice across the division.

Create an environment that demands everyone focus on customer needs.

Ensure that we have the right people in the right positions at the right time throughout the organization.

Provide resources and structure necessary to implement the divisional strategic priorities.

Strengthen our internal marketing expertise to support our strategic direction.

Clear, consistent, and relevant messages communicated inclusively that celebrate our successes.

decisive action to counter organizational inertia and the resistance to change from several individuals provides another example of how successful strategy execution requires strong leadership at the top.

Case Study on Strategic Themes in the Public Sector: The Strategy Map for Brazil's Economic Development

The Confederation of National Industries (CNI) in Brazil has led one of the most innovative and complex applications of theme-based strategy maps. CNI is an association of private-sector organizations seeking to improve the competitiveness of Brazilian industry. CNI lobbies for a better business environment, pro-market economic policies, good regulations, and a sound investment climate.

Jorge Gerdau, chairman of the Gerdau Steel Group and member of a CNI board, in a conversation with CNI president, Armando Monteiro, about the long-term perspectives of Brazil and the role of the private sector, suggested the use of the Balanced Scorecard to help push an agenda for growth. They wanted to reverse the continued poor performance of the Brazilian economy over decades. GDP growth had averaged only 0.7 percent per year, a growth rate that would require one hundred years for Brazil to reach the per capita income currently enjoyed by countries like Portugal. The low growth of the economy hindered Brazil's capacity to generate jobs and to foster the development of a fairer, equal-opportunity society.

Gerdau had already led a highly successful, Balanced Scorecard Hall of Fame program at Gerdau Steel.[4] He believed that a strategy map and scorecard at the national level could clearly define a coherent economic and social development agenda for Brazil that could be translated into action. CNI appointed its main policy advisory council, The National Industry Forum, to define the agenda and develop an execution program. Led by a consulting team from Symnetics, The Forum's fifty business leaders prepared an initial strategy map design for Brazil's economic development. They then shared the map and received feedback from more than three hundred people, including employees in The Forum companies, CNI councils, and staff. They produced a revised strategy map, as shown in Figure 3-7.

Brazil has a population of almost 200 million people. Yet its strategy map for sustainable social and economic development fit on one piece of paper. The label at the top of the map describes the vision that inspires the strategy: "Sustainable Economic Development" for the country. The map translates the vision into five tangible results, which are the high-level objectives for the strategy (the public-sector version of shareholder value):

FIGURE 3-7

Economic development strategy for the country of Brazil

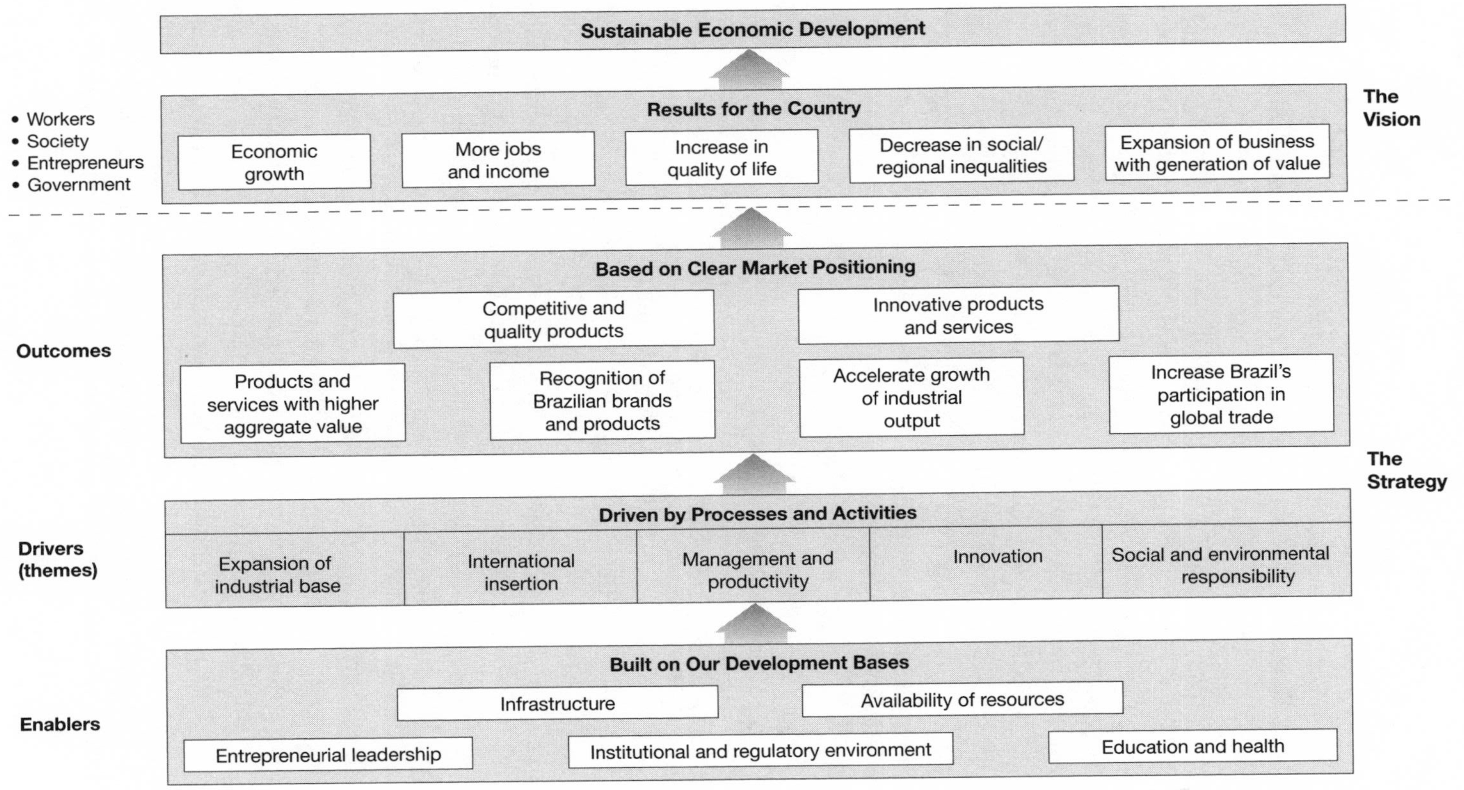

Sustainable Economic Development

The Vision

- Workers
- Society
- Entrepreneurs
- Government

Results for the Country

Economic growth	More jobs and income	Increase in quality of life	Decrease in social/ regional inequalities	Expansion of business with generation of value

The Strategy

Based on Clear Market Positioning

Outcomes

| Products and services with higher aggregate value | Competitive and quality products | Recognition of Brazilian brands and products | Innovative products and services | Accelerate growth of industrial output | Increase Brazil's participation in global trade |

Driven by Processes and Activities

Drivers (themes)

| Expansion of industrial base | International insertion | Management and productivity | Innovation | Social and environmental responsibility |

Built on Our Development Bases

Enablers

| Entrepreneurial leadership | Infrastructure | Institutional and regulatory environment | Availability of resources | Education and health |

- Economic growth reaching annual levels of 5.5 percent by 2010 and 7 percent by 2015
- More jobs and income for the citizens
- An increase in the quality of life
- A decrease in social and regional inequalities
- Expansion of businesses that generate sustainable value

Shown below these five high-level objectives are the strategic outcomes expected to deliver the desired results. CNI believed that only the private sector can generate sustained economic growth: "A climate which is unfavorable to investments discourages business persons and creates obstacles for generating the jobs that will finance social expenses and services for the benefit of society. Corporations are the engine of growth."[5]

For Brazil to achieve the desired results, the strategy map indicates a requirement to create a "clear market positioning" for Brazilian companies. The positioning would be measured by several business outcomes, including the following:

- Competitive and quality products
- Innovative products and services
- Products and services with higher aggregate value
- Recognition of Brazilian brands
- Accelerated growth of industrial output
- Increased participation by Brazil in global trade

The outcomes are driven by five drivers, or strategic themes: expansion of the industrial base, international insertion, management and productivity, innovation, and social and environmental responsibility. Supporting the key processes within these five strategic themes is a set of enablers, which the CNI collected under the theme, "Built on Our Development Bases," an equivalent to the BSC learning and growth perspective. This included infrastructure, availability of resources, entrepreneurial leadership, institutional and regulatory environment, and education and health.

The strategy map described in Figure 3-7 provides the overall architecture but by itself is not sufficient for execution. That requires another level of detail. Figure 3-8 shows how, for the innovation theme, the project team developed specific strategic objectives and the cause-and-effect linkages between them. The innovation theme is designed to create country-level results—economic growth, more jobs and income, and expansion of businesses that generate value—through two business outcomes: innovative

FIGURE 3-8

Cause-and-effect relations for Brazil's innovation theme

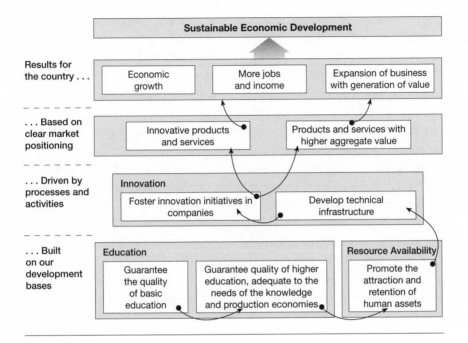

products and services, and products with higher aggregate value. These outcomes link to innovation programs and several learning and growth enablers. The cause-and-effect logic illustrated in Figure 3-8 clearly defines the set of activities and their interrelationships required to execute the innovation theme of the strategy.

This succinct description of Brazil's economic development strategy enabled the nation's leaders, for the first time, to clearly communicate the desired direction for the country. More than twenty thousand copies of the "Brazil Economic Development Strategy Map" have been printed and distributed. It has been presented on TV shows, radio, and newspapers and to targeted audiences including national ministers, supreme court justices, universities, and the business community.

CNI recognized that implementing the national strategy would require the cooperation of a broad audience. It created a new unit, called Institutional Relations, and redefined the role of its Operations Unit, with both reporting directly to the CEO. This change in structure had two goals: to increase the effectiveness of the strategy execution process and to deliver on the strategy map objective to build stronger coalitions with various stakeholders (such as government ministries and entrepreneurs) by aligning their efforts and putting pressure on them to accelerate the implementation of strategic projects. José Augusto Coelho Fernandes, executive director of CNI, observed, "The strategy map goals are beyond CNI's internal goals. It is a strategy for industry and for the country. As the execution is not under CNI's control, its main result will be that we can look back and say that we did our best. We could not control the results but we had a strategy and we managed it to be successful. The strategy map will certainly increase the probability of strategy implementation regarding social and economic outcomes."[6]

In summary, strategy maps provide a clear picture of both the desired outcomes of the strategy (in the financial and customer perspectives) and the critical processes and enabling infrastructure (people, systems, and culture) required to achieve those outcomes. When strategic themes are used as foundational building blocks, the strategy map becomes easier to communicate and understand. The themes more clearly indicate the causal hypotheses within the strategy and also provide a powerful structure for resource allocation, accountability, alignment, and reporting.

SELECT MEASURES AND TARGETS

The strategic themes clarify the logic of the strategy. They subdivide the overall strategy into logical, manageable, and understandable substrategies consisting of linked objectives within each theme. The next step in the strategy planning process establishes measures and targets for each objective.

Selecting Measures for Strategic Objectives

Our original objective when introducing the Balanced Scorecard in 1992 was to provide managers with a broader (more "balanced") set of measures for driving long-term value creation. Our interest in measurement as a way to drive performance improvements arose from a belief articulated more than a century earlier by a prominent British scientist, Lord Kelvin: "I often say that when you can measure what you are speaking about, and express it in numbers, you know something about it; but when you cannot measure it, when you cannot express it in numbers, your knowledge is of a meager and unsatisfactory kind."[7] If you cannot measure it, you cannot improve it.

We believed that measurement was as fundamental for managers as Lord Kelvin believed it was for scientists. If companies are to improve the management of their customer relationships, their operational and inno-vation processes, and their intangible assets (such as people, systems, and culture), they need to integrate the measurement of these items into their management system.

Strategic objectives and strategy maps clarify, in words and diagrams, the organization's objectives for the delivery of short- and long-term per-formance. But following Lord Kelvin's advice, we still need to make strategic objectives more meaningful and actionable by selecting mea-sures for them.

For example, consider Figure 3-9, which shows the strategy map for a bank's customer management strategic theme. For each strategic objective on the map, managers must select at least one measure. The act of mea-surement reduces the inherent ambiguity of language, such as, "Increase

FIGURE 3-9

The Balanced Scorecard provides actionable measures and targets for the customer management strategic theme

Strategy Map for a Customer Management Theme	Balanced Scorecard		
Objectives	**Measures**	**Targets**	
Broaden revenue mix	• Revenue mix	New = +10%	**Objective:** What the strategy is trying to achieve
	• Revenue growth	+25%	**Measure:** How success or failure (performance) against objectives is monitored
Increase customer confidence in our financial advice	• Share of segment	25%	
	• Share of wallet	50%	**Target:** The level of performance or rate of improvement needed by the strategy
	• Customer satisfaction	90%	
Cross-sell the product line	• Cross-sell ratio	2.5	
	• Hours with customer	1hr/Q	
Strategic job — Financial planner	• Human capital readiness	100%	
Strategic systems — Portfolio planning	• Strategic application readiness	100%	
Create organization readiness	• Goals linked to BSC	100%	

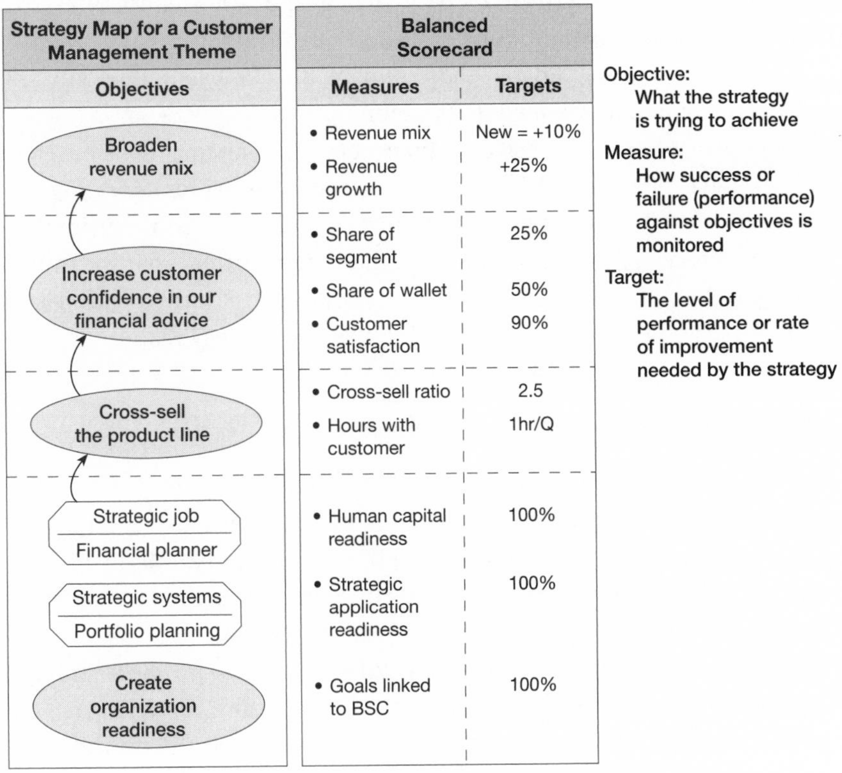

consumer confidence in our financial advice" and "Create organization readiness." Measures and associated targets express the objective in specific terms and enable the tracking of the organization's progress in achieving that strategic objective.

We remain committed to the importance of measurement. We have written extensively about it in our earlier articles and books. At this time, however, we don't have a great deal new to say about measurement. The focus of this book is to embed the performance measurement system into a comprehensive and integrated system for managing strategy and operations. So rather than recapitulate our prior writings on selecting measures, we refer you back to two earlier books—*The Balanced Scorecard* and *Strategy Maps*—where we discuss measurement in considerable detail.[8]

Selecting Targets

In developing targets for Balanced Scorecard measures, managers face the challenge of splitting the value gap established at the highest level (e.g., shareholder value) into logically consistent targets for customer, process, and learning and growth metrics, such as the performance of critical processes and the capabilities of key employees. Targets are consistent if their achievement will enable the company to close its value gap and achieve the outcome specified in its vision.

In contrast to our extensive writings about measurement, we have not written a great deal about how to set targets for measures. Selecting targets is a difficult task, although we have accumulated some insights to guide the process. Two techniques facilitate target setting: split the overall value gap into targets for each strategic theme, and set targets within each theme based on the cause-and-effect logic of the strategy map.

Assigning the Value Gap to Strategic Themes

Target setting originates in the vision statement, when the leader sets a high-level stretch target—a BHAG—for the organization. The target creates a *value gap* between aspiration and current reality: what would be achieved by continuing with the status quo, including the existing strategy. The strategy must close this value gap.

Executives can split the value gap into subtargets for each strategic theme. The themes create value in different ways, and, in aggregate, the values created by the individual themes should sum to the overall value gap. The targets established for each theme reflect the theme's relative impact on helping create and deliver the various components of the strategy.

For example, Consumer Bank, a composite of many retail banks we have worked with, established a value gap to increase its current operating income of $20 million by more than $100 million during the next five years (see Figure 3-10). At first, managers and employees were incredulous about closing this ambitious gap. Splitting the target among three strategic themes, however, enabled the company to demonstrate how the gap could be closed if each theme contributed its assigned share.

First, Consumer Bank set a target for the operational excellence theme to reduce the cost to serve each customer by 25 percent, while still delivering more consistent services. Second, it established a target for the customer relationship theme to raise revenue per customer by 50 percent by becoming the trusted financial planner for targeted customers and cross-selling them multiple banking products and services. For example, customers following the financial plan would purchase an integrated suite of financial products and services, including time and savings deposits, lending programs, insurance, brokerage, investments, and periodic financial planning updates. Third, the bank set a target for the growth through innovation theme to attract 400,000 new customers through superior performance and innovative products. If each theme delivered its targeted performance, the ambitious value gap would indeed be closed.

FIGURE 3-10

Decomposing the value gap into financial targets at Consumer Bank

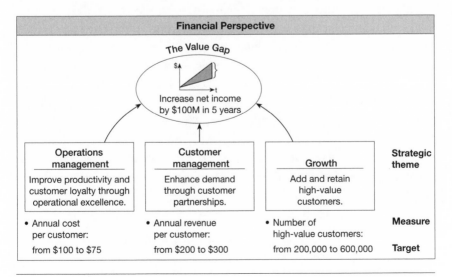

Consumer Bank forecast that its three strategic themes would deliver benefits over different periods of time, as shown in Figure 3-11. The operational efficiency theme was expected to generate its cost saving benefits relatively quickly, with 80 percent of the targeted savings realized in the first two years. Revenue enhancements from deepening relationships with existing customers would take somewhat longer, yielding most of the benefits in years 3 and 4. Growing the customer base through innovative new products and an enhanced brand image would take the longest time.

The timetable for results, by strategic theme, enabled managers to customize each strategic theme's performance targets based on realistic estimates of the time required for each to deliver benefits. By the end of year 5, if all three strategic themes achieved their targets, the company would reach its financial goal, specified in the value gap, for operating income to increase by more than $100 million from the current $20 million level.

Case Study on Target Setting: Cigna Property and Casualty

Recall (from Chapter 2) the vision set forth by the Cigna Property and Casualty division to achieve top-quartile industry profitability. With its current position at the bottom of the fourth quartile, the division needed dramatic improvements in its *combined ratio*, defined as the ratio of cash outflows from expenses and claims payouts to cash inflows from premiums. Cigna P&C's combined ratio at the start of its journey was 140; the ratio for a top-quartile performer was 103. Thus, Cigna P&C's new strategy had to close a combined ratio value gap of 37 points within five years.

Figure 3-12 illustrates how Cigna addressed the two high-level questions all managers ask: *where* the dramatic improvements to close the combined ratio value gap would occur, and *when* these improvements were expected to occur. The executive team split the overall strategy into four strategic themes, each representing a relatively independent value-creating process. The team estimated how much each of the four themes could contribute to closing the value gap, and the timetable for each theme's progress during the five year horizon of the strategy. This first pass showed the feasibility of achieving the vision's stretch target and laid the groundwork for detailed thinking about the objectives, measures, and targets within each of the four strategic themes.

Case Study on Target Setting: Ricoh

The experience of Ricoh provides another example of splitting a value gap into smaller, achievable substrategies at the start of the strategic planning

FIGURE 3-11

Establishing the value time line at Consumer Bank

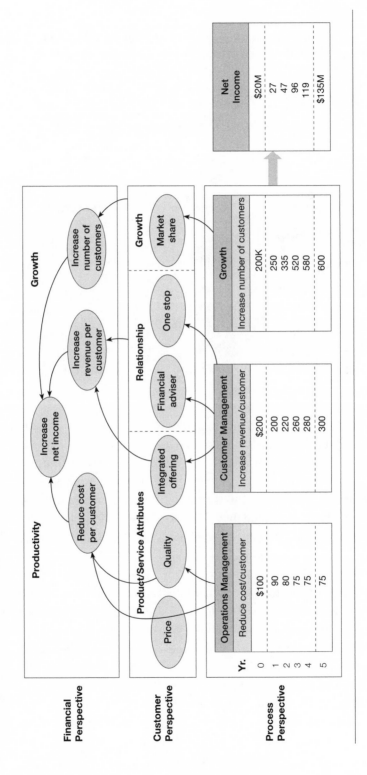

FIGURE 3-12

Cigna decomposed its combined ratio value gap into four themes around which they developed realistic stretch targets

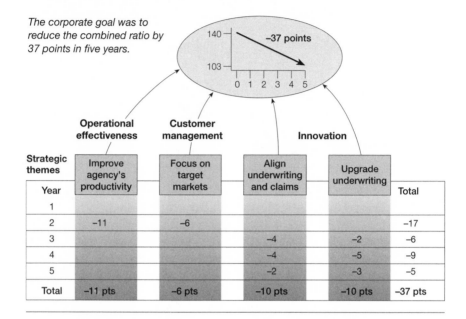

Strategic themes	Operational effectiveness	Customer management	Innovation		
Year	Improve agency's productivity	Focus on target markets	Align underwriting and claims	Upgrade underwriting	Total
1					
2	−11	−6			−17
3			−4	−2	−6
4			−4	−5	−9
5			−2	−3	−5
Total	−11 pts	−6 pts	−10 pts	−10 pts	−37 pts

process. As described in Chapter 1, Ricoh uses a formal planning process based on three-year plans, known as the Mid-Term Plan (MTP). In planning for the fifteenth MTP (encompassing April 2005 to March 2008), Chairman and CEO Susumu "Sam" Ichioka established an ambitious revenue growth target and mobilized four strategic teams to define key strategies and ultimately targets for each to achieve the aggregate sales target. Ichioka's ambitious challenge created a strong sense of urgency throughout Ricoh's leadership team.

Figure 3-13 summarizes the key elements of the strategy. The small matrix in the upper-left corner illustrates the simple logic of the strategy: growth through a combination of organic growth, new customers, new channels, and new products and services. The first strategic theme was "Organic growth," to be achieved by improving the quality of sales of existing products and services through current dealers and direct channels. The second theme, "Channel expansion," focused on the incremental sales generated by the addition of new dealers. "New products," the third theme, would generate growth by introducing new products and services to the dealer network, and the fourth theme, "New channels," would generate sales from new markets and alliances.

FIGURE 3-13

Ricoh decomposed its value gap into four themes

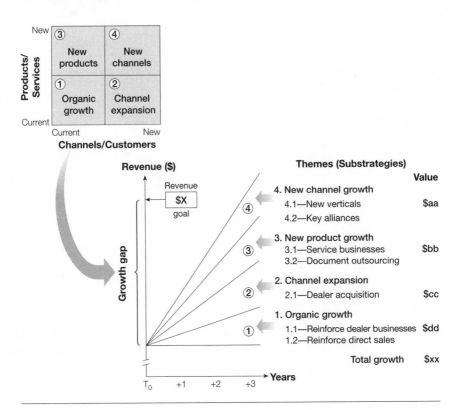

Over the next three years, the four strategies in aggregate would deliver sales growth sufficient to close the value gap established by the CEO. With key executives leading each of the four strategic themes, Ichioka had effectively mobilized the organization to formulate a new strategy to deliver breakthrough performance.

Using Cause-and-Effect Logic to Set Targets

The targets for each strategic theme need to be further subdivided into targets for the strategic objectives within the theme. The target for objectives within a strategic theme should not be set in isolation. Each target should be related to targets for other theme objectives in a chain of cause-and-effect logic.

Consider the customer service strategic theme illustrated in Figure 3-14. The target-setting process (shown on the right) starts with the value

FIGURE 3-14

Establishing targets based on cause-effect scenarios

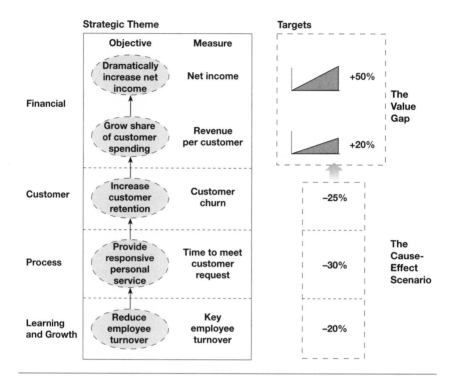

gap—a 50 percent improvement in net income—that the strategy must close. The theme's financial subobjective is to increase revenue per customer by 20 percent. This increase will contribute to achieving the targeted improvement in net income. From the many strategies that could accomplish this goal, the organization decides to focus on increasing customer retention by providing higher levels of responsive personal service. The improved customer service, in turn, requires an increase in the competency of the staff, an objective that can be achieved by reducing the departure of high-quality people. The linked hypotheses are that a 20 percent reduction in key employee turnover will deliver a 30 percent improvement in service levels. Such service improvements will reduce customer turnover by 25 percent, which, in turn, will generate the desired 20 percent increase in revenue per customer.

The cause-and-effect links in Figure 3-14 provide a bottom-up, clear, logical test of the strategy's feasibility. If the company deems the proposed strategy to be feasible, it launches the cause-and-effect scenario by developing initiatives to reduce turnover of key employees, which should create the sequence of events culminating in reduced customer churn and increased revenue of the desired amount.

Benchmarking Targets

Establishing the specific targets for the various strategic objectives remains a judgment call, especially the first time through the process. As organizations gain experience with a measure, they will better understand its properties and feasible rates of improvement.

External benchmarks for performance measures can be useful, but they need to be treated with care to ensure that the company's circumstances are comparable to the conditions under which the external performance occurred.[9] For the example illustrated in Figure 3-14, external benchmarks would likely be available for measures in all four perspectives. The company could attempt to learn, from public data and trade association or consultants' databases, the percentile performance it is trying to achieve in those measures. Are the targets at the 75th percentile performance level, or the 99th percentile level? These data establish the degree of stretch in the company's targets, assuming that circumstances are similar between the company and those in the external benchmarking survey.

Private-sector companies start their external benchmarking in the financial perspective. Because most competitors are likely to be public companies, the company has ready access to the detailed financial performance of others in its industry. Companies should strive for performance that will make them among the best in the industry in metrics such as return on capital, revenue growth, operating margins, and productivity. They should strive to be number 1 or 2 in such measures, or at least to achieve top-quartile or top-quintile performance, especially if their current performance is less than the industry median. Public-sector or nonprofit enterprises often access public data on financial performance of comparable organizations, such as ratios of operating expenses to the spending that directly benefits constituents.

Some customer outcome metrics, such as improvements in market share or growth in account share, are, by definition, externally focused and benchmarked against competitors. Companies can also ask key customers to rank their performance relative to that of competitive suppliers. The stretch target for that metric would be "to become (or remain) our customers' number 1 ranked supplier."

Companies with large numbers of homogeneous outlets, such as retail-store chains, hotels, banks, and quick-service restaurants, can use statistical analysis to determine their targets for processes and employee capabilities. This is an example of *internal benchmarking*. For example, we describe in Chapter 6 how a Canadian bank used multiple regression analysis on data collected from its hundreds of branches to set targets for each branch. The coefficients from the regression analysis measured the rates of increases in profitability, customer satisfaction, and loyalty that are associated with improvements in process performance and employee satisfaction. The bank used these coefficients proactively to estimate the levels of process and employee performance that were required, branch by branch, to yield the desired levels of customer and financial performance.

Companies can also use external, best-in-class benchmarks as targets for their process metrics, especially those related to the cost, quality, and cycle times of key processes. For example, suppose a retail bank has identified the approval of mortgages or loans as a key process. The bank might set a target to offer the shortest response time—from customer application to credit approval—in the industry. Another bank might strive to match or exceed the lowest ATM downtime percentage in the industry. Or a bank might wish to have the highest yield of new customers acquired through its promotional activities. For an innovation process, a manufacturing or software company might set a target of having the shortest product development times in the industry, measured from the time of idea generation to the time of commercial product availability. To use such external benchmarks for these key processes, of course, the company must have access to industry or trade association data, subscribe to a benchmarking service, or lead or participate in benchmarking studies.

Case Study on Target Setting:
Vista Retail

Vista Retail (disguised) uses internal benchmarking among its large number of retail outlets to establish targets for its Balanced Scorecard measures, which include the following:

- Earnings before interest, taxes, depreciation, and amortization (EBITDA)
- Revenue per outlet compared to competitors
- Customer loyalty
- Employee loyalty

Annually, Vista compares the performance of each of its more than one thousand outlets to that of the top performer for each measure. The difference between the two is the *gap to perfection*, a portion of which must be closed during the next year. Vista sets a corporate target for its properties to close the gap to perfection by a specified percentage—say, 25 percent—each year. For example, suppose a low-performing outlet has a current score of 45 on a particular metric, whereas the best performance score for a comparable property is 89. In this case, next year's target for the low-performing outlet would be

$$45 + [0.25 \times (89 - 45)] = 56$$

This approach acknowledges that Rome was not built in a day. Each outlet has stretch, but still achievable, goals. Vista's gap-to-perfection target-setting process also recognizes that it may be more difficult to realize improvements as outlets approach performance perfection. An outlet with a current rating of 75 would have next year's target at 78.5, a much lower percentage improvement than a low-performing outlet would be asked to achieve.

In addition to setting the targets based on achievable performance within its system, Vista identifies and studies the practices of its highest-scoring outlets. It then uses this knowledge to transfer best practices across the organization (we discuss best practice sharing more extensively in Chapter 6). Thus, an outlet not only calibrates its own targets against those of the best performers but also learns about the management practices of the high-performance units.

Case Study on Target Setting:
Mobil US Marketing and Refining

Setting stretch targets for strategic theme metrics is one thing. Having managers internalize the stretch targets and strive to achieve them is quite another task, perhaps a stretch target in its own right. Several companies have motivated managers to buy in to stretch targets by linking performance bonus percentages to the degree of stretch in the target.

Mobil US Marketing and Refining had managers establish targets for each Balanced Scorecard measure and also estimate a performance factor that represented the perceived degree of difficulty of target achievement. The maximum index score of 1.25 occurred when the target represented best-in-class industry performance. An average target received a performance factor of 1.00, and a factor score as low as 0.7 would be applied when the target represented poor performance or was deemed very easy to achieve.

Executives in the individual business units proposed the performance factors for each measure and explained and defended them in a meeting attended by the executive leadership team and the heads of shared-service units. Collectively, this group had a great deal of knowledge about each business and the degree of stretch in any proposed target, knowledge that served to discipline the optimism that managers might otherwise have built in to their performance factors.

Mobil US Marketing and Refining multiplied the performance factor by the actual value of the measure to arrive at a total performance score, in much the way a diving competition is scored. In a diving competition, someone who attempts an easy dive may execute it flawlessly and be awarded the top score of 10 on artistic merit. But because the degree of difficulty was low (say, 0.8), the total number of points awarded to the dive will be low (8). Another competitor may try an extremely difficult dive (triple reverse with two and a half spins, a difficulty factor of 2.8) and do it satisfactorily but not perfectly (and receive a score of 7.1), thereby earning a much higher total score (19.9) for the dive. Establishing performance factors based on degree of difficulty helps compensate unit managers on a more level playing field, with the targets' degree of difficulty made comparable across diverse geographical and product units.

Another aspect of setting a stretch target is to reward managers even if they fall a little short of achieving the target. Otherwise, managers will sandbag the target, selecting one that they are quite confident they can achieve, rather than risk falling a little short of a stretch target.[10] To mitigate the sandbagging effect, the payoff should be nonlinear with performance, but not binary. Managers who fall, say, 10 percent short of the target may experience a 30 to 50 percent reduction in payoff. But the partial payoff motivates managers to come as close to the target as possible, even when they expect their performance to fall somewhat short of it.

As a brief extension of the Brazilian CNI strategy map (shown earlier in Figure 3-7), the CNI team developed, for each strategic theme, a set of measures and targets. For example, the measure for the strategic objective "Foster innovation initiatives in companies" was "Private investment in innovation as a percent of GDP." The team set a target for this measure to increase the current level of 0.6 percent (in 2007) to 1.4 percent by 2015. The targets for many of the measures on the CNI strategy map came from the actual experience of comparable but best-practice countries around the world.

SUMMARY

In this chapter, we plan the strategy, formulated during the process described in Chapter 2. First, we translate the strategy into theme-based strategy maps, with linked objectives describing how value is to be created within each theme. We also describe how to select targets for each strategic theme, consistent with achieving the company's vision, and the targets for each Balanced Scorecard measure associated with each strategic objective.

The use of a strategy map as the organizing framework is the distinguishing feature of our strategy development and planning approach. Most approaches to strategy development focus on the desired *outcome* of the strategy. For example, the strategy describes the customer value proposition that the organization intends to offer to satisfy the customer's needs and also the niche in which the organization will compete. But the statement of the value proposition does not address how it will be achieved. Most of the popular approaches to business strategy define the *what* but not the *how*. A complete strategy should define the what and the how—or, in our terminology, the desired outcomes and the drivers of the outcomes.

The structure of a strategy map provides a comprehensive and logical framework for designing and executing a strategy. The strategy map is a managerial breakthrough that allows organizations to manage strategy more effectively and to achieve the execution premium from a successful implementation.

STRATEGY MAPS

A strategy map (see figure 3-A1) describes the process of value creation through a series of cause-and-effect linkages among objectives in the four Balanced Scorecard perspectives.[11]

- The ultimate goal of an organization is to create long-term value for shareholders (private sector) or stakeholders (public sector).
- Organization value is created by satisfying a customer value proposition.
- Internal processes create and deliver the value that satisfies customers, and they also contribute to the financial perspective's productivity objectives.
- Intangible assets (people, technology, and culture) drive performance improvements in the critical processes that deliver value to customers and shareholders.

The *financial perspective* describes the tangible outcomes of the strategy using familiar metrics such as return on investment, economic value added, operating profits, revenue per customer, and cost per unit produced. These outcomes or lagging indicators signal whether the strategy is working to deliver tangible results to shareholders.

The *customer perspective* includes customer outcome measures, such as satisfaction, retention, and growth, as well as metrics for the value proposition selected for targeted customer segments. The value proposition is the heart of the strategy. It describes how the company will differentiate itself in the eyes of the customer. It also defines the context for the rest of the strategy. A value proposition based on achieving the lowest cost for

FIGURE 3-A1

The strategy map describes the way the organization intends to create value for its stakeholders

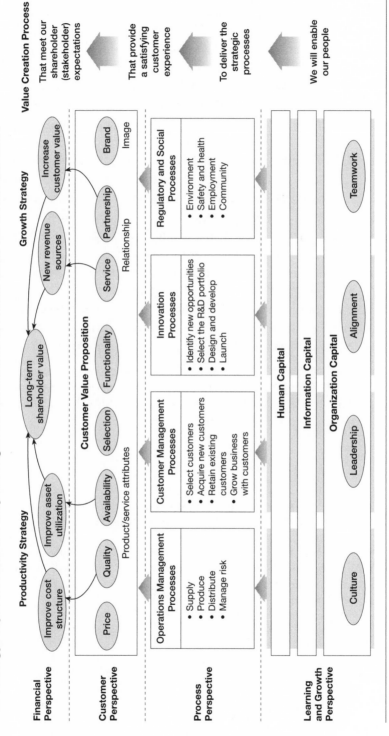

customers requires excellence in very different processes and human capital than does a value proposition intended to provide complete and customized customer solutions.

Together, the financial and customer perspectives in strategy maps and Balanced Scorecards describe what the organization hopes to achieve: increases in shareholder value through revenue growth and productivity improvements, and increases in the company's share of customers' spending through customer acquisition, satisfaction, retention, loyalty, and growth.

The *process perspective* identifies the critical few business processes that will satisfy the customer and financial objectives. Organizations perform hundreds of processes, from meeting the payroll and publishing quarterly financial statements to maintaining equipment and facilities and inventing new products. Although all processes must be performed adequately, only a few create the real differentiation for the strategy. The strategy map should identify those key processes so that managers and employees can focus on continually improving them.

The *learning and growth perspective* identifies the jobs (human capital), systems (information capital), and climate (organization capital) that support the value-creating processes. Taken together, objectives in two perspectives— the process perspective and the learning and growth perspective—describe how the organization will implement its strategy.

The strategy map's visualization of the causal relationships among strategic objectives has been widely adopted and is the starting point for all Balanced Scorecard projects.

NOTES

1. R. S. Kaplan and D. P. Norton, *Strategy Maps: Converting Intangible Assets into Tangible Outcomes* (Boston: Harvard Business School Press, 2004); and Kaplan and Norton, *The Strategy-Focused Organization* (Boston: Harvard Business School Press, 2000).
2. *Account share* is the company's share of a customer's spending in its category; e.g., share of financial transactions, share of wardrobe purchased, share of food or beverages consumed.
3. "Balanced Scorecard European Summit," Prague, June 2007.
4. "Gerdau Açominas," in *Balanced Scorecard Hall of Fame Report 2007* (Boston: Harvard Business School Publishing, 2007), 19–20.
5. "Growth: The Industry's Vision," National Confederation of Industry, Brasilia, 2006.
6. José Augusto Coelho Fernandes, speaking at BSC North American summit, San Diego, November 2006.
7. Lord Kelvin [William Thomson], "Electrical Units of Measurement," in *Popular Lectures and Addresses*, vol. 1 (London and New York: Macmillan and Co., 1894).

8. R. S. Kaplan and D. P. Norton, *The Balanced Scorecard: Translating Strategy into Action* (Boston: Harvard Business School Press, 1996), and Kaplan and Norton, *Strategy Maps*.

9. R. S. Kaplan, "Limits to Benchmarking," *Balanced Scorecard Report* (HBS Publishing Newsletter), November 2005.

10. The original meaning of *sandbagging* was literal: using bags filled with sand for protection against floods, gunfire, and explosions. It has come to mean the concealment of one's strengths to gain an advantage over a competitor. Sandbagging has come to be associated with the practice of deliberately understating your best estimate of a future outcome so that actual performance will almost surely be better than others have been led to expect.

11. Kaplan and Norton, "Strategy Maps," Chapter 3 in *The Strategy-Focused Organization*.

CHAPTER FOUR

STRATEGIC INITIATIVES

Launching the Strategy into Motion

IN CHAPTER 3, we described how to translate a strategy into strategic themes, objectives, measures, and targets that represent *what* the organization wants to accomplish. Strategic initiatives represent the *how*. Newton's First Law applied to organizations states that an organization at rest will remain at rest. Newton's Second Law states that a force is needed to accelerate a mass into motion. Strategic initiatives represent the force that accelerates an organizational mass into action, overcoming inertia and resistance to change. *Strategic initiatives* are the collections of finite-duration discretionary projects and programs, outside the organization's day-to-day operational activities, that are designed to help the organization achieve its targeted performance.

Although the need for linking the long-term strategy to immediate action plans seems obvious, our survey of management practices, reported in Chapter 1, indicates that 50 percent of organizations do not link strategy to short-term plans and budgets. A senior executive summarized many executives' frustration with the lack of strategic alignment between strategy and action plans when he said, "Half my initiatives achieve strategic goals. I just don't know which half."

Organizations use three processes to manage their portfolios of strategic initiatives, as summarized in Figure 4-1: select initiatives, provide resources for them, and assign accountability for executing them. We discuss each in turn.

FIGURE 4-1

Initiative management process model

Initiative Management Process	Objective	Barriers	Enabling Tools
1. Choose Strategic Initiatives *What action programs does our strategy need?*	To define the portfolio of initiatives needed to close each of the performance gaps	Strategic investments are justified on a stand-alone basis in different parts of the organization.	• Portfolios of initiatives for each strategic theme
2. Fund the Strategy *How do we fund our initiatives?*	To provide a source of funding for strategic initiatives that is separated from the operational budget	Cross-business portfolio funding is contrary to hierarchical, departmental structure of the budgeting process.	• STRATEX • Prioritized initiatives
3. Establish Accountability *Who will lead the execution of the strategic initiatives?*	To establish accountability for execution of cross-business strategic themes	Executive team members are generally responsible for managing within functional or business unit silos.	• Executive theme owners • Theme teams

CHOOSE STRATEGIC INITIATIVES

A strategic plan requires the coordinated management of multiple initiatives across the company, including processes that cross functions and business units. Yet in our original conception of the Balanced Scorecard, we encouraged companies to select initiatives independently for each strategic objective. Companies could perform a financial return analysis, such as net present value or return on investment—often combined with nonfinancial criteria, such as project risk, project duration, and cross-unit impact—to obtain a weighted index for ranking proposed initiatives. We came to realize, however, that selecting initiatives independently for each strategic objective ignored the integrated and cumulative impact of multiple related strategic initiatives.

Initiatives should not be selected in isolation from each other. Achieving a strategic objective in the customer or financial perspective generally requires multiple and complementary initiatives from various parts of the organization, such as human resources, information technology, marketing, distribution, and operations. We continue to recommend, as shown in Figure 4-2, that each nonfinancial objective have at least one initiative to

FIGURE 4-2

A portfolio of strategic initiatives should be developed for each theme

Strategic Initiative Portfolio

Strategy Map (Theme)	Balanced Scorecard		Action Plan	
	Measures	Targets	Initiative	Budget
Broaden revenue mix	• Revenue mix • Revenue growth	New = +10% +25%		
Increase customer confidence in our financial advice	• Share of segment • Share of wallet • Customer satisfaction	25% 50% 90%	• Segmentation initiative • Satisfaction survey	$XXX $XXX $XXX
Cross-sell the product line	• Cross-sell ratio • Hours with customer	2.5 1hr/Q	• Financial planning initiative • Integrated product offering	$XXX $XXX
Strategic job Financial planner	• Human capital readiness	100%	• Relationship management • Certified financial planner	$XXX $XXX
Strategic systems Portfolio planning	• Strategic application readiness	100%	• Integrated customer file • Portfolio planning application	$XXX $XXX
Create organization readiness	• Goals linked to BSC	100%	• MBO update • Incentive compensation	$XXX $XXX
			Total Budget	$XXX

drive its achievement but also that the initiatives be bundled for each strategic theme and considered as an integrated portfolio.

The customer management strategic theme shown in Figure 4-2 requires that the entire collection of initiatives be implemented if the theme is to achieve its performance objectives. For example, improving human capital readiness requires two initiatives: one to develop relationship management skills among employees, and the other to get employees accredited as certified financial planners. If these two initiatives are executed, they will achieve the target of 100 percent human capital readiness for employees who serve targeted customers.

However, if the initiatives for the other objectives are not effectively executed, the overall performance for this strategic theme will be degraded. Human capital readiness must be accompanied by the availability of new product offerings, new customer-centered information systems, and a new incentive system that will reward employees who create and grow complete customer relationships. A comprehensive program of managing portfolio initiatives requires the simultaneous implementation of all initiatives within a theme; any individual initiative is necessary but not sufficient.

Many companies can justifiably argue that they already have too many initiatives under way and that they don't have the financial or human resources to take on entire portfolios of new ones. But this is exactly the reason companies should first develop their strategy and strategic themes before deciding which initiatives they will accept. Consider, for example, the situation in the late 1990s in the online banking division of Wells Fargo.[1] This division was already the market leader in online banking and was continuing to experience explosive growth. Employees provided a continuing source of new initiatives, each of which seemed attractive, to support the division's rapid growth and market leadership position. At one point, the division had more than six hundred initiatives under way, and the senior management team met for a half day each week just to review and approve newly proposed initiatives, monitor the progress of existing ones, and decide which ones to cancel and how to reallocate people and funds among the remainder.

We continue to see many companies operating with the same problem of initiative explosion. It is a natural consequence of treating proposal and selection of initiatives as a sequence of individual and independent decisions, one that is not guided by a strategic framework. Companies get an immediate benefit from creating their first strategy map when they perform an initiative review and rationalization process, as shown in Figure 4-3.

In this exercise, managers create a matrix (a two-dimensional table) with BSC themes and objectives as rows, and existing initiatives as columns. For each existing initiative, they identify (with an x in the appropriate cell) those themes and objectives that are expected to improve significantly if the initiative is successfully completed.

As shown in Figure 4-3, one existing initiative has no impact on any strategic theme. Our experience suggests that as many as 20 to 30 percent of existing initiatives have this characteristic. These initiatives are prime candidates for consolidation or deletion, unless they are necessary to comply with regulatory requirements or provide short-term (less than a year) tangible financial paybacks through local operational improvements.

FIGURE 4-3

Companies test the alignment of their initiatives to strategic themes and objectives

Strategic Themes/ Initiative Portfolios (Programs/Projects)	Procurement redesign	Sales force training	Warehouse upgrade	Identification of quality needs	Product development funnel	Financial system restructuring	Customer call center connectivity	Initiative "n"
Enhance Service Delivery								
• Objective 1	X				X			
• Objective 2			*(Initiative serving no themes ↑↓)*					
Grow Partner Relationships								
• Objective 3			X				X	
• Objective 4								
Drive Future Value					X			
• Objective 5								
Meet Regulatory Standards			*(← Theme with no initiatives →)*					
Grow our customer focus capabilities								
• Objective 7		X					X	
• Objective 8								

This initiative rationalization process, which should be done as soon as the strategy map has been created, produces immediate financial savings that generally more than pay for the cost of implementing the BSC project. In the Wells Fargo online banking division, consolidating and delegating operational initiatives to various business and functional units reduced the number of initiatives actively supervised by the executive team from more than six hundred to about a dozen.

Similarly, despite having three or more times as many initiatives as objectives, companies find that some objectives may have no existing initiatives designed to improve them. These gaps identify the need for new strategic initiatives. Some of the best initiative ideas come from frontline employees. Once employees learn about the strategy through active communication of the strategy map and Balanced Scorecard, managers encourage and solicit them to generate new initiative ideas that can help the organization achieve its performance targets.

A designated group (typically a theme team, to be described in the next section) reviews all the new proposals that have been accumulated and conducts a formal assessment and ranking process.[2] Many organizations now have a standard initiative proposal template that includes the following:

- Description of the initiative
- The strategic theme or objective it is intended to support
- The expected results
- Resource, cost, and time requirements

The team then applies a formal process to evaluate and rank the initiatives. Figure 4-4 shows a typical process to screen existing and proposed initiatives and arrive at a quantitative score. The process has three criteria: strategic fit and benefit (weighted 50 percent), resource demands (weighted 30 percent), and organizational capability and risk (weighted 20 percent). Of course, each company should choose its own criteria and relative weighting.

Figure 4-5 describes a typical weighting scheme used to score an initiative on the three criteria in Figure 4-4. After scoring and ranking all

FIGURE 4-4

Scoring each initiative facilitates comparison

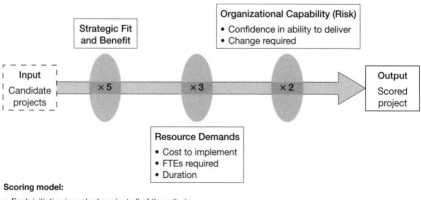

Scoring model:
- Each initiative is ranked against all of the criteria.
- The rating is then multiplied by the criterion's weight.
- The scores for the criteria are added together for the total score.

FIGURE 4-5

Scoring initiatives for a strategic theme's portfolio

Each initiative is scored on a 1 to 9 scale for the three criteria. Each criterion is weighted. The initiative's criterion score is multiplied by the criterion weight and summed across the criteria to arrive at a total score. The higher the score, the more promising the initiative.

Criterion 1 (50%) Strategic Relevance and Benefit	Criterion 2 (30%) Resource Demands	Criterion 3 (20%) Risks
• Screen for strategic relevance • Map to objectives and determine impact • Determine strategic benefit	**FTEs and** **Duration** **Cost** • Number of people • Investment • Quantity of • SG&A* resources • Project duration	• Project risk (complexity, multiple units, implementation, and operational issues) • Budget exposure • Staff and skills availability
1. Not well aligned to strategy, little strategic benefit 3. Aligned to strategy, modest strategic benefit 9. Aligned to strategy, major strategic benefit	1. Requires many valuable resources to implement and sustain 3. Requires some resources to implement and sustain 9. Requires few resources to implement and sustain	1. High risk 3. Medium risk 9. Low risk

*Selling, general, and administrative expense.

potential initiatives, the project team refers all the initiatives and their scores to a leadership team for final discussion, debate, and selection. The final approved list contains the critical few strategic initiatives that will be funded to drive performance.

At Canadian Blood Services, project teams score proposed initiatives for each strategic theme based on strategic fit, value provided, length of time to yield benefits, total cost to implement, project team availability, project risk, and depth and breadth of change involved (see Figure 4-6). The first three elements have a double weighting, and all others have a single weighting. This weighting places higher priority on initiatives with the highest strategic fit and potential benefits. The remaining factors tilt toward initiatives that will deliver benefits sooner, are lower cost, have a project team available, are lower risk, and impose relatively little change on the organization.

Case Study of Initiative Selection: University of Leeds

The University of Leeds, a U.K.-based education and research institute whose vision we briefly described in Chapter 2, has more than thirty

FIGURE 4-6

Initiative scoring at Canadian Blood Services

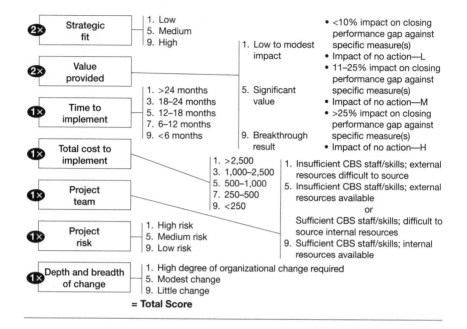

= Total Score

thousand undergraduate and graduate students.[3] Upon becoming vice-chancellor, Michael Arthur recognized the need to develop a strategy that would help the university achieve its vision of becoming a top 50 global university by 2015. The university's strategy team developed the strategy map shown in Figure 4-7. The strategy placed equal importance on research and education, with the differentiating feature being the integration of the two. Leeds based its strategy map on four strategic themes:

· Enhance our international performance and standing.
· Achieve an influential world-leading research profile.
· Inspire our students to develop their full potential.
· Enhance enterprise and knowledge transfer.

To accomplish its strategic theme of world-leading research, the university conducted a process to select the dozen or so *centers of excellence*, which would receive targeted funding to launch them into world-class status. Figure 4-8 illustrates the structure used to implement the third theme, "Inspire our students to develop their full potential." This theme would

FIGURE 4-7

University of Leeds strategic themes

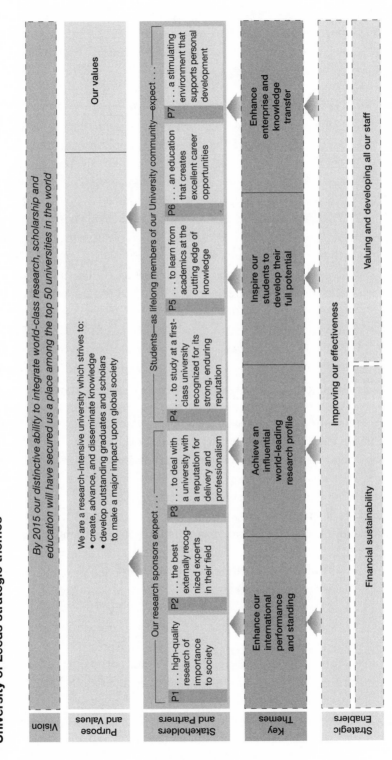

deliver on student expectations by providing an education that creates career opportunities and ensures that students learn from academics at the cutting edge of discovery and knowledge creation. This theme has four objectives:

1. *Deliver excellent and inspirational learning and teaching:* Teaching programs are constantly developed to keep them up to date; programs are reviewed against international norms and focus on the development of lifelong learning skills for the student, including several specialist opportunities such as international experiences, workplace learning, and entrepreneurialism.

2. *Translate excellence in research and scholarship into learning opportunities for students:* The university's research is the foundation of all teaching programs at all levels.

3. *Provide an exceptional student experience:* The university understands the student experience from the student's perspective and clearly communicates this through a student partnership agreement.

4. *Increase participation of those who can benefit:* Introduce a comprehensive approach to recruit students from all areas, including underrepresented and nontraditional students.

The University of Leeds project team quantified these four objectives with five measures, setting stretch targets for each, as shown in Figure 4-8. The theme's objectives, measures, and targets represent the combined input, debate, and consensus of the various university stakeholders.

Having defined the theme's destination, the project team next identified a set of programs to convert its strategic vision into reality. It bundled the programs into one overarching strategic initiative, "Students really matter," which would integrate the student perspective as partners and stakeholders in various academic structures. The specific programs within the initiative included the following:

- Conduct a *student satisfaction survey* to provide the primary feedback identified in the objectives and measures. The survey complemented a national survey used at other universities. The university worked with the University Union to ensure that the demands of the student population were acted upon.
- Improve the *learning and teaching process* through coordinated projects designed to enhance the educational experience through, for

FIGURE 4-8

University of Leeds strategy map (theme 3)

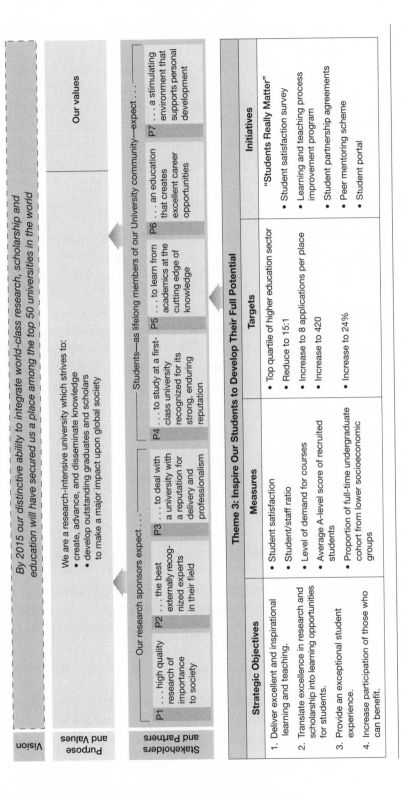

Vision

By 2015 our distinctive ability to integrate world-class research, scholarship and education will have secured us a place among the top 50 universities in the world

Purpose and Values

We are a research-intensive university which strives to:
- create, advance, and disseminate knowledge
- develop outstanding graduates and scholars to make a major impact upon global society

Our values

Stakeholders and Partners

Our research sponsors expect . . .

P1 . . . high quality research of importance to society

P2 . . . the best externally recognized experts in their field

P3 . . . to deal with a university with a reputation for delivery and professionalism

Students—as lifelong members of our University community—expect . . .

P4 . . . to study at a first-class university recognized for its strong, enduring reputation

P5 . . . to learn from academics at the cutting edge of knowledge

P6 . . . an education that creates excellent career opportunities

P7 . . . a stimulating environment that supports personal development

Theme 3: Inspire Our Students to Develop Their Full Potential

Strategic Objectives	Measures	Targets	Initiatives
1. Deliver excellent and inspirational learning and teaching.	• Student satisfaction • Student/staff ratio	• Top quartile of higher education sector • Reduce to 15:1	"Students Really Matter" • Student satisfaction survey
2. Translate excellence in research and scholarship into learning opportunities for students.	• Level of demand for courses	• Increase to 8 applications per place	• Learning and teaching process improvement program
3. Provide an exceptional student experience.	• Average A-level score of recruited students	• Increase to 420	• Student partnership agreements • Peer mentoring scheme
4. Increase participation of those who can benefit.	• Proportion of full-time undergraduate cohort from lower socioeconomic groups	• Increase to 24%	• Student portal

example, new course development, quality assurance, and research integration.

- Establish a *student partnership agreement*, a new, two-way process clearly defining what students can expect from their courses and faculty, as well as what the faculty can expect from the student.
- Launch a *peer mentoring scheme*, a student-to-student program aimed at successful induction and ongoing mentoring.
- Create a *student portal*, a technology-based initiative that would provide online registration, enrollment, payments, and other core learning and teaching functions.

The university's other strategic themes had their own sets of objectives, measures, targets, and initiatives. The new focus on executing the strategy created enthusiasm and results. Vice-Chancellor Arthur described the early progress: "It is early days but the signs are promising . . . There is a new confidence about our campus which is both attracting fantastic new staff and persuading others to reject tempting offers from elsewhere . . . The process of truly embedding the university's strategic goals into the working lives of all our staff is our highest priority."[4] The university's execution premium is summarized in the insert.

UNIVERSITY OF LEEDS' EXECUTION PREMIUM

- In November 2007, the THES-QC world university rankings placed the University of Leeds as number 80, a jump of 41 places in one year.[5]

To summarize, strategic initiatives are the short-term actions that launch an organization on a trajectory toward achieving its vision. The company screens and selects strategic initiatives by assessing their impact on achieving the targeted performance for strategic objectives and measures. Each strategic theme requires complete portfolios of strategic initiatives if its ambitious performance targets are to be achieved.

FUND THE STRATEGY

Linking strategy to action is not simple. The budget—the traditional management control system—focuses on the performance and accountability of responsibility centers (such as profit and cost centers) and functional departments. Each business unit, support group, and functional department has its own budget.

If the funding for strategic initiatives must come from these budgets, the success of the strategy will be put in jeopardy. For example, consider a company that requires the resources for a strategic initiative to upgrade specific employee competencies to come from the training budget in the human resource organization. The strategic initiative must compete for resources with other projects that the HR department wants to support. Such fragmentation of initiatives often dilutes and even destroys the accountability and funding required for executing the strategy. Instead of having one strategy with one level of funding to support the necessary strategic initiatives, a company's strategic initiatives draw upon multiple funding sources that have fragmented ownership and accountability. It is not unusual, in our experience, to see the execution of strategy fail because a department canceled or deferred funding for a strategic initiative to avoid overspending its budget.

Resources—people and funding—must be provided for each strategic theme's portfolio of initiatives. Determining the quantity of resources for each theme's portfolio generally involves a top-down process to establish total funding levels, and a bottom-up process to select the specific initiatives that will receive the funding. Figure 4-9 outlines the major components of this process.

First, the executive team establishes a designated—and, ideally, restricted—pool of funds to support the initiative portfolios for all the strategic themes. Business unit and functional managers, under pressure to deliver short-term results, often reallocate funds from initiatives designed to deliver long-term results to initiatives that yield short-term improvements. If you don't segregate the funding, managers can view the portfolio of strategic initiatives as discretionary and "nice to do" as long as short-term operations are delivering expected results. Managers with short time horizons are easily tempted to delay or transfer funds from strategic initiatives to focus available people, funding, and attention on improving near-term operational performance.

Companies have long distinguished between operational and capital funds to segregate spending that supports near-term improvements from that required to provide benefits over multiple periods. They classify spending in their financial system into either operating expenses (OPEX) or capital expenses (CAPEX). As mentioned earlier, we believe that a third category, strategic expenses (STRATEX), should be created to segregate

FIGURE 4-9

Funding strategic initiatives

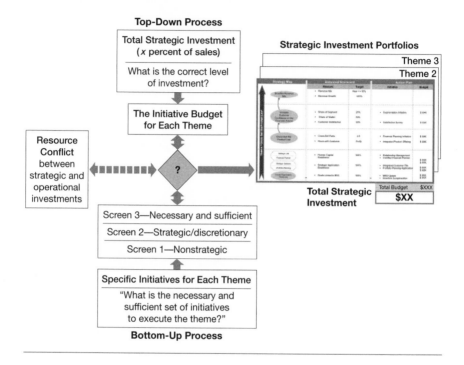

the resources required to implement initiatives that deliver long-term benefits.

Capital budgeting generally applies to a proposed investment in tangible property, plant, and equipment. Managers perform discounted cash flow calculations to assess whether future cash flow benefits from the investment will repay the initial investment and the opportunity cost of capital tied up in the investment. Capital budgeting works best when future cash flow benefits can be explicitly estimated from the new investment, although newer approaches can quantify somewhat uncertain or intangible benefits from investments in property, plant, and equipment.[6] STRATEX is designed to enhance the intangible assets that provide organizational capabilities, such as training and customer databases. A formal process to determine the level of STRATEX funding enables companies to subject strategic initiatives to rigorous, disciplined reviews just like those conducted for CAPEX spending on tangible assets. The estimated impact of these investments on revenue growth and productivity can then be incorporated into the company's updated rolling financial forecast, a topic we cover in Chapter 7.

For example, Nordea, the Nordic banking company we introduced in Chapter 1, runs a separate process for planning and resourcing its strategic initiatives. After the annual planning meeting that updates the strategy, strategy map, and Balanced Scorecard, the Nordea executive team identifies the strategic initiatives required to achieve the performance targets on the BSC. It funds these with a separate budget allocation (its version of STRATEX).

Of course, all funds, whether for operational, capital, or strategic purposes, come from a single source: the company's cash account. A company cannot spend unlimited amounts on new and expensive strategic initiatives. It needs a way to limit and ration the demand for such funds. We recommend that the senior executive team determine subjectively, from their experience and best judgment, a top-down funding level for all strategic initiatives. A good place to start is to accumulate all the spending on existing initiatives and see what percentage of total spending it represents. The new process for rationalizing existing initiatives and selecting new ones will enable the same level of spending to be applied to initiative portfolios having a greater impact, or to justify additional funding to complete a strategic theme's initiative portfolio.

The discretionary funding can also be guided by a rule of thumb—for example, 5 percent of sales. Executives use similar rules of thumb to establish funding levels for categories such as general and administrative expenses, selling expenses, and research and development expenditures. Such rules of thumb arise from industry benchmarks as well as the expectations of investment analysts about ratios of discretionary expense categories to sales.

Ideally, the targeted spending on strategic initiatives takes into account the benefits from funding future performance and balancing these against the risk of spending too much on initiatives whose future benefits do not yield an adequate return. If spending falls short of the STRATEX target, then the organization is underfunding its future growth. If spending exceeds this number, there might be a question about the adequacy of controls. Of course, to argue for a somewhat higher spending level than the targeted percentage allocated, a theme owner can make a convincing case that a somewhat more expensive portfolio of strategic initiatives will yield higher breakthrough performance for the company.

We believe that STRATEX funding for the portfolios of cross-business initiatives is so important that it deserves a separate authorized line item

FIGURE 4-10

Linking strategy to the budget through STRATEX

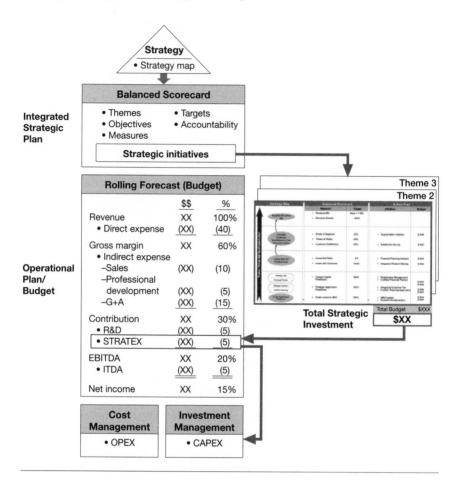

in the company's internal budget or financial forecast (see Figure 4-10). In this way, the funding for strategic initiatives will be shielded from the inevitable short-term pressures to reduce costs and constrain spending. The separate STRATEX line item allows the organization to balance long- and short-term considerations in its financial forecasting and operating processes.

Case Study on Initiative Funding: Ricoh

Ricoh creates a strategic investment fund for projects not included in its operational and capital budget. Working from the mid-term, three-year strategic plan, business and functional units prepare and submit detailed proposals for funding the initiatives identified in their respective plans. A team (consisting of the CEO and members of the Strategy and Planning Office) analyzes each proposal in depth and allocates Ricoh's strategic investment fund to those projects deemed most strategically important.

The CEO and SPO hold quarterly review meetings to assess the progress of the funded projects. For initiatives that span multiple years, the sponsor provides specific milestones about expected results for each year, milestones that must be met if funding is to continue in subsequent years. Before implementing the BSC, Ricoh's parent company determined the initiatives that would be funded. The new application, funding, and monitoring process has given the corporate parent sufficient confidence that it now allows the local company to make the decisions about funding the strategic initiative portfolio.

ESTABLISH ACCOUNTABILITY
FOR STRATEGIC INITIATIVES

The final step in the strategy continuum is to assign responsibility and accountability for execution of the strategy. Two factors make this step a challenge. First, the strategy has been divided into several strategic themes. Most strategic themes cross functions and business units. Therefore, they do not fall within the existing responsibility of any senior executive. Second, the strategic themes are still plans. They do not produce results until the required changes are executed at the operational and process levels.

Strategic themes require strong executive-level leadership if they are to obtain adequate resources and continued visibility, action, and review. Companies typically assign one or two members of the executive team to be the owners of each strategic theme, giving the *theme owners* the "night jobs" of overseeing execution of the assigned strategic themes in addition to their day jobs as heads of business or functional units. Such assignments give management team members a dual role. Their day job brings their business, technical, and functional expertise to management team meetings; their theme-owner night job role gives them a strategic view of and accountability for the company's success.

At Luxfer Gas Cylinders, theme owners have the following responsibilities:

1. Assess how well the theme's cross-functional strategic objectives are being executed across the *entire* business.

2. Identify key issues and situations that could affect strategic implementation, and propose appropriate actions and accountabilities.
3. Act as a center of theme competency, a mentor to his or her own team, and a liaison to other theme teams to facilitate teaching, learning, and understanding.
4. Ensure that theme measures and initiatives align with theme objectives, and propose changes when necessary in collaboration with other members of the team.
5. Sponsor new initiatives or changes to existing initiatives, and place these proposed changes on the management agenda.

Each theme owner leads a *theme team*—a collection of individuals drawn from multiple business, regional, and support units—whose job is to link the theme's strategic objectives to operational tasks. Theme team members can be dedicated to the strategic theme, or they may be part-time, with team membership added to their normal jobs and responsibilities. They join the team because of their competencies and process expertise. President John Rhodes described the roles of theme teams at Luxfer Gas Cylinders:

> *When we started working with cross-functional teams, we had considerable dissonance for a time. Teams pass through phases: forming, storming, norming, and—finally—performing. Sounds a bit like members of a rock band learning how to play together.*
>
> *We teach members of theme teams to be communicators, influencers, and persuaders—not dictators and demanders. The whole point of themes is to make people* want *to work differently, smarter, more collaboratively, and more productively together to accomplish our strategic objectives. People need to be* sold, *not just told.*[7]

Theme teams do not have authority over functions or businesses. They provide multiple perspectives, strengths, and talents—they are big thinkers, detail-oriented coalition builders, and hard-charging functional specialists—and strive to ensure buy in throughout the organization.

For example, Luxfer's product leadership theme team does not take over product development, but it does interact with various existing functions and processes. It helps out where needed and draws attention to any aspect of product development that is not aligned with strategic objectives. Being part of the theme team engages a wider group in managing the strategy and in making assessments of the issues and the impact of the organization's performance on achieving the strategic objectives. Luxfer has also found that the theme teams have been a great incubator of talent as well as a mechanism to continuously improve the level of competency in strategy management within the company.

The theme team has primary responsibility for identifying and funding (from the STRATEX allocation) the portfolio of initiatives required to execute the theme's strategy. After the theme team selects and allocates resources for the initiative portfolio, it identifies who will be assigned the task of accomplishing each initiative.

Often, the theme team can assign this responsibility to an existing organizational unit. For example, the information technology department would take on responsibility for an enterprise resource planning (ERP) application, whereas the human resource department would have responsibility for required training and competency development programs.

Some initiatives in the portfolio, however, are likely to be cross functional. In this case, the responsibility for these initiatives either remains with the theme team or is assigned to a centralized project management office that has particular expertise in large-scale project management. By giving high-level authority and accountability to senior executives (the theme owners), companies can achieve holistic implementation of its portfolios of strategic initiatives while still maintaining line-of-sight accountability to functional managers and the theme teams for the strategic initiatives that each has been assigned to execute.

The theme team also can translate the high-level strategic process objectives into detailed and actionable subprocesses. Often the theme team performs analytic studies that identify the key performance drivers of the team's strategic processes. These drivers then are formalized into operational dashboards that are the focus of and feedback for the team's actions.

The final process of linking strategic themes and short-term initiatives requires that the senior management team periodically review the execution and results of the strategic initiative portfolios. We cover in Chapter 8 the details of monthly strategy review meetings, at which senior managers review progress on the strategic initiatives. In this chapter, we focus more narrowly on the reviews conducted by theme owners and their theme teams.

The theme owner and team must monitor the performance of all the theme's initiatives; if any is abandoned or not executed effectively, the associated objective, measure, or target would be missed and the performance of the entire strategic theme would be jeopardized. Typically, theme owners meet with their teams monthly to review the progress of each initiative in the theme: those the team is doing or managing directly, and those that have been assigned to a functional department or project management office. Based on these meetings, the theme owner documents and reports to the executive committee, at the monthly strategy review meeting, on the progress of all strategic initiatives under way.

Case Study in Initiative Management: Serono

Serono, a Switzerland-based pharmaceutical firm, has made initiative management a competitive advantage. The initiative management process starts each year after the executive committee has crafted and updated the five-year plan for each of the company's four core therapeutic areas: multiple sclerosis, women's reproductive health, growth hormone, and psoriasis. From the plan, managers identify all the component projects required to implement the plan. The projects might range from the development of a new drug to the introduction of a new aspect of corporate governance. On average, managers identify one hundred fifty projects.

Serono has established strict criteria for launching a new initiative. Each objective and strategic theme must have at least one initiative that will drive the actions designed to achieve targeted performance. Also, all organizational units and functions must participate in at least one strategic initiative.

The executive committee sets priorities among all the projects and assigns one of its members to sponsor each project approved for funding. This practice ensures that a strategic initiative has been identified to support all the objectives on the company's Balanced Scorecard. The executive committee also assigns responsibility for each strategic initiative to an executive committee member. This person reports monthly on the progress and direction of his or her strategic initiative to cross-functional supervisory committees that monitor the successful execution of the company's strategy.

Serono uses a sophisticated project management system, called the Corporate Strategic Master Plan (CSMP), which is documented in its "Yellow Book." This online system establishes the procedures for monitoring and managing strategic initiatives and projects. The CSMP is updated daily by project managers, and progress can be tracked live through the online system. The executive committee conducts monthly reviews of all the projects in the Yellow Book. A centralized team—which reports to an executive committee member, the group compliance officer, and the head of corporate administration—acts as the custodian of the CSMP. The team ensures alignment and coordination between the strategy, the Balanced Scorecard, and the initiative management process.

To streamline the approval and supervisory process, projects are also organized into clusters of fifteen to twenty strategic initiatives that the executive committee reviews at least twice a year. Serono's corporate governance includes supervisory committees that meet monthly to review and recommend corrective actions for the strategic initiatives. The CEO reviews all strategic initiatives in formal semiannual project review meetings.

SUMMARY

After the executive team has translated its strategy into a strategy map and Balanced Scorecard, it must lead a process that selects, funds, and assigns accountability for theme-based portfolios of strategic initiatives. These initiatives set the organization into motion along a trajectory of successful strategy implementation. Companies use three processes to select and manage their strategic initiative portfolios:

1. *Choose strategic initiatives:* Identify, rank, and select new strategic initiatives for each strategic theme while rationalizing existing ones to strategic priorities.
2. *Fund the strategy:* Establish a budget for strategic expenditures (STRATEX) to fund the strategic initiative portfolios.
3. *Establish accountability:* Select theme owners and theme teams to execute the portfolios of strategic initiatives; review the performance of strategic initiatives in achieving targeted results.

These processes align short-term action programs with strategic and cross-functional priorities, and they provide high degrees of visibility and accountability to the programs.

The executive team can now move to the next stages of the management system: aligning organizational units and employees to the strategy, and linking strategy to operations.

NOTES

1. See R. S. Kaplan and N. Tempest, "Wells Fargo Online Financial Services (B)," Case 9-199-019 (Boston: Harvard Business School, 1998). This case illustrates a process of selecting strategic initiatives independently, without considering their interrelationships; see also R. S. Kaplan and D. P. Norton, *The Strategy-Focused Organization* (Harvard Business School Press, 2000), 297–300.
2. For a more extensive treatment of initiative generation and evaluation, see P. LaCasse and T. Manzione, "Initiative Management: Putting Strategy into Action," *Balanced Scorecard Report* (November–December 2007): 7–10, and T. Brown and

M. Gill, "Charting New Horizons with Initiative Management," *Balanced Score-card Report* (September–October 2006): 13–16.

3. University of Leeds Strategic Plan, 2006, www.leeds.ac.uk.

4. M. Arthur, "Foreword by the Vice-Chancellor," University of Leeds Strategic Plan, 2006, p. 2.

5. Rankings published at http://www.topuniversities.com/worlduniversityrankings/results/2007/overall_rankings/top_100_universities/.

6. T. Copeland and P. Tufano, "A Real-World Way to Manage Real Options," *Harvard Business Review* (March 2004); T. A. Luehrman, "Investment Opportunities as Real Options: Getting Started on the Numbers." *Harvard Business Review* (July–August 1998): 51–67.

7. J. Rhodes, speech at Balanced Scorecard European Summit, Prague, June 2007.

CHAPTER FIVE

ALIGNING ORGANIZATIONAL UNITS AND EMPLOYEES

OUR PRIMARY FOCUS in this book is the design of a management system for aligning business unit strategy with operations. But most organizations consist of multiple business and support units, so the management system must also address how strategy is integrated across these diverse organizational units. In addition to aligning organizational units with the strategy, the system must align employees with the strategy. Unless all employees understand the strategy and are motivated to achieve it, successful execution of the strategy is highly unlikely. Aligning organizational units and employees is stage 3 of the management system (see Figure 5-1).

In this chapter, we discuss the three subprocesses for aligning organizational units and employees with the strategy, as shown in Figure 5-2.[1] Our previous books, especially *Alignment* and *The Strategy-Focused Organization*, provide extensive discussions on aligning organizational units and employees with the strategy. In this chapter, we summarize the key concepts of the alignment processes described in these earlier works.[2]

ALIGNING BUSINESS UNITS

Corporate strategy describes how the company intends to create more value from its collection of business units than if the units operated independently with their own capital and governance structure. Collis and Montgomery summarize an effective corporate strategy: "An outstanding corporate strategy is not a random collection of individual building blocks

FIGURE 5-1

The management system: Align the organization

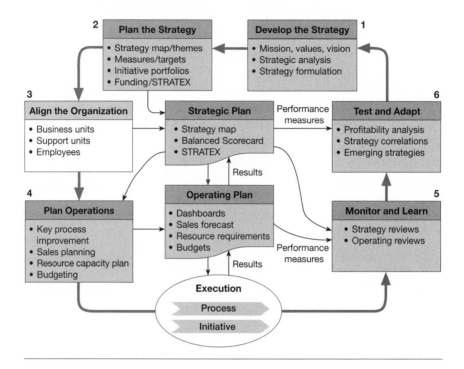

but a carefully constructed system of interdependent parts . . . In a great corporate strategy, all of the elements [resources, businesses, and organization] are aligned with one another. That alignment is driven by the nature of the firm's resources—its special assets, skills and capabilities."[3]

Corporate headquarters is like the coxswain in an eight-rower shell. Eight strong, motivated, skilled rowers, working independently, will make some progress along a race course. But if their individual efforts are unaligned and poorly coordinated with each other, they may actually progress more slowly than would a smaller shell with only a single rower. The coxswain adds value by understanding the competitive environment and the strengths and weaknesses of the individual rowers and using that insight to develop a coherent action plan. The coxswain's plan coordinates and leverages the strengths and contributions of the individual rowers so that they can outperform smaller and perhaps more nimble competitors.

Corporations achieve synergies from their collection of operating and business units in a variety of ways. The four perspectives of the Balanced

FIGURE 5-2

Align the organization

Alignment Process	Objective	Barriers	Enabling Tools
1. Align Business Units *How do we align business units to create corporate synergies?*	Cascade and embed corporate strategy into business unit strategies.	Business unit strategies typically are developed and approved independently, without the guidance of a corporate perspective; lack of integration across business units.	• Cascading of strategy maps to business units • Vertical and horizontal alignment
2. Align Support Units *How do we align support units to business unit and corporate strategies?*	Ensure that each support unit has a strategy that enhances the performance of corporate and business unit strategies.	Support units treated as "discretionary expense centers," with goals to minimize costs rather than to support enterprise and business unit strategies.	• Service-level agreements • Support unit strategy maps and scorecards
3. Align Employees *How do we motivate employees to help us execute the strategy?*	All employees understand the strategy and are motivated to help successfully execute the strategy.	Most employees are not aware of or do not understand the strategy. Their objectives and incentives focus on local, tactical performance, not strategic objectives.	• Formal strategy communication program • Employee objectives with clear line of sight to strategic objectives • Incentive and reward programs • Competency development programs

Scorecard provide a useful taxonomy for describing the various sources of corporate synergies (see Figure 5-3):

Financial synergies:
- Effectively acquiring and integrating other companies
- Operating an efficient internal capital market by using private (internal) information to allocate capital to productive opportunities
- Conducting excellent monitoring and governance processes across diverse enterprises
- Leveraging a common brand (Disney, Virgin) across multiple business units
- Achieving scale or specialized skills in negotiations with external entities such as governments, unions, capital providers, and suppliers

FIGURE 5-3

Building the corporate scorecard

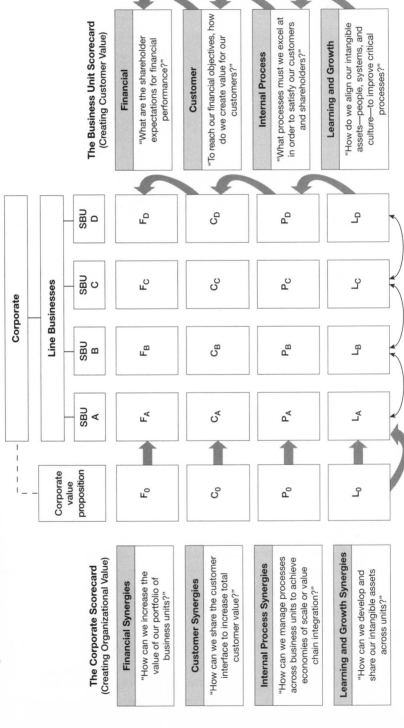

Customer synergies:
- Consistently delivering a common value proposition across a geographically dispersed network of homogeneous retail, wholesale, or distribution outlets
- Leveraging common customers by combining products or services from multiple units to provide customers with a distinctive value proposition—low cost, convenience, or customized solutions

Process synergies:
- Exploiting *core competencies* that leverage excellence in product or process technologies across multiple business units[4]
- Achieving economies of scale through shared manufacturing, research, distribution, or marketing resources

Learning and growth synergies:
- Enhancing *human capital* through excellent HR recruiting, training, and leadership development practices across multiple business units
- Leveraging a *common technology*, such as an industry-leading platform or channel for customers, that can be shared across multiple product and service divisions
- Sharing best-practice *capabilities* through knowledge management that transfers process quality excellence to multiple business units

Strategy maps and the Balanced Scorecard turn out to be ideal mechanisms to help corporate headquarters align multiple organizational units for superior value creation. The headquarters executive team, in its corporate strategy map and scorecard, articulates the theory of the enterprise: how the enterprise generates additional value by having business units operate within its hierarchical structure. Once defined, the corporate strategy map can be cascaded to divisions, business and support units, and departments to coordinate the value-creating activities at all these organizational units. Figure 5-4 shows how strategy maps are cascaded to achieve vertical and horizontal alignment throughout the enterprise.

Consider, for example, the experience of Marriott Vacation Club International, the company we profiled at the start of Chapter 1. MVCI started by defining its enterprise strategy map and Balanced Scorecard, which emphasized the benefits to be gained by coordinating multiple business lines and functions. It then cascaded the enterprise map to its four business lines. In turn, the four key process-based organizational

FIGURE 5-4

Enterprises require vertical and horizontal alignment

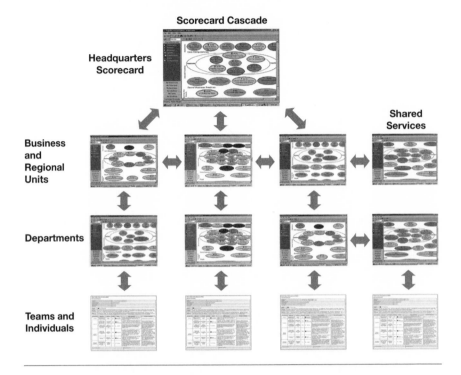

units, land development, sales and marketing, the mortgage bank, and resort management and service developed integrated strategy maps.

Each cascaded map reflected what the unit had to do locally to create outstanding performance while still including objectives that related to integrating with other units at the same level (horizontal integration) and being responsive to business-line and enterprise strategic priorities (vertical integration). Each process unit cascaded its strategy to business-line support services—finance and accounting, human resources, information resources, legal, and resort services—as well as to regional business units and then to individual sites. In this way, MVCI created alignment across multiple business lines, key business processes, support services, and regions and individual resort sites.

Figure 5-5 illustrates the range of integration required by various corporate strategies. On the left, holding corporations—such as private equity firms and family business groups like India-based Tata—allow complete autonomy in the strategies of their various operating companies. Each

FIGURE 5-5

Corporate role in the cascading process depends on corporate type

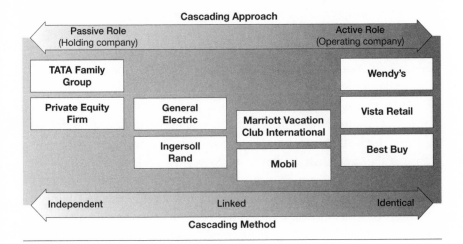

operating company generates its own strategy, strategy map, and score-card. Corporate headquarters reviews and approves each unit's strategy, map, and scorecard and then holds the units accountable for delivering the performance. Passive holding corporations gain their synergies from an ability to allocate capital effectively across the diverse units and oper-ate an effective governance process. Most feel little need to create a corpo-rate-level strategy map and scorecard, because most of their relevant metrics would be financial.

At the right in figure 5-5 are corporations that operate a system of vir-tually identical retail units, such as quick service restaurants, like Wendy's, and retail outlets, like Best Buy, and local bank branches. To reinforce the brand during every shopping transaction, these corporations want the con-sumer experience to be identical in each unit. Corporate headquarters defines the customer value proposition and translates the corporate strat-egy into key metrics for financial performance, the consumer experience, the critical processes at which each decentralized unit must excel, and the recruitment, development, and retention of employees. The strategy maps and scorecards at each unit are identical, facilitating the monitoring and benchmarking of the units' performance.

Between these two polar situations—complete operating unit autonomy and complete adherence to corporate-determined strategy and metrics— are the majority of other companies, such as MVCI. These companies have a corporate strategy, but the strategies of operating units reflect a mixture of local competitive excellence as well as objectives that relate to coordination and integration with other operating units and corporate-determined strategic themes. The strategy maps and scorecards of such operating units contain many objectives that are unique to local operations, but they also contain several that reflect corporate-level priorities and objectives shared with other operating units. The operating unit head must maintain a balance between local optimization, as if the unit were an autonomous company, and the unit's contribution to corporate and other business units' objectives that generate the corporate synergies.

Consider a utility corporation consisting of three units: generation, transmission, and distribution. The corporate strategy might articulate strategic themes concerning safety, environmental protection, responsiveness to consumer requests, and management of government regulatory issues. But the transmission business has been deregulated a decade ago, so its strategy map would not have objectives relating to governmental regulatory affairs. In contrast to the other units, the transmission business would have a value proposition and objectives to increase market share with other generation and distribution companies.

Cascading Through Strategic Themes

The development of strategy maps built around strategic themes (described in Chapter 3) provides a great structure for cascading corporate-level strategy and for integrating the operations of diverse business units. Consider the example of Canadian Blood Services (CBS), which we initially described in Chapter 2. The CBS leadership team identified three strategic themes for its strategy map: safety, operational excellence, and plan for tomorrow.

Figure 5-6 shows the CBS strategy map of linked objectives within each of the three process-based strategic themes; each theme is supported by a learning and growth theme to develop strategic assets that are most valuable for that theme. CBS selected two members of the strategy council to head up each of the three themes, along with a theme team drawn from across the enterprise, following the guidance described in Chapter 4.

Having defined the corporate strategy using the strategy map shown in Figure 5-6, the strategy council then led the process to cascade the strategic themes to each of CBS's operating units (including regional as well as product-line units). Each operating unit's strategy map had the same structure as the enterprise-level map, with the mission at the top and the

FIGURE 5-6

Theme-based stratgy map at Canadian Blood Services

Canadian Blood Services operates Canada's blood supply in a manner that gains the trust, commitment, and confidence of all Canadians by providing a safe, secure, cost-effective, affordable, and accessible supply of quality blood, blood products, and their alternatives.

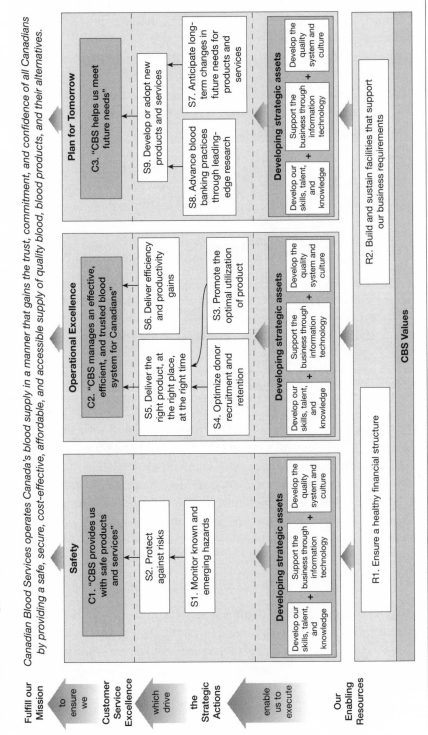

three vertical strategic themes (safety, operational excellence, and plan for tomorrow) in the center, supported by the theme to develop the strategic assets (see Figure 5-7).

Managers of the enterprise felt that some objectives and measures, such as safety, were so critical to the mission and strategy that they mandated a common safety objective and measure for each operating unit's strategy map. CBS also wanted every unit to use the same objectives and measures for the "enabling strategic assets" theme:

- Human Capital Readiness identifies the specific families of jobs and skills that drive this theme, assesses the degree to which the organization possesses the skills, and guides the strategy for acquiring the required skills.
- Information Capital Readiness identifies the *specific* information capital requirements (information technology, systems, etc.) that are required to build the capacity to enable this theme to be executed.
- Quality System Readiness identifies the *specific* quality systems and processes required to ensure that each theme can be executed in a state of control and with overall process excellence.

Apart from these enterprise-mandated objectives and measures, each unit had the discretion to develop objectives and measures within the three strategic themes that were most relevant to that unit's environment and experience. In this way, all units were aligned with the enterprise's strategic priorities while having the freedom to develop and implement locally determined strategies. The common theme-based structure of all strategy maps also promoted internal benchmarking and knowledge sharing. Many global companies now use the strategic theme structure in their strategy maps to align the operations and contributions from their geographically dispersed regional units.

Vertical Alignment Sequencing

We have described the alignment of business units with the corporate strategy as a top-down process. In effect, the output of this alignment step—stage 3 in the corporate management system—becomes the input to the strategy development process (stage 1) for the business units. This process assumes that the corporation and business units have aligned strategy maps and Balanced Scorecards from a previous cascading process.

FIGURE 5-7

Every division uses the same common architecture for its strategy map

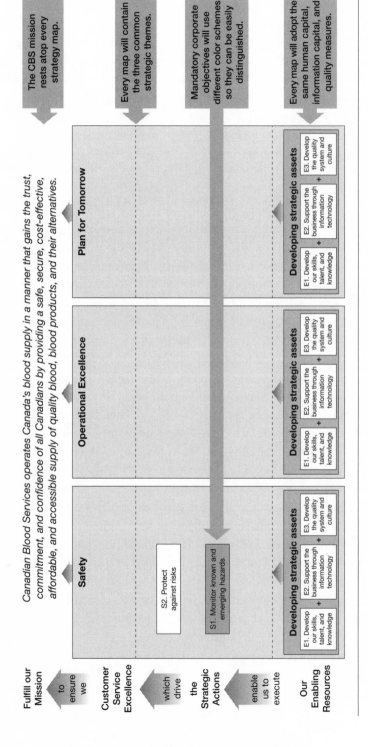

Canadian Blood Services operates Canada's blood supply in a manner that gains the trust, commitment, and confidence of all Canadians by providing a safe, secure, cost-effective, affordable, and accessible supply of quality blood, blood products, and their alternatives.

For companies doing their initial Balanced Scorecard implementation, few follow a top-down sequence. Most of them introduce the initial Balanced Scorecard strategy execution system in one or two business units, because either the initial champion for the new system is at the business unit level or the corporation wants to pilot and prove the concept at a business unit level before attempting to deploy it across the enterprise. In the latter case, after doing several business unit implementations, the corporate office establishes a project team for itself to develop and translate the corporate-level strategy into a strategy map and scorecard that it can then cascade to the business units, as described in this chapter.

ALIGNING SUPPORT UNITS

Support and shared-service units, such as human resources, information technology, finance, and planning, develop their strategy maps and Balanced Scorecards to enhance the strategies of the operating units they support. For example, the corporate strategy may require that the human resource department create synergy by developing new programs to recruit, train, retain, and share key personnel across all organizational units. If corporate strategy dictates an emphasis on risk management, then the finance and information technology departments will each incorporate a strategic theme to manage and mitigate the risks they can influence. Internal support units must understand the corporate and operating unit strategies before they can align their activities with those strategies.

Support units follow a systematic set of processes to create alignment that helps business units and the enterprise achieve their strategic objectives. First, the support units develop a clear understanding of enterprise and business unit strategies, as revealed by the line organization strategy maps and Balanced Scorecards. Next, they align their strategies with the business unit and corporate strategies by determining the set of strategic services to be offered. Often, this is formalized with a *service-level agreement*, a performance contract between the support unit and the business unit or units. Figure 5-8 shows a service-level agreement in a commercial bank.

Once a support unit understands how it can contribute to business- and enterprise-level strategy, it creates a strategy map and Balanced Scorecard to align its internal organization for executing the strategy. A support unit, like a business unit, has a mission, customers, services, and employees. Some support units, such as the information technology departments of financial service organizations, have budgets that would place them on the *Fortune* 1000 list of largest companies.

FIGURE 5-8

Example of a service-level agreement for a credit and loan support unit at a commercial bank

---

**Agreement to provide Credit Administration and
Loan Operations Services to RidgeStone Bank**

Scope of Services

RidgeStone Bank Credit and Loan Operations agrees to provide the following key services as described below:

Commercial and Personal Banking

Credit Administration Services

1. For new commercial loan requests, provide accurate and timely turnaround of credit analysis package within five (5) business days from receipt of complete analysis request.
2. Provide ninety (90) days from maturity notification on credits to the Lending Office.
3. On approved renewals, gather information from client and provide review packages thirty (30) days prior to maturity to the Lending Officer.

Documentation Services

4. Complete and accurate loan documentation ready for review 24 hours before closing to enable the lender to proof documents.
5. Maintenance of accurate and timely loan information detail in the Loans-in-Process tracking system.
6. Staffing availability during closings for documentation, check preparation, and copying as needed.

Loan Servicing

7. Complete, timely, and accurate maintenance of loan accounts within 24 hours of receipt of request from either SBUs or external clients, with rework and service defects completed same day or as soon as system allows.
8. Complete and accurate data entry of loan activity onto ITI by conclusion of next business day after closing, including all third-party payments and filing of collateral perfection and lien filing documentation.
9. Personal Banking: accurate, timely booking and shipping of complete fundable package to investors by next business day from closing or date of rescission, with no avoidable errors or omissions.

Quality Control

10. Monitor daily activity for loan non-posts, exceptions, paid loans, and new loans.
11. Within three (3) business days of booking a loan, the editing of the documentation and system input coding will be cross-checked for accuracy.

At the highest level, the support unit should have the same overarching goal as the enterprise—some measure of shareholder value (or its equivalent in nonprofits). It is essential that all employees, whether in line or support units, understand the ultimate measure of enterprise success. The support unit's financial perspective contains objectives that reflect how the unit contributes to the company's cost reduction, revenue growth, or asset utilization objectives.

The support unit's primary customers are the business unit managers to whom it provides services and support. Some support units have additional customers; for example, the human resource group provides services to employees, and the finance unit provides reports and disclosures to external stakeholders, including investors, the board of directors, analysts, regulators, and tax authorities. In crafting the objectives on its strategy map and Balanced Scorecard, the support unit must identify how it contributes to the value-creating strategies of its business unit partners and any other constituencies it serves.

The process perspective of a support unit scorecard typically has three themes that enable it to achieve its financial and customer objectives. An operational excellence theme emphasizes lowering the cost of operating the unit and delivering its services. Another theme deals with how the function manages the relationship with its internal customers. A third theme might describe the unit's strategic support to the business, including providing business units with new capabilities that enhance their strategies.

The learning and growth perspective reflects the specific needs of the functional staff for training, technology, and a supportive work climate.

Case Study of a Support Unit Strategy Map: Lockheed Martin Enterprise Services Internal IT Group

Lockheed Martin Corporation, with 140,000 employees, became the country's largest defense contractor after the merger of Lockheed and Martin Marietta in 1995. Sales in 2007 were $41.9 billion. Its largest customer is the U.S. Department of Defense, with other customers including nondefense government, international sales, and domestic commercial.

Lockheed Martin's Enterprise Services Internal IT Group division has more than five thousand employees working at sites in forty-seven states and overseas. Internal IT Group is responsible for about two-thirds of the spending on information technology across the enterprise; the rest is embedded in four decentralized business areas.

Lockheed Martin Enterprise Services Internal IT Group adopted a "complete customer solutions" strategy, with the goal of becoming a credible innovator and supplier of cutting-edge, Net-based capabilities that would make it the preferred IT service supplier for Lockheed Martin business units. It also wanted to provide support to external Lockheed Martin customers by helping win large IT-related contracts from the government, such as those expected from the U.S. Department of Homeland Security and the Department of Defense.

Figure 5-9 shows the Internal IT Group strategy map. The map identifies Lockheed Martin's business and technology leaders as its key customers.

FIGURE 5-9

The Internal IT Group strategy complete customer solutions strategy map

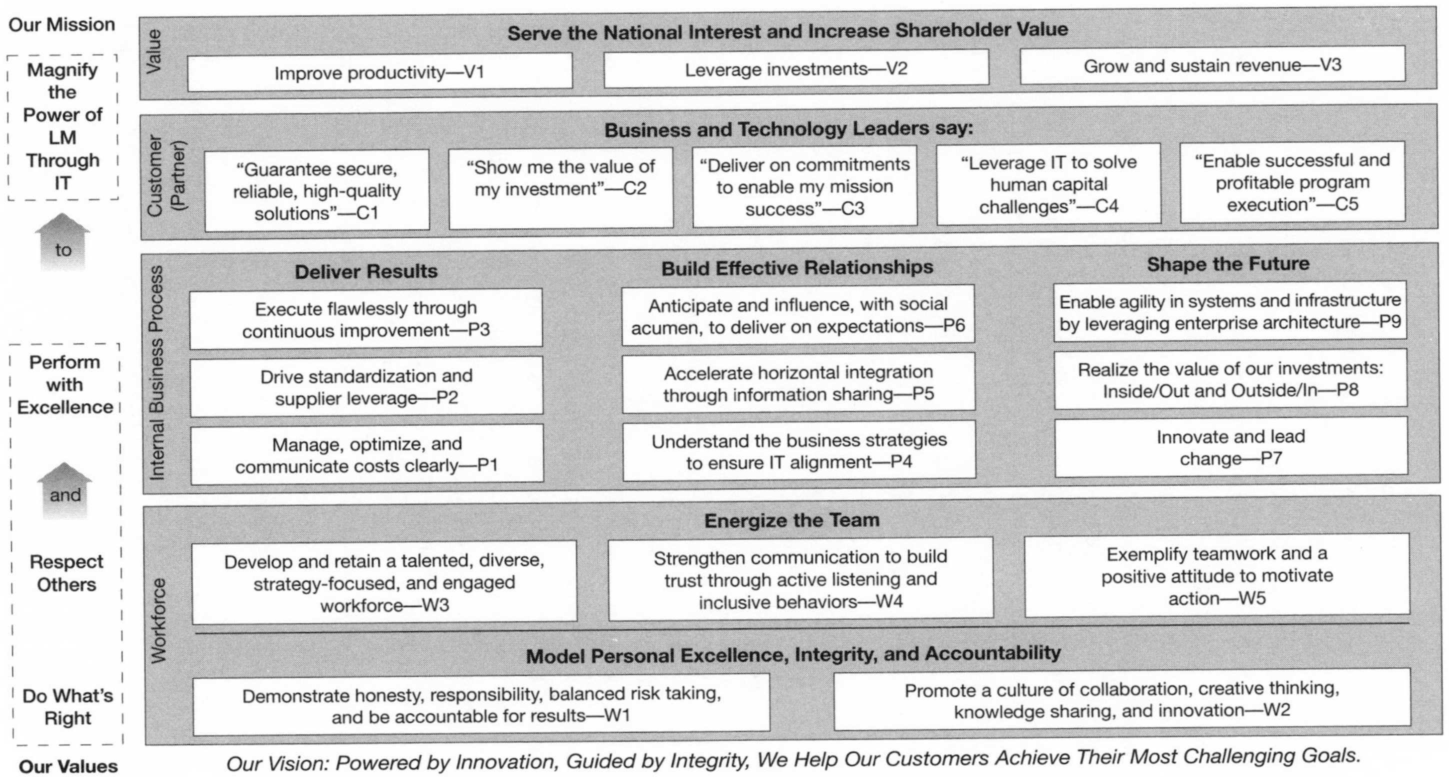

Our Mission
Magnify the Power of LM Through IT
to
Perform with Excellence
and
Respect Others
Do What's Right
Our Values
Value
Serve the National Interest and Increase Shareholder Value
Improve productivity—V1
Leverage investments—V2
Grow and sustain revenue—V3
Customer (Partner)
Business and Technology Leaders say:
"Guarantee secure, reliable, high-quality solutions"—C1
"Show me the value of my investment"—C2
"Deliver on commitments to enable my mission success"—C3
"Leverage IT to solve human capital challenges"—C4
"Enable successful and profitable program execution"—C5
Internal Business Process
Deliver Results
Execute flawlessly through continuous improvement—P3
Drive standardization and supplier leverage—P2
Manage, optimize, and communicate costs clearly—P1
Build Effective Relationships
Anticipate and influence, with social acumen, to deliver on expectations—P6
Accelerate horizontal integration through information sharing—P5
Understand the business strategies to ensure IT alignment—P4
Shape the Future
Enable agility in systems and infrastructure by leveraging enterprise architecture—P9
Realize the value of our investments: Inside/Out and Outside/In—P8
Innovate and lead change—P7
Workforce
Energize the Team
Develop and retain a talented, diverse, strategy-focused, and engaged workforce—W3
Strengthen communication to build trust through active listening and inclusive behaviors—W4
Exemplify teamwork and a positive attitude to motivate action—W5
Model Personal Excellence, Integrity, and Accountability
Demonstrate honesty, responsibility, balanced risk taking, and be accountable for results—W1
Promote a culture of collaboration, creative thinking, knowledge sharing, and innovation—W2
Our Vision: Powered by Innovation, Guided by Integrity, We Help Our Customers Achieve Their Most Challenging Goals.

The five customer objectives are stated in the voice of the customers. Reading from left to right, these objectives move from table stakes ("Guarantee secure, reliable, high-quality solutions," "Show me the value of my investments," "Deliver on commitments to enable my mission success") to objectives for delivering value by integrating IT into the business unit solutions for their customers.

The process perspective themes stress that Internal IT Group must deliver results, build effective relationships, and shape the future. The foundational objectives in the learning and growth perspective are to live by the company's values and develop a culture that will energize the team to model personal excellence, integrity, and accountability.

Although the strategy map is a relatively recent development at Internal IT Group, its leadership estimates that alignment benefits from its strategy will generate significant cost avoidance and millions of dollars of productivity savings during the next five years. It also projects additional savings from improved customer focus and IT-to-business alignment.

Managing Alignment as a Process

Alignment, like the other strategy execution processes, crosses organization boundaries. To be executed effectively, alignment requires the integration and cooperation of individuals from different organizational units. This poses a dilemma because most organizations have no natural home for cross-business processes. In Chapter 10, we present the case for establishing a new office of strategy management (OSM) to perform and coordinate the multiple processes required for successful strategy execution. Taking responsibility and accountability for an effective organizational alignment process is a natural task for the OSM. Among its responsibilities is to ensure that the strategy maps and scorecards of all business and support units are aligned with each other and with the enterprise-level strategy, as illustrated with the Canadian Blood Services example.

MOTIVATING EMPLOYEES

Ultimately, effective strategy execution requires that employees be personally committed to helping their enterprise and unit achieve strategic objectives. The process to align employees with the strategy requires three steps:

1. Communicate and educate employees about the strategy.
2. Link employees' personal objectives and incentives to the strategy.

3. Align personal training and development programs to provide employees with the knowledge, skills, and competencies they need to help implement the strategy.

Communicate and Educate About the Strategy

Leaders unleash enormous internal creativity and energy when they can appeal to employees' desire to work for a successful organization that makes a positive contribution to the world. Employees want to take pride in the organization in which they spend much of their waking lives. They should understand how the success of their organization creates benefits not only to shareholders but also to customers, suppliers, and the communities in which it operates. Employees should feel that their organization functions both efficiently and effectively. No one enjoys working for a failing, underperforming enterprise. Employees should be reassured that the organization does not squander resources in pursuit of its mission. Poorly functioning organizations, bureaucracies that hamper decision making, and turf battles arising from the narrow-mindedness often spawned by functional silos are visible to everyone and demoralizing to all.

Communication of mission, values, vision, and strategy is the first step in creating motivation among employees. Executives can use the strategy map and Balanced Scorecard to communicate strategy—both *what* the organization wants to accomplish and *how* it intends to realize its strategic outcomes. Taking all the objectives and measures together provides a comprehensive picture of the organization's value-creating activities.

This new representation of strategy communicates to everyone what the organization is about: how it intends to create long-term value and how each individual can contribute to organizational objectives. Employees can come to work each day energized about doing their jobs differently and better, helping advance the organization's success and realizing their personal objectives.

Communication also helps shape the culture. In Chapter 2 we describe how leaders can use a strategic change agenda to communicate concerns about the existing culture and processes and to share the vision of what the organization aspires to become. Cultural messages might include a commitment to performance and accountability, a focus on customers, and a relentless passion for continuous improvement, or creativity and innovation.

At the Bank of Tokyo-Mitsubishi, Americas, the leadership team used a modified strategic change agenda (see Figure 5-10) to show the challenges

FIGURE 5-10

Bank of Tokyo-Mitsubishi, Americas, had to bridge two distinct cultures

Japanese companies		American companies
Vague	Mission and Vision	Defined
Incremental	Strategy Formulation Process	Grand Design
Operational Efficiency	Competitive Edge	Differentiation/Uniqueness
Bottom-Up (or Middle-Up-Down)	Decision Making	Top-Down
Implicit/Nonverbal/Closed	Communication Style	Explicit/Verbal/Open
Process Orientation	Performance Evaluation	Outcome Orientation
Single Culture/ Cooperative	Work Culture	Diversified Culture/ Competitive

it faced in bridging the different cultures of Japanese and U.S. employees. It encouraged employees to leverage the best of the two worlds to develop a unique culture at the company.

Communication by leaders is critical. Employees cannot follow if executives do not lead. Executives at our conferences regularly report that it is not possible to overcommunicate the strategy; effective communication is critical for the success of their BSC implementations. One CEO told us that if he were to write a book describing his successful transformation of a large insurance company, he would definitely include a chapter on the Balanced Scorecard; it played an invaluable role in the turnaround. But he would devote five chapters to communication, because he spent most of his time communicating with business unit heads, frontline and back-office employees, and key suppliers such as insurance brokers and agencies.

Jack Klinck, former vice chairman and president of Mellon Financial's Investment Manager Solutions (IMS) group, based in London, made it a practice when visiting a regional office to stop, seemingly at random, at an employee's workstation. He would pull a document—the IMS strategy map—out of his inside jacket pocket and ask the employee three questions about it.

1. "Do you know what this is?" (A bad answer reflected more on the employee's manager than on the employee.)
2. "Can you explain it to me?"
3. "How will the work you were doing, just before I interrupted you, have an impact on one or more of the objectives shown on this document?"

Initially, not all the responses were satisfactory. But one can only imagine the e-mail traffic that must have run around the group, alerting everyone that when Klinck visited an office, you should be prepared to talk with him about the strategy and how you are linking it to your every-day operations. This type of leadership is priceless in communicating the priority that the CEO places on having every employee understand the strategy and contribute to its successful execution.

Managers report that they must communicate seven times, in seven different ways. They regularly use multiple communication channels to get the message out: speeches, newsletters, brochures, bulletin boards, in-teractive town hall meetings, intranets, monthly reviews, training pro-grams, and online educational courses.

Figure 5-11 shows one company's plan to communicate the strategy multiple times in multiple ways to employees who were highly diverse and geographically dispersed. Figure 5-12 shows the annual strategy commu-nication plan used by Marriott Vacation Club International to ensure that employees got messages throughout the year, through various chan-nels, about the unit's strategy.

The communication best practices we have observed in the most suc-cessful enterprises have certain characteristics. Senior executives person-ally lead the communication process. The communication group develops a plan to ensure that the right information is communicated at the right time, the message is relevant to the intended audience, and the message is delivered through a variety of media. The group periodically surveys em-ployees to ensure that they understand the message, not just whether they saw or heard it.[5]

Case Study in Communication

Lockheed Martin Internal IT Group has developed an award-winning com-munication program that includes leadership briefings, internal company news articles, posters, videos, Webcasts, framed strategy maps for execu-tive conference rooms, mounted strategy maps for all other conference

FIGURE 5-11

One company's strategy communications plan

Objective: Identify specific messages for each targeted audience and the mix of channels through which messages will be conveyed.

Approach: Leverage the in-house communication team and existing communication vehicles to deliver a strategically planned flow of information that will communicate and reinforce a complex message to a diverse and geographically spread audience over an extended period.

Vehicle	Type of Communications	Comments
Small Group Meetings	Staff meetings, one-on-one reviews, weekly status updates	• Generate involvement and enthusiasm • Labor intensive
"Social" meetings	Overlay with refreshments, relevant entertainment	• May not reach all shifts
MG News, Local Newsletters, Publishing	Companywide newsletters, division newsletters	• Dedicated scorecard column • Include relevant BSCol articles • Newsletter
Local Intranets	Internal Web site	• Not everyone has access • Includes links to Meganet and BSCol
PowerPoint Presentations	Template designed to provide overview, updates, resources, etc.	• Widely used and accepted
Posters/Bulletin Boards/Racks	Posters, brochures posted in coffee rooms/kitchens, conference rooms, lobby	• Accessible to all
Permanent Framed Posters	Corporate/division scorecard displayed in high-traffic areas, primary conference rooms, etc.	• Top-of-mind every day • Post measures, goals, trends • Signed by CEO
Video	CEO states importance of initiative; reinforces commitment	• No "talking heads" • Effective training tool • High-energy opening/closing or updates

Two basic but critical requirements of effective communication:

• Every communication had to answer the WIIFM employee question, "What's in it for me?"

• Each distinct phase or initiative had to be synchronized with the cascading of the Balanced Scorecard to that unit or department.

Source: Balanced Scorecard Report, May–June 2002.

rooms, interactive strategy maps on the portal, and personal copies of functional strategy maps distributed to all four thousand employees.[6]

The communication program started with a poster campaign (see Figure 5-13). The almost blank initial poster contained only the phrase "Got Strategy?" in the middle of a pentagonal-shaped figure. Successive posters, which appeared at periodic intervals, filled in the blank spaces, eventually articulating the five strategy-focused organization principles, with special emphasis on principle 4, "Make Strategy Everyone's Job." The next phase of the poster campaign (see Figure 5-14) featured the strategic themes on

FIGURE 5-12

MVCI BSC communication plan

Communication Channel	Q1	Q2	Q3	Q4
One-to-One Consulting		As needed		
Strategy Planning Brochure	✔			
Webinar	✔			
Strategic Performance Report	✔	✔	✔	✔
Poster Series	✔	✔	✔	✔
Weekly Update	✔	✔		✔
myHR Newsletter	✔		✔	✔
Communication Forum		✔		✔
Strategy Refresh			✔	

the Internal IT Group strategy map, helping employees learn about the objectives and issues for each theme.

The communication team created a customized version of the strategy map (see Figure 5-15). This diagram shows the company's strategy map, surrounded by brief descriptions of the major initiatives, each pointing to the strategy map objective it supports. This chart enables all employees working on initiatives to see where and how they contribute to the unit's

FIGURE 5-13

Internal IT Group poster campaign, phase 1—Awareness

FIGURE 5-14

Internal IT Group poster campaign, phase 2—Execution: "Think strategically, act locally"

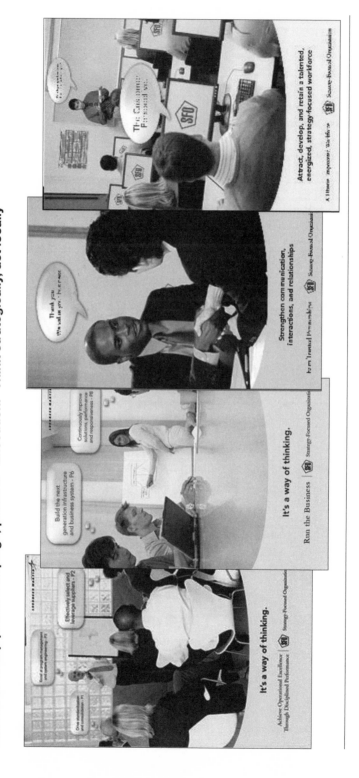

FIGURE 5-15

Internal IT Group illustrates the connection of each strategic initiative to the EIS strategy map

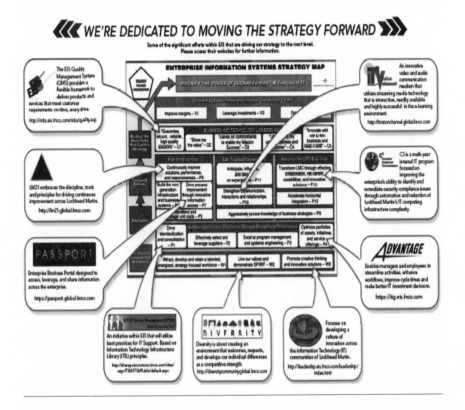

strategy. They could now see why the various initiatives were needed and how they all fit together to help implement the Internal IT Group strategy.

To reinforce the message, the Internal IT Group communication team gave every employee a pen that contained a pullout (a printed plastic sheet on a spring-loaded spindle). On one side, the pullout shows the Internal IT Group strategy map under the caption, "Make Strategy Everyone's Job," and on the other side it shows key components of the IT strategy.

The communication team also manages a customized strategy "iViews" component on the company's portal. The page has a link to "Strategy News," which contains weekly updates of the latest strategy news and hot objectives as well as articles about the strategy. It contains strategy training and resources, links to all strategy maps, and views—including video clips—of what individual employees are saying about their understanding of the strategy. A Web page, "Internal IT Group Customers," has links to customer service-level agreements and account managers. A "Contact

Us" page contains links to employees who can answer questions about the strategy or receive feedback.

The "Internal IT Group Strategy and Business Planning" navigation bar has buttons linking to the following pages:

- *Strategy maps:* Drop-down menus allow employees to access and view line-of-business and functional strategy maps.
- *Quarterly Strategy Reviews (QSRs):* A drop-down menu enables employees to access QSRs from 2005 to the current date.
- *Initiatives:* The page includes links to the Quality Management System (QMS), with links to quality news and resources and internal initiatives.

Internal IT Group measured the success of its communication program using periodic employee surveys. In late 2006, 90 percent of Internal IT Group employees rated the strategy communication and training program as "very important" or "important." Here are some of their comments from the survey:

- "Top-down explanation of the strategy map from management to the foot soldier."
- "Easy to understand and I can see where I fit into the picture."
- "How individual Internal IT Group employees can contribute to its goals."
- "What I can do for the strategy—it helps explain the strategy of each functional organization and how and where the company is going."

Internal IT Group earned an execution premium summarized in the insert below:

LOCKHEED MARTIN INTERNAL IT GROUP'S EXECUTION PREMIUM

- Internal IT Group achieved 15% productivity savings through stronger alignment of objectives with customer needs and elimination of ineffective efforts.
- Further savings came from reductions in the number of non-essential IT initiatives, products, and services.
- Use of Internal IT Group products and services has enabled internal customers to achieve 10% productivity savings.

- Lockheed Martin operating divisions gained new business owing to Internal IT Group's improved program knowledge.
- Customers' perceptions of Internal IT Group's strategic alignment improved, as measured by survey ratings of leadership commitment, organizational climate and culture, workforce strategy and development, and customer relationship management.

All results 2004 to 2006.

Link Personal Objectives and Incentives to the Strategy

The most successful Balanced Scorecard implementations have occurred when organizations skillfully melded the intrinsic motivation emanating from its leadership and communication program with the extrinsic motivation created by aligning personal performance objectives and incentive compensation. After receiving communication, education, and training about the strategies of their unit and enterprise, employees develop personal objectives that are aligned with the strategic objectives (see Figure 5-16). Personal objectives create a clear line of sight between strategic objectives and the work that each employee does every day.

Annually, employees validate their personal strategic objectives with the help of their supervisors and human resource professionals. Several organizations encourage employees to develop personal Balanced Scorecards, with each employee setting targets to improve a cost or revenue figure, boost performance with external or internal customers, improve a process or two that will deliver customer and financial value, and enhance a personal competency to drive process improvement.

For example, consider the machine operator at the end of the line of sight in Figure 5-16. He might express his personal objectives using the Balanced Scorecard framework:

Machine Operator # 452	Personal Objectives
Financial	Reduce cost of downtime.
Customer	On-time transfer of finished goods to next workstation.
Process	Reduce changeover times. Reduce machine breakdowns.
Learning and Growth	Obtain certification in machine maintenance.

FIGURE 5-16

Employees develop personal objectives aligned with strategic objectives

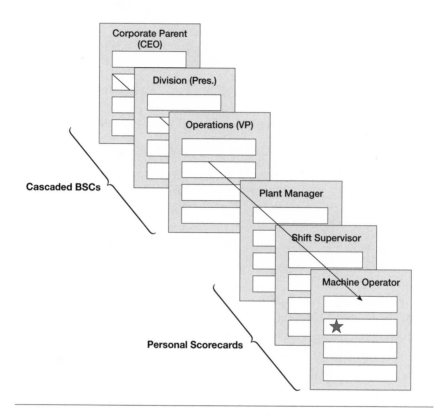

The operator's supervisor reviews the objectives with him to ensure that they align with departmental, facility, business unit, and corporate objectives. She also discusses the performance targets for each measure to set an appropriate degree of difficulty for each objective. Annually the supervisor reviews performance with the machinist and recommends whether it merits a promotion or bonus payment.

Most companies also link incentive compensation to targeted scorecard measures. In that case, managers see a significant increase in employees' level of interest in the details of the strategy. The philosophy of such a link is that if the company does well, the employees should share in the value they helped create. Also, by linking incentives to performance on Balanced Scorecard metrics, the company signals that it is serious about the strategy the scorecard represents. It is not focused only on short-term financial outcomes; it wants employees to enhance relationships with customers (external and internal), improve key processes, and develop competencies that will drive future value creation in the firm.

Incentive plans vary widely across organizations. Generally, they have an individual component and a business unit and enterprise component. Plans that calculate awards only on business unit and enterprise performance signal the importance of teamwork and knowledge sharing, but they also may encourage individual shirking and free rider problems. Plans that reward only individual performance generate strong employee incentives to improve their personal performance measures, but they inhibit teamwork, knowledge sharing, and suggestions to improve performance outside the employee's immediate accountability and control.

Typical plans therefore include two or three kinds of awards: (1) an individual award based on achieving targets established annually for each employee's personal objectives and (2) an award based on the employee's business unit, along with, perhaps, (3) an award tier for divisional or enterprise performance.

To avoid paying bonuses when financial performance is weak, companies often set a minimum financial hurdle that must be achieved before bonuses are paid. The hurdle might be measured by, say, achieving profits as a targeted percentage of sales, or achieving a minimum return on capital, or achieving breakeven in an economic-value-added calculation. Once the financial hurdle has been exceeded, some portion of the excess is committed to a bonus pool, with actual bonuses based on performance of BSC metrics and a majority of weight on measures in the three nonfinancial perspectives.

Some companies create excitement around Balanced Scorecard performance by introducing contests. Vista placed $1 million in a bonus pool that was distributed equally to all employees in units that hit the performance stretch targets for the key BSC metrics.

Develop Employee Competencies

One final step is required to align employees with strategy. Employees must develop the competencies—the knowledge, skills, and values—that enable them to excel:

- *Knowledge* is *what* an individual knows, an understanding gained through education and experience. It represents mastery of a field of study, a professional or technical discipline, or a focused area of expertise.

- *Skill* is the knowledge of *how* to do something in a consistent and efficient manner, such as running a complex machine, performing an audit, developing a customer's financial plan, facilitating a meeting, or executing a sales call.
- *Values* are the behaviors, traits, and motivations that people bring to the tasks they perform. Values can be described as customer focused, pragmatic, innovative, or goal oriented.

The company can develop knowledge and skills among its employees through training and development programs, along with career planning that gives employees experiences in various tasks, businesses, regions, and functions. Instilling values is more complex. It requires a combination of taking good inputs through careful recruitment and selection programs—in addition to extensive training and communication of corporate mission and values—to inspire the behaviors that the corporation desires.

In previous work we have described how to identify strategic job families.[7] These employees, generally encompassing only a small percentage of the total workforce, are in a position to improve dramatically the performance of the processes that are most important for creating value for customers and shareholders. They create the differentiation in the strategy for sustainable competitive advantage. Given their importance, the company's human resource department places a high priority on developing the desired competencies among all employees in the strategic job families. Of course, the HR processes eventually need to ensure that all employees have competency development programs in place that will give them the knowledge, skills, and values they need in order to achieve the targeted performance on their personal scorecards.

Case Study in Employee Competency Development: KeyCorp

KeyCorp's Corporate and Investment Banking (CIB) team represents a best-practice example of developing employee competencies.[8] The CIB project team consisted of a partnership between the executive leaders of each line of business and the senior corporate HR managers. The team started by developing a detailed list of the skills and competencies required for each critical job position and the learning needs for each job to close gaps in foundational skills in sales and client management, as well as functional, product, and technology skills. Based on CIB's new business model, which combined corporate and investment banking functions, the team identified, for each position, the skill levels that were necessary for the employee to make an immediate impact.

As shown in Figure 5-17, to function as an industry leader or a senior banker an employee needed to be an expert—capable of teaching others—in prospect identification, competition assessment, presentation skills, and development of the institutional perspective. A junior banker, in contrast, needed to have only working-level skills in these areas but needed expert skills in negotiations to close deals that had been identified and sold by senior bankers and the industry leader.

The project team identified training courses that could bring all individuals up to the required skill levels for their positions. It tracked the enrollment and performance of employees in the various training courses that were offered. KeyCorp soon saw the results of its comprehensive competency development program, which was linked to critical strategic objectives. Unlike earlier training initiatives, KeyCorp's training courses had 100 percent attendance at every session, with no empty seats.

Employees responded with evaluations such as this one: "The course I just completed is immediately applicable to the work I am now doing . . . When is the next course on [skill xyz] being offered? . . . Finally, training

FIGURE 5-17

KeyCorp matrix of required employee capabilities, by job position

This matrix is an excerpt from a much broader skills grid.

	Industry Leader			Senior Banker			Junior Banker			Associate		
	Knowledge Level			Knowledge Level			Knowledge Level			Knowledge Level		
Skill/Competency—Sales	E	W	L	E	W	L	E	W	L	E	W	L
Negotiation (back-end process)		X			X		X					X
Prospect identification and prequalification	X			X				X				
Prospect identification and prequalification (research)							X				X	
Pricing (process and market knowledge), includes price set and selling it	X				X			X				X
Developing the institutional perspective (external)	X				X			X				X
Competition (understand who else is in the game)	X				X			X				X
Presentation (conceptual and delivery)	X				X			X				

KEY: E: Can teach others
W: Well rounded—can fly alone
L: Limited—may need support

that fits my job." The returns from enhancing the CIB key employee competencies came soon in the form of higher scores for customer loyalty and greater sales and income for the division.

KeyCorp's execution premium is shown in the insert below.

KEYCORP'S EXECUTION PREMIUM

- KeyCorp's share price jumped from a low of $15.69 in 2000 to a high of $35 in 2005. The company's ROE rose to 15.42% in 2005, from 13.75% the previous year.
- Net income improved by $217 million, from $903 million in 2003 to $1.12 billion in 2005, the highest net income in the company's history.
- Employees' "willingness to go the extra mile" increased from 3.78 in 2001 to 4.26 in 2004 (on a scale of 1 to 5, with 5 as the highest), according to the company's employee survey.
- Retail client retention rates rose 5% from 2002 to 2004.
- Nonperforming loans decreased for 11 consecutive quarters over the past several years. Net loan charge-offs, as a percentage of average loans, remained at their lowest level since Q4 1995.

SUMMARY

Alignment of organizational units and employees is critical for successful strategy implementation. The alignment and communication process should start as soon as the high-level corporate strategic themes and objectives have been determined. Vertical alignment enables each business unit and department to contribute to higher-level strategic objectives while simultaneously striving to implement its local strategy for success in its competitive environment. Horizontal alignment with other business units enables the corporation to realize synergies from the following:

- Delivering an integrated customer value proposition across multiple business units
- Reinforcing the corporate brand during each customer buying experience
- Achieving economies of scale by sharing production, technology, distribution, or sales resources and corporate staff functions
- Sharing knowledge and best practices across the corporation
- Enhancing employees' capabilities through common training and managed career development plans

Cascading strategy maps down and across the organization helps business units internalize their dual roles of local optimization and corporate contribution.

Aligning employees starts with leadership-driven communication programs. The strategy communication program should be planned and managed as carefully as any company advertising, branding, and marketing campaign. The communication plan must deliver the message each year at least seven times in seven different ways. Once employees are aware of and understand the strategy, the company can reinforce the message by asking local employees to set personal objectives that have a clear line of sight to business and corporate-level strategic objectives.

Many companies gain even more employee awareness and commitment to the strategy by linking incentive and bonus awards to the attainment of employee, business unit, and corporate objectives. In addition, human resource departments work closely with employees and their supervisors to craft customized training and experience-building programs so that employees can develop the competencies that help them achieve their personal objectives and contribute to business unit and corporate success.

NOTES

1. If you are implementing the management system at a single business unit, you can skip the first section (aligning business units) and concentrate on the next two sections (aligning support units and employees).
2. Greater detail about organizational and employee alignment can be found in R. S. Kaplan and D. P. Norton, *Alignment: Using the Balanced Scorecard to Create Corporate Synergies* (Boston: Harvard Business School Press, 2006); and *The Strategy-Focused Organization: How Balanced Scorecard Companies Thrive in the New Competitive Environment* (Boston: Harvard Business School Press, 2000).
3. D. J. Collis and C. A. Montgomery, "Creating Corporate Advantage," *Harvard Business Review* (May–June 1998): 72.
4. *Core competencies* have been defined as the "pool of experience, knowledge and systems within the corporation that can be deployed to reduce the cost or time to create or extend a strategic asset"; strategic assets are the "imperfectly imitable, imperfectly substitutable, and imperfectly tradable assets that promote cost advantage or differentiation." Constantinos Markides, "Corporate Strategy: The Role of the Centre," Chapter 5 in *Handbook of Strategy and Management*, 1st ed., eds. A. Pettigrew, H. Thomas, and R. Whittington (Thousand Oaks, CA: SAGE Publications, 2001).
5. An excellent short summary of a company's strategy communication process can be found in L. Johnson, "Common Sense in Strategy Communication: Four Lessons from Canon USA," *Balanced Scorecard Report* (May–June 2007): 6–7.

6. Lockheed Martin Internal IT Group's strategy communication program received the 2006 Magellan Award of the National League of Communications Professionals.

7. R. S. Kaplan and D. P. Norton, "Measuring the Strategic Readiness of Intangible Assets," *Harvard Business Review* (February 2004): 52–63, and Kaplan and Norton, *Strategy Maps: Converting Intangible Assets into Tangible Outcomes* (Boston: Harvard Business School Press, 2004), 199–248.

8. The KeyCorp experience was initially reported in Kaplan and Norton, *Alignment*, 273–277.

CHAPTER SIX

PLAN OPERATIONS

Align Process Improvement Programs

MANY ORGANIZATIONS have achieved one-time performance break-throughs without the use of a formal management system. Charismatic leadership and the art of management are powerful and frequently effective forces. Performance that depends on the power of individual leaders, however, is generally not sustainable over the long term. Unless an organization links its strategy to its governance and operational processes, it won't be able to sustain its successes.

Figure 6-1 shows the positioning of the process that links strategy to operations within our comprehensive closed-loop management system. Figure 6-2 describes the two key subprocesses used to accomplish this linkage. The first subprocess links business process improvements to strategic priorities. The second links strategy to forecasts of resource capacity and the spending on operating and capital resources that will be required to deliver on the strategic plan. We discuss the linkage of strategy to process improvements in this chapter, and the development of the complete operating plan—including the sales forecast, resource capacity, operating budget, and projected profit-and-loss statements—in Chapter 7.

IMPROVE KEY PROCESSES

Strategy execution requires alignment and execution of both strategic initiatives and process improvement programs. In Chapter 4, we described

FIGURE 6-1

The management system: Linking strategy to operational planning

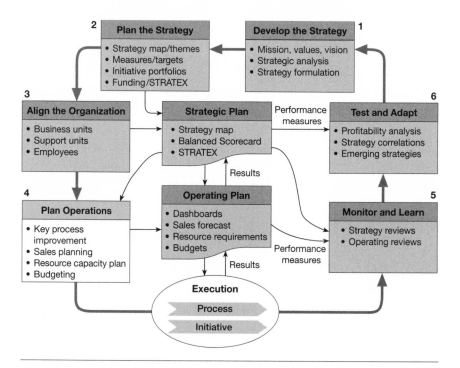

FIGURE 6-2

Plan operations

Strategy Execution Process	Objective	Barriers	Representative Activities
1. **Improve Key Processes** *What business process changes does the strategy require?*	Ensure that changes required by the strategic themes are translated to changes in operational processes	No alignment between strategic priorities and quality and continuous improvement programs	• Total quality management • Business process improvement • Key success factors • KPIs/dashboards
2. **Develop the Resource Capacity Plan** *How do we link strategy to operating plans and budgets?*	Ensure that resource capacity, operational plans, and budgets reflect the directions and needs of the strategy	Forecasts, budgets, and operating plans developed independently from strategic plan	• Rolling forecasts • Activity-based costing model • Resource planning • Budgeting (OPEX/CAPEX) • Pro forma financials

how companies identify and execute portfolios of strategic initiatives—short-term, finite-length projects (up to twelve to eighteen months)—designed to drive improvement in Balanced Scorecard measures. In this chapter, we describe how to align ongoing process improvement programs with strategic objectives.

Quality and process improvement programs existed well before the introduction of the Balanced Scorecard. Japanese companies, in the 1970s, demonstrated the power of their total quality management (TQM) approaches, which built on earlier innovations by Deming, Shewhart, Juran, and others. Western versions of Japanese TQM showed up in the 1980s, including lean management, just-in-time, and six sigma.

The U.S. Congress established the Malcolm Baldrige National Quality Award in 1987; several leading European companies founded the European Foundation for Quality Management (EFQM) in 1988. The EFQM organization created a model similar to Baldrige's for judging applicants for a European Quality Award. The reengineering movement occurred simultaneously with the introduction of the Balanced Scorecard in the early 1990s. By the early 1990s, almost all enterprises were implementing quality and process improvement initiatives built on these developments.

Organizations can use the strategic objectives on their strategy maps and scorecards to enhance and align their process management programs. Quality models, by themselves, often focus on local, tactical, and unlinked process improvements. Quality resources are committed to processes that have been identified as falling short of best practices. This allocation process, however, occurs independently of strategic priority setting. The BSC provides explicit causal links from quality and process improvements to successful outcomes for customers and shareholders. The cause-and-effect relationships in a strategy map and the strategic objectives on the Balanced Scorecard highlight the process improvements that are most critical for successful strategy execution. The BSC provides the guidance that organizations need to redeploy their scarce resources of people and funds away from improving vital processes that are already operating satisfactorily and toward those processes most critical for implementing the strategy.

As one executive noted, "The BSC provided a unity and focus to our TQM efforts, and also to our annual and long-range planning. We had a lot of teams doing a lot of things, but the efforts were ad hoc. The BSC brought this all together into a unified, systematic approach. Now when we assign responsibilities to departments, we do it within a framework."

Aligning quality and process improvement programs with strategy starts with the value proposition—the heart of a strategy. For example, companies offering a low-cost value proposition to customers will focus on reducing the cost, improving the quality, and shortening the cycle time of supply-chain, production, distribution, and service delivery processes. Companies focused on offering complete solutions and relationships will home in on improving the processes that select and deepen relations with targeted customers, such as analyzing a customer's needs and cross-selling multiple products and services to achieve a complete solution to the customer's problem. And companies following an innovation strategy will get the greatest return on their process improvement spending when they focus on improving their innovation and product development processes.

Case Study on Key Process Management: LowCost Airlines

Consider the situation of LowCost Airlines, a generic discount airline with a strategic theme of operational excellence, as illustrated in Figure 6-3. The theme's high-level financial measures are net income and return on assets. LowCost has also identified two additional financial metrics—revenue growth and asset utilization (operating fewer planes)—that drive its high-level financial metrics. If LowCost can increase utilization of its airplanes and flight crews, it can earn higher revenues without having to spend more on these expensive resources.

The theme's customer perspective expresses LowCost's value proposition to offer passengers both the lowest prices and the most reliable departure and arrival times in the industry. LowCost measures these customer objectives by benchmarking its prices, on-time departures, and arrival performance against industry best practices.

The reduction of ground turnaround time is the key process objective for the operational excellence strategic theme. LowCost uses two measures for this critical process objective: the average time its planes spend on the ground between flights, and the percentage of flights that depart the gate on time. By reducing the time its planes spend on the ground, LowCost enables its planes to depart on time (meeting a key customer expectation) and gets better use of its most expensive resources—airplanes and flight crews. These practices enable LowCost to earn profits even at prices that are the lowest in the industry (a key financial objective). The theme's learning and growth perspective has an objective to train and motivate ground crews for fast ground turnarounds, much like the training of an Indianapolis 500 race car pit crew, which can change four tires in less than fifteen seconds.

As noted, LowCost's critical operating process objective is to reduce ground turnaround time. Using language from the TQM and lean man-

FIGURE 6-3

Operational excellence strategic theme for LowCost Airlines

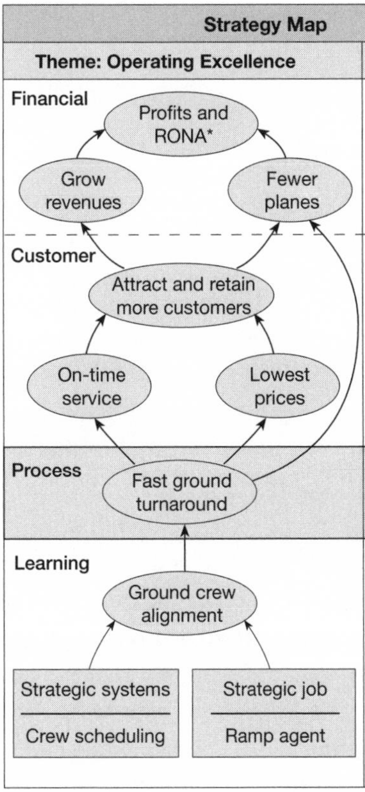

Strategy Map			Balanced Scorecard	
Theme: Operating Excellence		Objectives	Measurement	Targets
Financial — Profits and RONA*, Grow revenues, Fewer planes		• Profitability • Grow revenues • Fewer planes	• Market value • Seat revenue • Plane lease cost	• 30% CAGR** • 20% CAGR • 5% CAGR
Customer — Attract and retain more customers, On-time service, Lowest prices		• Flight is on time • Lowest prices • Attract and retain more customers	• FAA on-time arrival rating • Customer ranking • Number of repeat customers • Number of customers	• #1 • #1 • 70% • Increase 12% annual
Process — Fast ground turnaround		• Fast ground turnaround	• On-ground time • On-time departure	• 30 minutes • 90%
Learning — Ground crew alignment, Strategic systems / Crew scheduling, Strategic job / Ramp agent		• Ground crew aligned with strategy • Develop the necessary skills • Develop the support system	• % ground crew stockholders • Strategic awareness • Strategic job readiness • Information system availability	• 100% • 100% • Yr 1—0% Yr 3—90% Yr 5—100% • 100%

*Return on net assets.
**Compound annual growth rate.

agement movements, the time an airplane spends on the ground is "waste," much like the setup time on a machine. No one pays an airline to have its planes on the ground. Only when planes are flying, transporting passengers and freight from one location to another, is the airline adding value for its customers.

Also, as discussed in Chapter 2, an airline such as LowCost competes not only against other airlines but also against other transportation forms, such as buses, trains, and automobiles. LowCost must deliver prices and departure reliability that are comparable to these other forms of transportation if its strategy is to succeed. LowCost's ability to (1) make money while offering the lowest prices in the airline industry and (2) match the on-time reliability of cars, buses, and trains depends critically on eliminating waste in all its forms. LowCost's strategy clearly requires that its processes for rapid ground turnaround and on-time departures have industry-leading performance.

LowCost decides to focus its process improvement capabilities on delivering this desired performance. Ground turnaround time is determined by the longest of three parallel processes performed by employees:

1. Plane unloading, cleaning, and reboarding
2. Luggage unloading and reloading
3. Ground maintenance and refueling

A plane cannot leave the gate for its next departure until the arriving passengers and their luggage leave the plane, the plane is cleaned, maintained, and catered for the next flight, the flight crew for the departing flight and all the new passengers board the plane, the departing passengers' luggage has been stowed on the plane, and the plane is refueled and declared mechanically fit to fly. To reduce ground turnaround from the current industry average of more than fifty minutes to the targeted level of thirty minutes, all three processes must be performed dramatically better.

Figure 6-4 shows a simple decomposition of the first of the three ground turnaround processes: unloading, cleaning, and reboarding the plane. This process starts when arriving passengers depart from the plane. Then a ground crew cleans and caters the plane, and, finally, the new passengers and flight crew board for the departing flight.

The analysis reveals that a rigorous commitment to improve this process can eliminate existing delays and waste sufficiently to achieve the stretch target for the first of the three subprocesses for ground turnaround. A similar analysis can be done for the two other ground turnaround processes. If targeted performance cannot be achieved within the desired time frame through continuous improvement of the existing process, the company would then consider a complete reengineering of the process, in effect designing an entirely new process to achieve the performance target.

Identifying Strategic Processes for Improvement

In addition to improving existing processes, a newly created strategy map often identifies entirely new processes at which the company must excel. For example, a construction company shifted from an operational excellence, low-cost strategy to a differentiated, customer intimacy strategy. For this strategy to be successful, it needed to execute a new process: work

FIGURE 6-4

Can process improvements close the performance gap?

Ground turnaround activities	Turnaround time between flights		Process improvements
	Current minutes per step	Best practice minutes per step	
Wait for airline door to open	3:16	0:00	A. Agent anticipates plane arrival time;
Unload passengers	6:41	4:38	waiting at jetway for plane to dock
Wait for cleaning crew to board	0:24	0:18	B. Stricter controls on carry-on bags,
Clean airplane	10:48	7:40	fewer passengers moving back in aisle to find bags
Wait for cabin crew to board	4:11	0:00	C. Cleaning crew in position ahead of time
Wait for first passenger to board	4:06	0:00	D. Standardized workflow, timing, and methods, such as prearranged kits
Load passengers	17:32	14:00	E. Visual signal from cabin crew to agent when plane is ready to board
Wait for passenger info list	1:58	0:13	F. Active management of overhead storage bins by flight crew
Close aircraft door	0:57	0:09	G. Passenger information list delivered by agent following last passenger on board
Detach boarding ramp	1:39	0:43	H. Agent ready at aircraft to close door
Total cycle time	51:34	27:41	

closely with targeted customers to anticipate their future needs. The company had never done such a process before. Previously, it waited for customers to request project bids before responding. It now realized that it had to excel at the new process of building a long-term, trusting relationship with its targeted customers to understand and anticipate their future needs.

Similarly, at a financial services company, frontline employees had to shift from being reactive transaction processors to becoming proactive financial planners. With only a quality scoring model to guide them, the employees could have scored high with their performance on speedy, responsive, zero-defect processing of customer transactions. But this process, soon to be automated, was no longer critical to the new customer relationship strategy. Instead, employees would have to excel at an entirely new set of processes:

- Anticipate and understand customers' emerging financial needs.
- Develop a deep and comprehensive knowledge of new financial products and services.
- Enhance capabilities for customizing and selling products and services tailored to the individual customer.

In both companies, the Balanced Scorecard identified the criticality of the new processes, enabling the companies to deploy their best improvement teams to design and enhance the processes' performance.

Quality and process improvement projects will generate the highest payoffs when they are selected based on criteria linked to the company's strategic objectives. Quality programs designed to improve a local process or a quality score on a business excellence model are fine. In general, a company is better off when more of its processes are done better, faster, and cheaper. But a collection of better, faster, cheaper local processes does not a strategy make. Companies should emphasize improving those processes that contribute the most to the success of the company's strategy.

Strategic Versus Vital Processes

Figure 6-5 shows a 2×2 contingency table that explains the link between process improvements and Balanced Scorecard strategic priorities. The columns classify the organization's existing processes as either "excellent" or "needs improvement" according to, say, EFQM or Baldrige process excellence criteria. The rows distinguish between processes identified on the Balanced Scorecard as strategic—contributing to the differentiation of the company's strategy—and those that are vital: necessary for the company's success but not creating a strategic difference.

Examples of vital but not strategic processes are processing the payroll, closing the books each period, providing basic housekeeping, grounds maintenance, and security, and operating the phone system and computer network. The company needs its employees to be paid, its financial books closed on time and properly, its properties cleaned, maintained, and se-

FIGURE 6-5

Using the quality assessment and balanced scorecard together

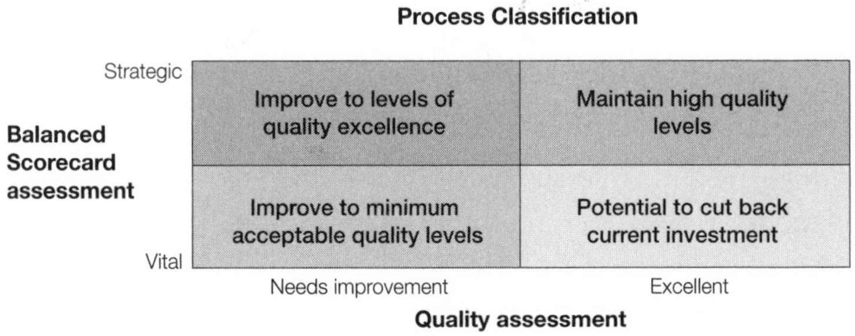

Process Classification

		Needs improvement	Excellent
Balanced Scorecard assessment	Strategic	Improve to levels of quality excellence	Maintain high quality levels
	Vital	Improve to minimum acceptable quality levels	Potential to cut back current investment

Quality assessment

cured, and its phone system and computer network operating. But being the world's best at any of these vital processes does not create innovative products, a differentiating experience for customers, or a productivity breakthrough for financial performance.

Vital processes are analogous to vital human processes such as those that determine body temperature, blood pressure, and heart rate. If any of these is erratic or out of control, the body cannot function and immediate corrective action must be taken. But an individual with superb control over body temperature, blood pressure, and heart rate still has not created the conditions required for a long-term successful career in a chosen profession.

Starting in the lower-left cell of Figure 6-5, we encounter the vital (nonstrategic) processes that the company currently performs poorly. The company needs to invest resources to improve these processes to competitive levels, or at least to a level where its performance does not detract from successful strategy execution. Proceeding counterclockwise in Figure 6-5, the lower-right cell represents nonstrategic processes currently being performed excellently. The company should strive to maintain current performance but can consider withdrawing quality improvement resources from these processes because they are already at satisfactory levels.

The cell in the upper-right corner represents strategic processes currently being performed excellently. The company can celebrate its success with these processes and can maintain a perhaps lower but still sustaining quantity of quality resources to continually improve them. Some quality experts claim that quality improvement is like riding a bicycle; if you don't continue to move forward, you fall down.

The cell in the upper-left corner is the critical area for management concern. The processes in this cell have been identified as critical for successful strategy implementation but are currently being performed poorly, or at least their current performance is far from targeted levels. It is here that significant resources, six sigma black belts, and management attention must be devoted. If these processes are not improved to best-in-class performance, the company is not likely to deliver a distinctive value proposition to customers nor the productivity improvements demanded by financial objectives.

This analysis of the 2×2 contingency table in Figure 6-5 illustrates what a quality expert once told us: "Quality (six sigma) teaches you *how* to fish. The Balanced Scorecard teaches you *where* to fish."

Because the strategic processes are featured in the Balanced Scorecard's process perspective, they will receive continual review and attention from senior management in their monthly strategy review meetings (as discussed in Chapter 8). These reviews are an important component of what Bob Simons calls the company's *interactive system:* the system that managers use to regularly and personally involve themselves in the decision activities of subordinates.[1]

The performance of the vital processes—those classified in the bottom row of Figure 6-5—is also important. The organization will benefit from improving any process, whether strategic or vital. The reporting and feedback on the performance of the vital processes are included in Simons's *diagnostic system.* Management establishes clear local performance targets for employees and then does not intervene unless the system alerts them when performance on a vital process falls outside established control limits (analogous to blood pressure or body temperature becoming too high or too low). The diagnostic system thus conserves management attention by operating under *management by exception.*

Several companies provide good illustrations of linking strategic objectives in the Balanced Scorecard process perspective to their quality improvement activities.

Case Study on Linking Strategy to Quality: Information and Communications Mobile

Information and Communications Mobile (ICM), a producer of mobile phones and networks, took a comprehensive approach to aligning its quality improvement programs with strategic priorities. The mobile communications marketplace was experiencing high growth and rapid change. ICM had to introduce a major new mobile phone every quarter, reach the market quickly with new products, respond rapidly to customer requests, and achieve scale economies by expanding its global reach.

ICM organized its operations around three core customer-to-customer processes: "idea to market" (innovation); "offer to cash" (operations); and "problem to solution" (customer management). It also included several support processes: strategy, human resources, and finance. Its Balanced Scorecard objectives reflected the three critical strategic themes: innovation, speed, and volume growth.

ICM used a catchball process (see Figure 6-6) to cascade the BSC business objectives in the three themes to operational objectives that could be addressed by frontline employees. *Catchball* is an element in the Japanese *hoshin kanri* policy-deployment process in which employees conduct two-way discussions with those above and below them. Through these discussions, the employees establish goals that support those at the

FIGURE 6-6

Using the Balanced Scorecard with the catchball process

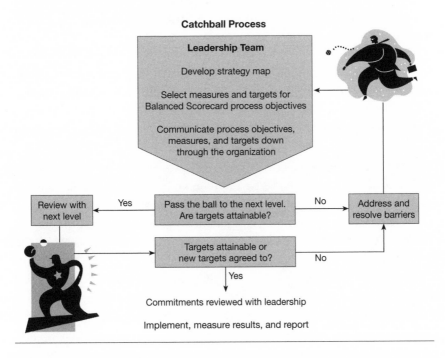

Catchball Process

Leadership Team

Develop strategy map

Select measures and targets for
Balanced Scorecard process objectives

Communicate process objectives,
measures, and targets down
through the organization

| Review with next level | ← Yes | Pass the ball to the next level. Are targets attainable? | No → | Address and resolve barriers |

Targets attainable or new targets agreed to?   No

Yes

Commitments reviewed with leadership

Implement, measure results, and report

level above them; these goals are also the outcomes of the goals set at the level below them.

Senior management at ICM started the catchball process by communicating strategic objectives, articulated in the divisional Balanced Scorecard, to all business units. Each business unit established goals to achieve the division's strategic objectives. The process continued with the business units linking their objectives and commitments to operational objectives at the department level, just below the business unit. The departmental objectives were then cascaded successively down until they had become translated into targets for local six sigma project teams.

Take, for example, the offer-to-cash business process, represented by a BSC objective for end-use consumers to experience an easy, speedy purchase. The catchball mechanism cascaded this objective from the consumer business group to a mobile phone manufacturing plant, which accepted two catchball objectives to improve on-time delivery and reduce order lead times. The catchball process cascaded this plantwide objective to various functional departments. One of them, the purchasing department, developed an objective to establish a six sigma project team that would strive to reduce replenishment times. In this way, the BSC objective for a transparent, speedy customer ordering process was now linked to a front-line work team's project to improve replenishment times for purchased materials.

Another BSC objective, in the problem-to-solution business process, was to reduce *nonconformance cost* (NCC), a term drawn from the cost-of-quality literature. NCC refers to the cost of handling and repairing device failures in the field. The BSC project team cascaded to manufacturing and design units the high-level objective of reducing NCC. A project team within engineering and design discovered that defective battery contacts caused a high fraction of field failures. The project team accepted a catch-ball objective to improve the battery charge contacts of mobile phones and launched a six sigma project to solve this problem.

The cascading process at ICM focused all departments and employees on projects that had the greatest impact on processes at the heart of the company's strategy. It also aligned every department and employee with company objectives. Employees learned how they contributed to their business unit's—and, ultimately, the company's—objectives.

As a third example, consider a BSC objective within ICM's problem-to-solution business process: to solve customers' complaints quickly and responsively. ICM committed staff and money to help it reduce the time required to resolve customers' complaints, including developing metrics that measured performance of this objective. But solving problems that arise in the field is costly, even if done well. ICM also shifted recurring customer complaint problems to its idea-to-market business process. The process owner formulated a "design for six sigma" project to eliminate the root cause of recurring failures. ICM understood that improved and more robust designs are a much more effective solution than reducing the time to resolve customer complaints after they experience defects.

ICM converted its BSC-level target to reduce its NCC into targets for each of its three major business processes. The conversion soon led to more than forty six sigma projects. Within one year, the division had completed more than fifty projects and realized a median saving of €150,000 per project.

When ICM benchmarked its six sigma programs against those of other companies, it learned that its average project payback was among the highest. It had used the Balanced Scorecard to align its quality improvement projects with the areas that yielded the greatest benefits for the company.

Case Studies: Thai Carbon Black, Motorola GEMS, Mobistar (Orange)

Thai Carbon Black (TCB) is one of the world's largest producers of carbon black, with six of the top ten tire makers among its customers. TCB's strategy was to become the lowest-cost producer of carbon black in the world. It developed a Balanced Scorecard to define and map its strategy. The Balanced Scorecard's financial perspective had a key objective to reduce manufacturing cost. The customer perspective included objectives to improve quality and delivery performance. The process perspective, of course, stressed continuous process improvements.

TCB, like ICM, integrated its Balanced Scorecard with total quality management and hoshin kanri methodologies. In TCB's hoshin kanri catchball process, department heads translated BSC measures into specific measures for their units; then, via catchball, they cascaded those down to the next managerial level within each department, and then down to supervisors and local employee project teams. Each cascading stage used two-way communication between managers and their direct subordinates to agree on measures and targets. This systematic cascading process created alignment throughout the organization. Aggregate measures at one level, such as "reduce manufacturing costs," became more detailed measures, such as "reduce consumption of lubricating oil," at the next lower level.

Thai Carbon Black's alignment of process improvements with strategy contributed strongly to earning the execution premium shown below:

THAI CARBON BLACK'S EXECUTION PREMIUM

- TCB's gross profit margin (almost 25 percent) is 12–15 percentage points higher than its nearest competitor.
- For 2007, return on net worth has grown to 16.7 percent.
- In 2007, TCB realized $2 million in savings from cost improvements.
- Overall plant effectiveness reached 97.2 percent in 2007.
- In 2003, Hewitt Associates judged TCB to be the Best Employer in Thailand and among the Top Five in all of Asia.
- From 2000 to 2006, employee satisfaction rose 23 percentage points to 92 percent.

For several years, Motorola Government and Enterprise Mobility Solutions (GEMS) used a performance excellence model, adapted from the Baldrige Criteria, to organize its continuous improvement activities, helping it realize best-in-class processes and results. An internal assessment, however, revealed a shortfall in the strategy and business planning process.

After a benchmarking study of leading practices used by Baldrige Award winners, GEMS adopted the Balanced Scorecard to provide an organizing framework for its six sigma and continuous improvement efforts. It formed a Performance Measurement Council of twenty-two members from the company's various regions, product groups, functions, and support areas, including several six sigma master black belts. The group developed a strategy map, Balanced Scorecard, and reporting system (called a "digital cockpit") for the GEMS strategy.

One BSC learning and growth objective was to "make six sigma the way we work." This objective led to evaluating all six sigma projects on their potential impact on high-level scorecard objectives, including customer satisfaction, quality, operating earnings, operating cash flow, and strategic sales growth. Motorola GEMS is an excellent example of a company with a highly developed six sigma and performance excellence program that gained substantial new benefits by using the Balanced Scorecard to align its existing program with strategic priorities. In 2003, Motorola GEMS became a Malcolm Baldrige National Quality Award winner. Its execution premium is described in the insert.

MOTOROLA GEMS' EXECUTION PREMIUM

- Return on net assets skyrocketed from about 16% in 2001 to 137% in 2004.
- From 2002 to 2004, sales rose 11% annually and GAAP operating earnings as a percentage of sales rose from 8.7% to 16.4%.
- Market share is twice as large as that of its nearest competitor.
- The division's call centers have achieved world-class performance results.
- Employees' job satisfaction, strategic awareness, and understanding of their contributory roles have risen greatly since 2001.

Mobistar, a leading mobile communications company in Belgium (now part of the Orange Group), began as a global system for mobile communications telecom in 1996.[2] From its beginning, Mobistar adopted the EFQM performance excellence model as its management system. Mobistar's focus on innovation and customer service led to rapid initial growth.

Like Motorola GEMS, however, Mobistar soon realized that even though it had many excellent local process improvement initiatives under way, it lacked a mechanism to align its workforce with its strategy. Mobistar adopted and integrated the Balanced Scorecard into its existing management processes. It used the acronym MASC to refer to the "Mobistar aligned scorecard," while also defining the acronym as "measurable, achievable, simple, and concrete."

Mobistar customized the scorecard to its culture; for example, rather than refer to the "process" perspective, it used the term *enabler* to associate this perspective with the leading indicators—the drivers—of performance results in the EFQM excellence model. It added a "partner" perspective to highlight the importance of managing relationships with its suppliers and external partners, and a "society" perspective to incorporate the EFQM objective to integrate corporate social responsibilities with a company's business goals. Also, Mobistar replaced the "learning and growth" perspective with one labeled "management by objectives" to adapt its well-developed existing MBO process for identifying individual employee objectives to align with Mobistar's strategy.

Mobistar's execution premium is summarized in the insert.

MOBISTAR'S EXECUTION PREMIUM

- Mobistar's share price has consistently outperformed its peers in the Dow Jones telecom index, becoming the index's best performer in 2002.
- Since November 2002, Mobistar has been included in the BEL 20 composite index, the leading corporate index of the Brussels Stock Exchange.
- Mobistar slashed operating expenses as a percentage of revenue by 70%, to 30%, in 2003.
- The BSC has helped Mobistar become strategically focused—and consistent—in a fast-growing and turbulent market that frequently spurs reactive behavior by competitors.
- Mobistar has dramatically increased its subscriber base by successfully wooing competitors' customers. From October 2002 to March 2004 alone, it gained 71,500 subscribers, while competitors lost 86,600.

In these three cases—Thai Carbon Black, Motorola GEMS, and Mobistar—the companies already had strong quality management programs. Rather than continue to use these programs to make continued, but unrelated, local and isolated process improvements, each adopted the Balanced Scorecard to focus and align its performance improvements on those processes that would have the greatest impact on meeting business and company strategic objectives.

SET PRIORITIES FOR PROCESS MANAGEMENT

Companies without a strong total quality management culture do not need to instill this culture before aligning process management with strategy. The Balanced Scorecard framework features the processes most critical for successful strategy execution. To make the framework operational, companies can focus on achieving the critical process objectives that are shown on the strategy map, as well as the learning and growth objectives that drive the key process improvements.

Symnetics, our South American consulting affiliate, has developed a formal approach for linking process management to strategic objectives.[3] The approach starts by comparing the existing customer value proposition to the proposed one. Consider a company that adopts the Balanced Scorecard to help it implement a new strategy based on providing a full range of services to meet a customer's needs. The previous strategy had the company competing by offering low prices and speedy service. The new strategy requires the company to develop capabilities for rapidly developing and introducing new products and services and for providing post-sales maintenance, support, and training. The company identifies the gap between its existing process capabilities, developed to support the previous strategy, and the process performance required for the new offering. The company must close this strategy gap by enhancing existing processes and introducing some entirely new ones.

The company continues to drill down to process management by identifying the key process objectives (on the strategy map) that drive the achievement of the customer and financial targets (see Figure 6-7). The company then identifies the key performance (process) indicators (KPIs) that drive process excellence. In this example, the company has selected a BSC innovation process objective to "be agile and effective in developing customer-oriented solutions." It defines two metrics for this objective: a research and development effectiveness index (RDEI)—which equals the ratio of new products' profits to the products' R&D investment costs—and time-to-market, a metric of speed for the idea-to-market innovation process (see Figure 6-8). The ambitious three-year targets are to improve

FIGURE 6-7

Linking process managment to BSC strategic processes

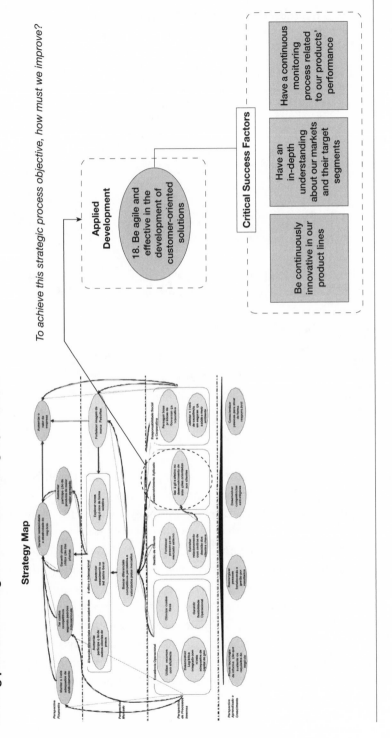

To achieve this strategic process objective, how must we improve?

Applied Development

18. Be agile and effective in the development of customer-oriented solutions

Critical Success Factors

Be continuously innovative in our product lines

Have an in-depth understanding about our markets and their target segments

Have a continuous monitoring process related to our products' performance

Strategy Map

FIGURE 6-8

Linking a balanced scorecard R&D strategic objective to critical success factors and metrics

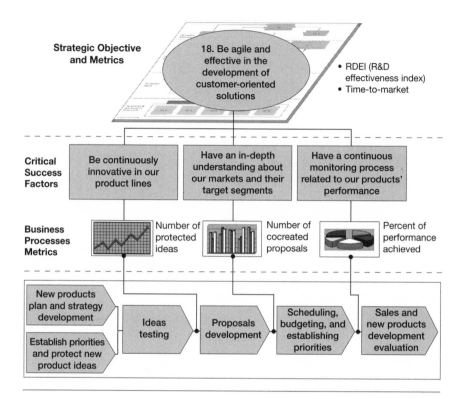

the RDEI ratio by 50 percent and to reduce time to market by 55 percent.

The two BSC metrics are outcome (or lagging) indicators, which provide feedback about whether the company successfully introduced new products that will more than repay their development costs and whether the introduction was accomplished rapidly. But to improve the design and development process, employees need process indicators that motivate and track whether existing projects are on track to achieve success. Employees cannot wait until the products have been introduced to learn whether they succeeded. They need more contemporaneous indicators.

In the next step, the company identifies the critical success factors (CSFs) for employees to strive to achieve while performing the process. The company selects the following three CSFs along with metrics to make the CSFs operational.

Critical Success Factor (CSF)	CSF Metric
Be continuously innovative in our product lines.	Number of protected ideas
Have an in-depth understanding about our markets and their target segments.	Number of proposals cocreated with targeted customers
Have a continuous monitoring process related to our products' performance.	Percentage of performance achieved by newly introduced products

The metrics can be displayed on a process dashboard to improve the performance of subprocesses within the overall idea-to-market innovation process, as shown earlier in Figure 6-8. Dashboard metrics are the operational performance indicators that lead, via a cause-and-effect relationship, to process excellence. They can serve as the basis for a service-level agreement between, in this case, the R&D function and the business unit. The agreement specifies how the support function (R&D) can contribute to delivering the targeted performance of critical process objectives in the business unit's strategy map.

USING DASHBOARDS

Companies enhance their process improvements by designing and deploying local operational dashboards. These *dashboards* are collections of key indicators that provide feedback on local process performance. Automated dashboards reflect business intelligence and data integration infrastructure, which facilitate the visual representation of the underlying data. They enable employees to drill deeper into the data for interactive analysis. Although all processes benefit from systematic measurement and reporting, dashboards are most effective when they highlight the processes from the unit's Balanced Scorecard process perspective (see Figure 6-9).

For example, LowCost Airlines, discussed earlier in the chapter, should develop dashboards for the employees who perform passenger deboarding and reboarding, luggage handling, and ground maintenance. In that way, the employees would receive continual feedback and learn which of their process innovations produces the greatest and most reliable improvements in reducing ground turnaround time, the critical process in the operational excellence strategic theme.

FIGURE 6-9

Linking strategic objectives to process dashboards

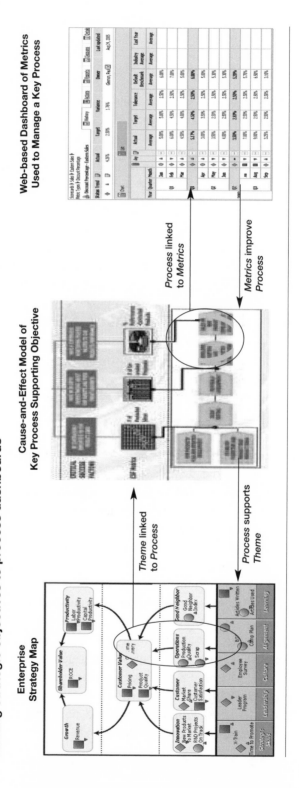

Dashboards differ from Balanced Scorecards in several ways.[4] Dashboards are operational, not strategic. Consequently, they may not have financial or customer metrics, or metrics of the department's human capital development activities. Dashboards focus on process metrics that employees can affect in their daily actions. Whereas most BSC metrics are outcomes, which are updated monthly or quarterly, dashboards can reflect daily and even hour-by-hour performance so that employees receive rapid and timely feedback about recent performance. Such rapid feedback helps employees learn from their experience.

Dashboards also focus on local departmental, functional, and process performance, in contrast to the cross-business and cross-functional outcome indicators on the Balanced Scorecard. Dashboards inform the problem-solving and continuous improvement of employees who work in the same department, function, or process. Dashboard data, apart from their value in managing and improving day-to-day processes, also are the prime informational input for focused operational review meetings, which we discuss in Chapter 8.

Case Study on Dashboards: TD Canada Trust

As an example of using statistical analysis (multiple regression analysis) to select the best operational (process) metrics, consider the example of TD Canada Trust (TDCT), a company formed by a merger between Toronto Dominion Bank and Canada Trust.[5] The Canadian regulatory authorities approved the merger only after Toronto Dominion Bank's CEO made a public commitment to maintain high customer service standards and deliver "comfortable" and convenient banking experiences to all customers. TDCT already used a dashboard of twenty-six metrics (see Figure 6-10) to track customer satisfaction (three metrics), customer loyalty (two metrics), and the presumed drivers of satisfaction and loyalty (twenty-one metrics). The management team had three concerns:

- The dashboard had too many metrics for branch personnel to focus on.
- The metrics had no associated weights or priorities.
- The bank had never validated that the twenty-one driver metrics correlated at all with customer satisfaction and loyalty.

Moreover, at a fundamental level, the bank was unsure what "comfortable" banking meant, despite having just made a highly public commitment to deliver it.

FIGURE 6-10

TD Canada Trust's existing customer dashboard

TD Canada Trust

2003 TARGET: 81.8

CSI Quarterly Report
BRANCH # 1020
KING & BAY PAVILION
MEASUREMENT PERIOD: AUG'03 to OCT'03

	Measurement At ... Level							Regional	National
	Branch							Regional	National
	Year End 2002	Nov'02 to Jan'03	Feb'03 to Apr'03	May '03 to Jul '03	Aug '03 to Oct '03	Year Ending Oct '03	Net ** Change	Year End 2003	Year End 2003
Base: Total # Interviews	200	50	50	50	50	200		26934	194514
	%	%	%	%	%	%	%	%	%
Customer Satisfaction:	Percent who give a rating of 6 or 7 on a 7-point numeric scale where 7=Excellent and 1=Poor								
Overall In-Branch	75.7	69.6	79.7	69.3	89.9	*77.1*	+1.4	81.5	85.6
At Teller*	76.9	72.3	77.5	70.0	92.9	*78.2*	+1.3	81.9	85.9
At Side-Counter+	70.8	58.3	88.9	66.7	77.8	*72.9*	+2.1	80.2	84.3
Customer Commitment:	† Percent giving 4 or 5 rating based on 5 point scale								
Recommend TD/CT To Friend or Colleague†	68.6	78.0	75.1	65.0	81.6	*74.9*	+6.3	76.2	79.3
Continue using TD/CT Over Next 12 Months†	86.0	89.9	86.0	81.5	88.1	*86.4*	+0.4	88.4	90.6
Did The Teller/Representative (Side-Counter)....?									
Appreciate your business	86.6	90.2	91.8	85.6	95.6	*90.8*	+4.2	91.9	93.3
Process your transaction quickly*	95.0	92.7	95.1	97.4	100.0	*96.3*	+1.3	96.0	97.3
Have the ability to handle your request		96.0	98.1	95.7	95.7	*96.4*		95.8	96.7
Wait time acceptable	91.0	87.7	87.7	86.2	94.1	*88.9*	-2.1	84.8	89.9
Give you his/her individed attention	93.4	91.8	87.7	98.1	97.8	*93.8*	+0.4	91.6	95.1
Make you feel like a person not number*		92.5	94.9	94.9	100.0	*95.6*		92.9	95.1
Smile	89.1	96.0	92.3	90.0	96.0	*93.6*	+4.5	91.8	93.6
Handle accts & transactions accurately+		88.9	88.9	88.9	100.0	*91.7*		95.0	95.8
Process your transaction accurately*		97.4	95.1	95.1	97.4	*96.2*		96.6	97.6
Appear knowledgeable about services		90.0	89.7	89.9	94.0	*90.9*		91.6	93.5
Show interest in you as a person+	88.2	77.8	91.7	88.9	88.9	*86.8*	-1.4	89.2	92.1
Promptly acknowledge your presence+	85.4	88.9	69.4	100.0	100.0	*89.6*	+4.2	84.2	86.7
Greet you pleasantly	96.6	98.1	100.0	97.9	100.0	*99.0*	+2.4	96.7	97.8
Encourage you to ask questions+	86.1	77.8	72.2	77.8	58.3	*71.5*	-14.6	73.7	75.7
Explain services ...easy to understand+	84.0	88.9	88.9	88.9	100.0	*91.7*	+7.7	92.2	93.4
Treat you in a respectful manner	98.0	97.8	97.8	97.8	100.0	*98.4*	+0.4	97.8	98.6
Address you by name	70.9	62.4	63.8	65.6	82.2	*68.5*	-2.4	71.9	73.2
Thank you for your business	84.9	90.0	87.5	85.9	90.0	*88.4*	+3.5	87.6	86.8
Give advice or...based on your needs+	86.1	77.8	61.1	69.4	69.4	*69.4*	-16.7	77.6	79.6
Conduct banking privately	93.6	93.7	91.6	93.8	96.0	*93.8*	+0.2	92.4	94.6
Recommend additional services+	72.9	61.1	55.6	77.8	50.0	*61.1*	-11.8	54.8	53.3

* Base: Among those who completed a transaction with a teller

+ Base: Among those who completed a transaction at the side-counter. CAUTION: The number of side counter interviews per branch is extremely small - about 10 interviews per quarter.

** Net Change is the Year Ending Oct '03 minus the Year End 2002 results.

Chris Armstrong, executive vice president of marketing in 2005, led a project to perform rigorous and systematic testing of the drivers and outcomes of customer satisfaction. The project team started with in-depth surveys, covering each dimension of service, with customers who had just had a branch interaction. The team then performed statistical analysis to estimate the impact of each service attribute on customer satisfaction.

The team retained an overall customer satisfaction index (CSI) and the two customer loyalty metrics of "likely to recommend" and "likely to continue as a TDCT customer." It replaced two other customer satisfaction metrics with a new dissatisfaction metric: the percentage of customers who scored the experience between 1 and 3 on a 10-point scale.

The team's major finding was that ten of the twenty-one driver metrics had no effect or only a negligible effect on customer satisfaction, loyalty, and branch profitability. It eliminated these ten metrics, resulting in a more streamlined and validated report, as shown in Figure 6-11.

The project team also used statistical analysis to streamline the dashboard by estimating the impact of improvements in the customer satisfaction drivers. For example, the team learned that customers valued a feeling of being appreciated more than speed of service:

An increase of 1% in measures related to comfortable banking *(percentage of customers who were satisfied that the teller made them feel their business was appreciated) led to a 1.7% increase in customer satisfaction, which in turn led to a 0.4% increase in branch profitability.*

A 1% increase in speed of service *(percentage of customers satisfied that their transaction was processed quickly) led to only a 0.8% increase in customer satisfaction, which, in turn led to a 0.2% increase in branch profitability.*[6]

Armstrong's team, with its knowledge of the value of increasing performance along each dimension of service, listed the service indicators on the branch scorecard in order of their relative performance. That enabled each branch employee to quickly grasp the most important service quality indicators.

The team also discovered that satisfaction had a nonlinear S-shaped response to improvements in most service measures. Improvements in a customer service level had little impact until a critical threshold was reached. Thereafter, the impact accelerated rapidly with improvements, but eventually satisfaction responded less strongly to further improvements. This insight helped direct attention away from metrics where most of the potential

FIGURE 6-11

TD Canada Trust's post-analysis customer satisfaction tracking report

Teller CSI

	Teller CSI	YTD	Performance Levels (1)	(2)	(3)	Current Tri-Monthly	Previous Tri-Monthly	vs Previous Tri-Monthly
1	CSI Score	86.9						
2	Satisfied (Bottom 3 Box)	1.9						
3	Likely to recommend	79.8						
4	Likely to continue	90.7						
5	Make you feel they appreciate your business	91.6	*					
6	Process your transaction quickly	96.3	*					
7	Have the ability to handle your request	96.3		*				
8	Wait time acceptable	91.6		*				
9	Greet you pleasantly	97.2		*				
10	Address you by your name	77.6		*				
11	Give you his or her undivided attention	96.3		*				
12	Thank you for your business	86.9	*					
13	Process your transactions accurately	97.2			*			
14	Treat you in a respectful manner	98.1		*	*			
15	Conduct your banking privately	93.5			*			

(1)-Need to Improve (2)-Room to Improve (3)-Maintain

gains had already been achieved and toward those indicators where improvements would yield significant improvements. The response curve served as the basis for a feedback report to each branch that helped the branch manager focus attention on those areas where performance improvements would be most valuable.

The TDCT experience is a sophisticated example of the design and use of dashboards. Many companies automate and display entire collections of operating metrics without first identifying the metrics expected to have the greatest influence on aggregate performance. In contrast, TDCT conducted front-end statistical analysis (multiple regression analysis) to identify which operating metrics apparently had the greatest impact on the performance of their decentralized units. These metrics could then be featured, trended, and benchmarked on the first page of each branch's electronic dashboard. In general, capturing and displaying a few key operating metrics on a dashboard, especially when the metrics are benchmarked against comparable internal or external units, provides great focus and feedback to employees' process improvement activities.

SHARING BEST PRACTICES

Companies should not view process improvement activities as local projects. They should leverage their process improvement capabilities by sharing best-practice experiences across all organizational units.

Vista Retail uses a formal process to review and compare performance across all outlets in its chain. The company encourages retail units to share best practices, such as dealing with customer complaints, improving customer service, and offering a speedier purchase cycle. Regional directors, on their periodic visits to outlets, search for best practices and then disseminate them to other units in the region.

The company established a nonmonetary recognition program at each outlet, Vista Pride Award, to reward people and teams for submitting great value-creating ideas. Each outlet selects and announces the first-, second-, and third-place prize winners each quarter. It submits the first-place winner to corporate for a quarterly contest whose grand prize is a trip for two for a six-night, seven-day resort stay and $500 spending money. Vista's Office of Strategy Management collects and posts the best-practice case studies on the company intranet. The company also asks its outside auditors and vendors for best practices that they have observed in companies in different industries.

Ricoh organizes visits by executives from one business unit to another as part of BSC review sessions, during which best practices are observed and studied. Ricoh's performance excellence (PE) unit manages a formal annual process for identifying and sharing best practices. Each business unit in a region submits its best practices, as measured by a Baldrige evaluation template, to the PE group. PE holds a Best Practice Sharing Rally, where the CEO and the presidents of the business units in the region select the three best practices to be submitted to and assessed, using the Baldrige Criteria, by a senior international internal consulting group. Those scoring higher than 50 percent are named as Ricoh Best Practices and entered into an international database that is shared across all regions.

Ricoh also organizes a Kaizen Process Improvement Sharing Rally to showcase the best quality-control and six sigma projects. It selects the best project to compete in a regional kaizen rally. The assessment criteria include the degree of sharing of the project's best practices with other organizational units, and the extent of implementation of the practices in areas of the business other than the one where it was developed.

Hillside Family of Agencies is a nonprofit organization, based in Rochester, New York, that offers child-centered and family-focused services through an integrated system of care. Services provided by Hillside affiliates include child welfare, mental health, juvenile justice, education, developmetal disabilities, and youth development in locations throughout central and western New York. It strives to be the leader in translating leading-edge research into practical solutions that are replicable across Hillside's service offerings. The Strategic Planning and Quality Assurance team serves as the link between national researchers and Hillside affiliate operating managers for sharing best practices. Successful implementation of research into practical solutions requires deploying best practices to multiple levels: individual practitioners, the organization, the payers, the community systems, and the consumers. Hillside, in turn, provides back to researchers a valuable perspective regarding the needs of the children and families and what families want for their children.

Hillside utilizes a collaborative, co-creation process to integrate evidence-based practices into existing service models. The design of services is finalized based on customer feedback and program evaluation. In this way, all managers are kept aware of the state of the art and continually search for ways to put the new ideas into the solutions they deliver to children and their families. Hillside has earned the execution premium shown:

HILLSIDE FAMILY OF AGENCIES' EXECUTION PREMIUM

- Hillside has exceeded its three-year revenue growth target for 11 consecutive quarters (2004 to 2007).
- From 2002 to 2007, the number of families served increased 37%, from 5,804 to 7,950.
- Hillside Work-Scholarship Connection continues to graduate high school students at significantly higher rates than among comparison sample students not exposed to the program.
- Hillside Work-Scholarship Connection provides an economic return on investment of $2,263,646 per 100 program participants (to age 30).
- The average length of time elapsed from referral to service initiation has decreased 50% over 2 years, falling from an average of 6.2 to 2.7 weeks.
- Positive Behavioral Interventions and Supports (PBIS) implementation has resulted in a significant decrease in the number of safety holds and support room referrals in Residential and Day Treatment programs.

SUMMARY

Process improvements are a critical part of any strategy execution program. The objectives and measures in a Balanced Scorecard's financial and customer perspectives describe the desired outcomes of a successful strategy. The objectives and measures in the process perspective describe how the strategy will be executed. Excellent performance in the processes identified on a company's strategy map and scorecard creates the differentiation in the strategy and also generates the desired productivity improvements in the financial perspective.

Quality and other process improvement programs play a critical role in enabling the strategic processes to achieve their performance targets. An organization should analyze each strategic process to identify the critical success factors and metrics that employees can work to improve in their daily activities. Dashboards provide the feedback on the metrics expected to drive process improvements. Finally, formal knowledge sharing—some of it based on cross-sectional, quantitative comparison of decentralized unit performance—enables successful process innovations to be quickly disseminated throughout the organization.

NOTES

1. R. Simons, *Levers of Control* (Boston: Harvard Business School Press, 1995), 91–124.
2. Mobistar material excerpted from "Mobistar," *Balanced Scorecard Report Hall of Fame 2005* (March 2005), 27–28.
3. We are grateful to Reinaldo Manzini for contributing these experiences from the Symnetics, Brazil, practice.
4. W. W. Eckerson, *Performance Dashboards: Measuring, Monitoring, and Managing Your Business* (Hoboken, NJ: John Wiley & Sons, 2006), provides an excellent and comprehensive treatment of dashboards. We use a slightly different terminology than Eckerson by restricting the term *dashboards* to what he calls operational or tactical dashboards, and retaining the term *Balanced Scorecard* for what he calls a strategic dashboard.
5. We are indebted to Professor Dennis Campbell for the TD Canada Trust case study; see D. Campbell, "Choose the Right Measures, Drive the Right Strategy," *Balanced Scorecard Report*, May–June 2006, 14–16.
6. Ibid., 15.

CHAPTER SEVEN

PLAN OPERATIONS

Sales Forecasts, Resource Capacity, and Dynamic Budgets

A COMPANY'S SPENDING on the strategic initiatives and process improvements discussed in Chapters 4 and 6 is essential for effective strategy implementation. But the spending on initiatives, projects, and process improvements typically accounts for only 10 percent or less of overall corporate spending. The remaining 90-plus percent enables the company to produce and deliver products and services to customers and to perform corporate support functions. In this chapter, we present an integrated approach for linking the strategic plan to forecasts for spending on operating and capital resources. This process (described in the second row of Figure 6-2 in Chapter 6) ensures that resource capacity, operational plans, and budgets reflect the direction and needs of the strategy.

BUDGETS AND BEYOND

In the 1920s, General Motors introduced operating and capital budgets, an important management innovation that has persisted to current times.[1] The mantra of General Motors CEO Alfred Sloan and his CFO, Donaldson Brown, was "decentralized management with centralized control." They used budgets to coordinate and control the diverse business units in the General Motors system. Budgets became most companies' central management system by performing the following functions:

- Forecasting future revenues and expenses to facilitate financial planning and managerial coordination
- Generating managerial commitment to deliver the budgeted results
- Authorizing managers to spend up to the budgeted amount for each line item in the budget
- Evaluating the performance of managers and divisions

But the budgeting process in many companies has become a costly, time-consuming, and inflexible control system for rewarding and punishing business managers. Harold Geneen, former CEO of ITT, became the stereotype of the command-and-control corporate executive. Geneen's highly centralized and idiosyncratic management style placed enormous pressure on managers to achieve budgeted performance. Geneen's style was emulated by Al Dunlap, who used budgets to force managers to achieve either ambitious sales goals or major line-item expense reductions; the intense pressure eventually led to major financial reporting problems.[2] Another notorious budget user was Bernie Ebbers of WORLDCOM, of whom it was said, "You would have a budget, and he would mandate that you had to be 2% under budget. Nothing else was acceptable."[3]

Several companies in northern Europe, such as Svenska Handelsbanken, Borealis, Statoil, and Nordea, have abandoned the use of budgets entirely. Practicing members of the "beyond budgeting" movement, these companies replaced the budget with a new set of forecasting and control processes.[4] Bjarte Bogsnes, a senior manager at Statoil and a leading practitioner in the beyond budgeting movement, states, "With today's dynamic, unpredictable, and demanding environment, managers require more freedom and responsibility. Processes must be more continuous and responsive, and managers must have more discretion on how to achieve results, not just meet budgeted performance."[5]

The beyond budgeting advocates argue that a budget has the following fatal weaknesses:

- Creating a budget takes excessive time and money.
- A budget motivates managers to make lowball estimates of revenues and income for fear of the consequences from Geneen-, Dunlap-, or Ebbers-type managers if they fall short on any budgeted target.
- It stifles innovation.

- It quickly becomes obsolete in a rapidly changing, globally competitive business environment.

Consider the experience of Borealis, a company formed by the merger of the petrochemical divisions of two Nordic oil companies: Statoil of Norway and Neste of Finland.[6] Bogsnes, who moved to Borealis from his position as head of budgeting at Statoil, wanted to use the creation of a new company as an opportunity to introduce a new management approach to replace the budget: "Traditional budgets serve too many different purposes—for instance, both forecasting and target setting. Forecasts should be realistic, targets should be challenging. They should not be the same number."[7]

Thomas Boesen, financial controller at Borealis, supported Bogsnes's mission. Boesen recalled the frustrations that managers had with the budget: "People worked hard to produce a detailed document, put the document in a large binder, and, sadly, never looked at it again. Our products and supplier markets were changing so fast that the budget was out of date within weeks."[8]

Bogsnes and Boesen replaced the budget at Borealis with an integrated suite of four targeted management control processes. As portrayed in Figure 7-1, the new Borealis management system delivered the capabilities of the traditional annual budget (the inner box) while also providing a much broader set of capabilities. It achieved these broader capabilities at lower cost and without budgeting's dysfunctional aspects, such as low-balling or sandbagging of budgeted revenues.

We examine each of the four processes in detail.

Rolling Financial Forecasts

Each quarter, Borealis generated rolling forecasts for the next five quarters to give a clear, simple picture of anticipated financial performance. The forecasts were intended to provide an unbiased estimate of future sales and expenses and had no implications for the measurement of managerial performance.

Managers in each business unit used the most objective data they could find to create a new set of forecasts each quarter. The data included price information from corporate planning, expected sales volume from the sales force, fixed costs and depreciation from the manufacturing sites, and exchange rates, inflation, and loan information from corporate finance. The forecasts were not elaborate exercises; they were basically back-of-the-envelope calculations, including updates of the main profitability drivers: volumes and prices.

FIGURE 7-1

The new Borealis management system offered capabilities well beyond those of the traditional budget

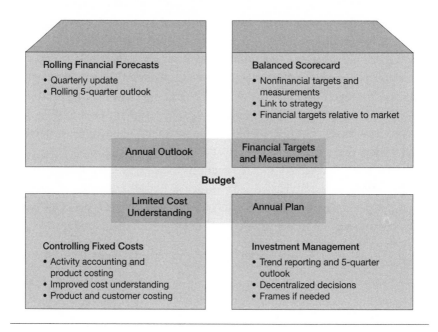

Bogsnes noted that although managers had done forecasting previously, the new purpose was different: "The rolling financial forecasts literally gave us more for less: better reliability because of no gaming and frequent updating, and significantly less data collection and number crunching."[9]

Balanced Scorecard

Borealis used the Balanced Scorecard to communicate strategic objectives and measures to employees. It encouraged employees to set personal objectives that would be linked to corporate strategy. Rather than communicate corporate performance through budgets and variances, the company now tracked performance against key performance indicators related to the business.

Thus, the Balanced Scorecard, and not the budget, became the primary performance management tool at Borealis. Performance of business units on the key indicators was benchmarked internally among comparable units, and externally using industry and competitor data.

Controlling Fixed Costs

Under the former budget process, Borealis controlled capacity-related (fixed) costs through budgets and variances for each expense line item. It also traced and monitored the costs of each operating department. Borealis replaced the budgeted line-item expense and departmental cost controls with activity-based costing (ABC), a cost management tool that is described later in this chapter.

The ABC model traced and accumulated line-item operating expenses into process costs and then to product and customer costs. ABC provided a common language for describing costs and for benchmarking process costs across plants and with other companies. The plants' employees found the activity-based cost information to be much more intuitive and understandable than the line-item expenses reported previously in the budget. Now employees could see how and where to control costs for maximum impact.

Investment Management

Borealis eliminated centralized capital budgets and gave decision making and control to the managers and employees who were closest to the marketplace and customers. It segregated investment project approval by size of project. Small investments, less than US$1.65 million (10 million Danish krona [DKK]) could be approved by the division, plant, and function that proposed the project.

Borealis tracked the cost of these small investments as a component of the twelve-month moving average of activity-based costs. Medium-sized investments (between US$1.65 and $8.25 million [DKK10–50 million]) had to exceed a hurdle rate that corporate management set each period in accordance with the financial projections from the five-quarter rolling financial forecast. If cash flow was going to be tight, management increased the hurdle rate. The executive board approved centrally the largest investment projects, those that exceeded US$8.25 million (DKK50 million). Bogsnes commented on the improved investment approval process: "Before, investment projects had to be calculated twice: once to get them approved in the budget, and once again before final approval and project start. By then market assumptions might have changed completely, requiring a full new investment appraisal."[10]

Borealis financial managers believed that the four new management control processes accomplished the traditional budget's objectives in a manner that was better, faster, and cheaper. Line managers now had a high degree of freedom in the way they achieved challenging targets that were benchmarked against leading global competitors. The managers did not have to seek preapproval to spend money to improve performance. They just had to deliver the performance. This clear accountability for results fostered increased responsibility and decision making.

The following table summarizes how the new processes at Borealis performed the roles previously done by the budget.

Budget Role	Borealis Process
High-level financial and tax planning	Rolling financial forecasts
Target-setting and performance evaluation	Balanced Scorecard
Controlling fixed costs	Activity-based costing Trend reporting External benchmarking
Authorizing and allocating capital expenditures	Small projects: trend reporting, localized Medium projects: varying hurdle rates Major strategic projects: done by the board on case-by-case basis

By introducing the new processes, Borealis managers focused on improving process costs and managing total project costs rather than on reporting and explaining a myriad of cost variances each month. They were evaluated on achieving strategic objectives, not on their compliance with monthly spending limits, and they avoided the annual burden of the rigid, time-consuming budgeting process.

LINKING THE STRATEGIC PLAN TO A RESOURCE CAPACITY PLAN AND OPERATING BUDGET

The Borealis example provides the platform for a new integrated planning and resource allocation process that tightly links strategy to operations. In the remainder of this chapter, we describe a comprehensive framework that integrates strategic planning with resource allocation, financial forecasting, and, ultimately, a dynamic budgeting process.

The framework's key innovation is a time-driven activity-based cost (TDABC) model to link strategic planning to operational and capital budgeting. The framework consists of five steps:

1. Use driver-based revenue planning to obtain sales forecasts for future periods.
2. Translate the high-level sales forecasts into a detailed sales and operating plan.
3. Enter the sales and operating plan, as well as projected process efficiencies, into a TDABC model that forecasts demand for resource capacity.
4. Derive dynamic forecasts (budgets) for operational and capital spending (OPEX and CAPEX).
5. Estimate pro forma financial profitability by product, customer, channel, and region.

In the remainder of this chapter, we discuss each of the five steps.

STEP 1: USE DRIVER-BASED REVENUE PLANNING TO OBTAIN SALES FORECASTS

Chapters 2 through 6 describe how companies develop their strategies and select the strategic initiatives and process improvements that will drive near-term actions. Based on these planned actions, and in light of the growth targets for financial and customer BSC metrics, companies need to forecast their near-term revenues and mix. To remedy the rapid obsolescence of an annual sales forecast, and following the recommendations of the beyond budgeting movement, many companies now forecast sales at least quarterly, and the forecast period goes beyond the current fiscal year (typically five or six quarters ahead), as illustrated in Figure 7-2.

Companies need updated forecasts for several purposes. First, public companies want to avoid unfavorable surprises with their investing and analyst communities. Companies that unexpectedly announce sales and earnings that fall short of market expectations experience severe price declines and often forced turnover in the ranks of senior executives. The unfavorable reaction comes from two sources. First, markets are disappointed whenever financial performance falls short of expectations. But sophisticated investors understand that companies operate in uncertain, challenging environments. Not all earnings expectations can be met even

FIGURE 7-2

Rolling forecast process

5-Quarter Rolling Forecast

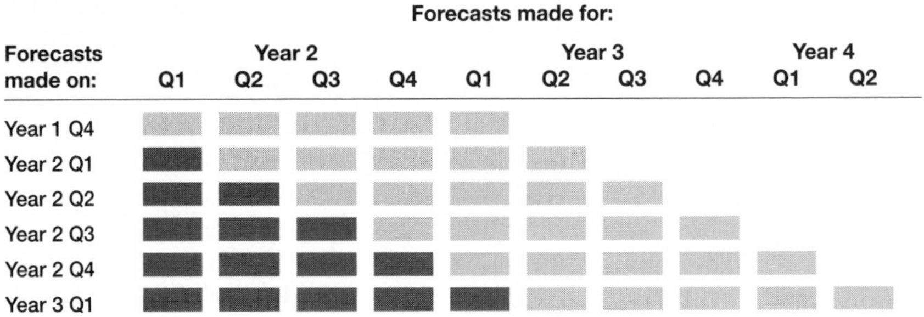

| Forecasts | Year 2 | | | | Year 3 | | | | Year 4 | |
made on:	Q1	Q2	Q3	Q4	Q1	Q2	Q3	Q4	Q1	Q2
Year 1 Q4										
Year 2 Q1										
Year 2 Q2										
Year 2 Q3										
Year 2 Q4										
Year 3 Q1										

Forecasts made for:

Light rectangle indicates a forecast period; dark rectangle indicates actual results known at time of forecast.

when companies have some discretion to postpone bad news by managing reserves and controlling the timing of revenue and expense recognition. The second source of the unfavorable market reaction to earnings shortfalls is that investors do not expect senior executives to be surprised by the content of their own earnings announcements. Unanticipated sales and earnings shortfalls imply that senior executives lack adequate information and control systems to detect when actual performance is falling short of forecasts. An unhappy surprise leads to loss of confidence in senior executive teams. So, at a minimum, companies should continually reforecast their results to keep market expectations in line with the most likely reported financial performance.

Valid forecasts are vital for short-term financial planning. Changes in sales and expenses affect the receipt and disbursement of cash. The company's treasury office must manage cash balances and draw upon banking or credit lines so that the company does not run short of cash. The treasury office needs accurate forecasts of near- and intermediate-term cash receipts and expenditures. It cannot operate from a monthly plan derived from a budget prepared six to twelve months earlier that no longer reflects current economic and market conditions.

A *quarterly rolling forecast* process also forces managers to be forward-looking, at least once per quarter, to scan the external environment and recent internal performance to identify new opportunities, respond quickly to new threats, and revise action plans to address performance shortfalls.

Using quarterly rolling forecasts allows companies to incorporate the most recent information and insights about the marketplace.

Managers can respond to new information by slowing discretionary expenditures—such as research and development, training, promotion, capital expenditures, and new market introductions—if the sales opportunities anticipated when these initiatives were planned and authorized turn out not to be occurring or are now seen to occur further in the future than previously anticipated. Conversely, if demand is stronger than previously forecast, the company may wish to accelerate capital spending, training, and new hiring so that it can bring capacity onstream sooner to support the higher sales levels.

The quarterly rolling forecast update is not a budget done four times a year. Managers forecast only a few high-level revenue items and perhaps— for manufacturing companies—gross margins. In many companies, the rolling forecast can be submitted on a single piece of paper (or computer page). Managers do not have to forecast line-item expenses. As we show later in the chapter, managers can derive costs and expense forecasts directly from a detailed revenue forecast.

Forecasting revenues, however, remains a difficult process, much more complex than forecasting costs. A revenue model is a forecast about what a myriad of economic agents *outside* the company, including customers, competitors, and government officials, will do in forthcoming periods. Companies use many approaches to forecasting.[11] We have seen several companies get excellent results from an approach called *driver-based planning*, in which managers build a structural model, typically using extensive nonfinancial data, to predict sales. The models can consist of multiple equations that incorporate macroeconomic variables, current market position of the company and its competitors, levels of advertising and promotional spending, and market penetration models of adopters, diffusers, and repeat customer purchases.

To produce a driver-based revenue model, each company must develop its own analytic capabilities. The factors most important for predicting sales will vary by industry, and even company by company within an industry. Consider, for example, the analytic sales-forecasting process used by a company producing frequently purchased consumer personal care products. The company has excellent knowledge of its existing customer base. It knows the total population in the countries where it currently sells, and the percentage of people who use the product regularly. The company also knows its existing market share, country by country and region by region. It also knows the distribution of its total sales in the product line by brand and by SKU (size, flavor, formulation, etc.) within each brand. See Figure 7-3 for an overview of the forecasting process.

For the upcoming period, the company attempts to quantify the impact of its marketing programs, such as new product launches, advertising, promotions, distribution of samples, in-store displays, and product-line extensions. The company estimates the impact of each of these marketing elements on retaining existing customers, persuading existing customers to try new products, and acquiring new customers. All these statistical relationships are aggregated into sales forecasts, by product and perhaps even SKUs within each product category, for end-use consumers. In summary, the company develops its sales forecast from the following six key drivers:

1. *New product performance:* The percentage of the targeted population (those willing to try) who would convert to the new product even before major marketing investments
2. *Advertising performance:* The impact of advertising spending on repeat and new purchases

FIGURE 7-3

Developing a driver-based forecasting model at a consumer goods company

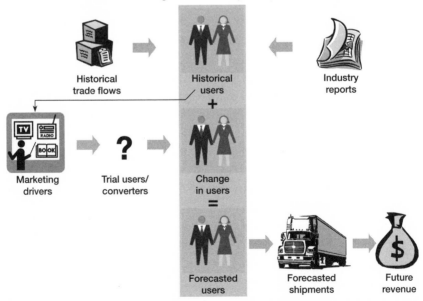

A volume forecast begins with an analysis of past trade flows . . .

| Historical trade flows | Historical users | Industry reports |

Marketing drivers → **?** → Trial users/converters

Change in users

Forecasted users → Forecasted shipments → Future revenue

. . . and ends with forecast shipments.

3. *Sales promotion:* The impact of in-store promotions on product sales
4. *Price performance:* The impact on demand of price changes, either plus or minus
5. *Sampling performance:* The impact on steady-state demand of delivering product samples directly to end-use consumers
6. *Distribution:* The impact on end-use sales of retail product availability

The company also models the existing stock of products held by the trade channel (distributors, wholesalers, and retailers) and by end-use consumers. Most consumers will not purchase a new item until they deplete their current stock of the item. Using estimates of end-use forecast demand and of the existing stock of products in the supply-chain pipeline, the company then estimates its production and distribution plan for the upcoming period.

While the process described above works well for a fast moving consumer goods company, a company in a different industry—say, a business-to-business industry or one selling durable consumer goods rather than consumable goods—will have a completely different revenue model, a different supply chain, and different causal and macroeconomic factors that influence customers' purchasing decisions.

Thus, driver-based revenue planning is far from trivial. It requires excellent databases and information systems as well as highly skilled model-builders and statisticians. Driver-based revenue planning must also incorporate knowledge about the industry's economics, competitors, customers, suppliers, and technologies.

Admittedly, we are not experts in how to deliver objective, fact-based sales forecasts. But we do recognize that accurate revenue forecasting is a key capability for creating an integrated planning, resource allocation, and budgeting process.

Forecasting Costs and Expenses: The Role of Activity-Based Costing

The section above focused on forecasting revenues, not expenses. Although many companies also forecast product costs and other expenses in the quarterly reforecasting process, we recommend that they derive the cost and expense estimates directly from the sales forecast. Once managers and planners have produced a sales and production forecast, they can enter the forecast into a time-driven activity-based (TDABC) model that analytically forecasts the supply, and hence the costs, of the internal resources that will provide the capacity to deliver on the sales and production forecasts.

We illustrate the chain of logic from sales forecasting to resource spending with the example of Towerton Financial Services (TFS), a hypothetical composite of several financial services firms with which we have worked. TFS is a brokerage firm historically focused on stock trading and mutual funds. It recently diversified into two new product lines, investment management and financial planning. Most of its expenses stem from supplying several categories of professional and support employees; its main tangible assets are office space and technology. Figure 7-4 summarizes TFS's current personnel and technology resources..

The senior management team has forecasted the following future monthly revenues for its four business lines:

Product Line	Sales
Stock Trading	$3,644,000
Mutual Fund Trading	2,031,000
Investment Management	113,000
Financial Planning	169,000
Total	$5,957,000

In summary, the first step in the planning operations stage concludes with managers producing a high-level sales forecast for upcoming periods. This forecast drives the sales and operating plans that are developed in the next step.

FIGURE 7-4

Towerton's resource base

Number	Resource
225	Brokers
18	Investment account managers
20	Financial planners
30	Principals
42	Customer service representatives
76	Computer servers

STEP 2: TRANSLATE THE SALES FORECAST
INTO SALES AND OPERATING PLANS

Towerton Financial Services needs to translate its aggregate sales forecast into a more detailed expected operating plan for its next period of operations, as shown in Figure 7-5. This figure shows how TFS expects to achieve its high-level sales forecast (displayed in the top row): how many trades must be executed, how many new accounts must be opened, and how many customer meetings must be held. For the aggregate sales forecast to be achieved, TFS must supply sufficient resources to handle these forecasted demands for service.

A detailed operating plan like the one shown in Figure 7-5 provides the essential input into a resource capacity planning model. The operating plan specifies the expected quantity, mix, and nature of individual sales orders, production runs, and transactions. For example, the operational implications of $10 million in sales coming from 100 orders of $100,000 each are far different from generating the same $10 million in sales from 100,000 orders averaging $100 each. The latter plan requires the company to process three orders of magnitude (10^3) more transactions, a much more complex and costly operating environment.

Technology can play a helpful role here. Companies with well-functioning enterprise resource planning (ERP) systems have a historical record of product and customer mix and transaction patterns that they can draw upon for forecasting. Rather than start each forecasting period with a blank sheet of paper (or spreadsheet), an ERP-equipped company can use a baseline of recent experience from which to project into the future.

FIGURE 7-5

Towerton Financial Corporation's forecast of sales and operations

	Stock trading	Mutual fund trading	Investment management	Financial planning
Forecasted monthly sales (000)	$3,644	$2,031	$113*	$169
Number of transactions	275,000	49,000	2,600	
Number of new accounts opened	595	255	40	90
Number of calls to customer service center	47,600	11,475	600	480
Number of meetings servicing existing accounts	3,570	765	200	400

*Based on average account balance of $125,000.

For example, to reach the forecast level of sales in each product and service line, the company could assume the same distribution of order size and frequency experienced in the past, but increased by the assumed percentage rise in sales. From this naïve extrapolation, the company's planners would modify the distribution to reflect planned changes in sales and ordering patterns. If the company has raised the minimum order size, then planners would eliminate small orders and increase the frequency of larger orders, especially around the new minimum. If, as in Towerton's case, the company has launched a strategic initiative to increase mutual fund sales, then the planners would increase the distribution of sales to this service line to reflect the new priorities.

This is not an exact process. To reflect the inherent uncertainty in forecasting a detailed ordering, production, and delivery schedule, managers should embrace scenario planning by developing optimistic, most likely, and pessimistic forecasts. Much of the planning data are already in electronic form, enabling planners to run multiple scenarios quickly and inexpensively. The deliverable from this second step is a sales and operating forecast (or forecasts) sufficiently detailed to translate into resource requirements.

STEP 3: FORECAST RESOURCE CAPACITY BY ENTERING SALES AND OPERATING DATA INTO A TDABC MODEL

This step is the key innovation in linking a strategic plan to an operating plan. It requires that a company have a time-driven activity-based costing model in operation. TDABC is a new costing approach that is faster, simpler, and more flexible than traditional activity-based costing.[12] TDABC assigns costs to products, services, and customers based on two fundamental parameters:

1. The cost of supplying resource capacity in each operating department and process, measured as the costs of resources supplied to the department divided by the practical capacity (measured typically by the time available for productive work each period)
2. The capacity (time) required from each department or process to handle the product or customer transaction

In general, a company will already have built a TDABC model to measure and manage the profitability of its products, services, and customers. The appendix to this chapter presents the fundamentals of building a TDABC model, using Towerton Financial Services as the example. In step 3, managers realize a major additional benefit of the company's TDABC model: an ability to quickly forecast and budget the needed supply of resource capacity.

Assuming that a TDABC model exists, the planning group modifies the model to reflect process improvements expected to occur in the forecasted period. This step links the quality and process improvement activities described in Chapter 6 to the planning and budgeting process described in this chapter. In this way, the company's continuous improvement activities become embedded in the budgeting process. For example, TFS might forecast that through training and better access to customer databases, the time it takes to handle a customer service call on a stock trade will be reduced from five minutes to four minutes. Perhaps the time required to prepare an initial financial plan will be reduced from ten hours to nine hours. These expected improvements will decrease the quantity of resources required to handle a given quantity of demands.

After the model's resource consumption estimates have been adjusted for the forecast process improvements, the planners enter the detailed sales and operating plan for the forecasting period (such as that shown earlier in Figure 7-5) into the model. This use of a TDABC model reveals a highly significant shift in the model's purpose. Typically, activity-based costing models operate with historic data. They calculate costs and profitability based on previous periods' operations. But companies now can use their ABC models in a much more powerful way: to forecast and influence the future.

By feeding forecast sales and operations data into the TDABC model, planners transform ABC from a snapshot-taking exercise to a management tool for influencing *future* costs and profitability. Accountants are often ridiculed for providing information while looking at a rearview mirror. When managers provide forecast data as input to a TDABC model, however, the cost accountant looks through the front windshield and helps managers navigate more profitably into the future.

Figure 7-6 shows how the TDABC model has enabled Towerton Financial to translate its sales and operating plan into forecast demand for capacity (time) for all its personnel and computing resources.[13] The demand for computing resources arises from customers' trading activities, inquiries, account statement preparation, and analytic support of account representatives. Figure 7-7 continues the process by dividing the total demand for capacity of each resource by the quantity of capacity supplied by each unit of the resource each month (for example, 130 hours

FIGURE 7-6

Towerton Financial estimates of resources required to fulfill the operating plan

Time Utilization (hours)

Resource Category	Stock trading	Mutual fund trading	Investment management	Financial planning	Total hours
Brokers	24,702*	4,593			29,295
Account managers			793		793
Financial planners				1,500	1,500
Principals	2,391	451	187	90	3,119
Customer service representatives	4,086	1,007	82	107	5,282
Peak MIPS utilized	420,000	56,200	28,800	11,500	516,500
Off-peak MIPS utilized	89,500	198,000	26,000	12,200	325,700

*Total hours of broker usage for stock trading = 5 minutes × (# transactions on existing accounts) + 60 × (# accounts opened) + 20 × (# meetings with existing customers)
= [5 × 275,000 + 60 × 595 + 20 × 3,570]/60 = **24,702 hours**

per month for brokers); in this way, the TDABC model forecasts the quantity of resource units required to implement a future period's operating plan. The quantities in the column, "Resource Units Required," represent the resources demanded by the operating plan. In effect, it is the "bill" that the company must pay to deliver on its sales plan.

The calculations in Figures 7-6 and 7-7 use a single-point forecast of the operating plan. The company's planners should likely explore a variety of possibilities, not just a single forecast, to give them a sense of the range of resources required to meet a likely range of outcomes. At a minimum, they might consider an optimistic, a most likely, and a pessimistic sales forecast. After examining the resource requirements under diverse assumptions, the company can authorize the level of resource supply to be carried into the next period. Because each resource unit has a known cost per period, the decision about the level of resource supply automatically leads to an authorized or budgeted level of spending on each resource category, as calculated in the next step.

In general, companies should supply somewhat more capacity than that forecast by the deterministic TDABC model. Resource demand is not uniform throughout the period, and some demand may take longer to process than the average amount. To avoid queuing and delays, some

FIGURE 7-7

Towerton calculates the quantity of resources required to implement next period's operating plan

Resource category	Total hours	Available hours/month per resource unit	Resource units required	Resource units supplied	Capacity utilization
Brokers	29,295	130	225.3	230	98%
Account managers	793	130	6.1	7	87%
Financial planners	1,500	130	11.5	12	96%
Principals	3,119	130	24.0	25	96%
Customer service representatives	5,282	140	37.7	40	94%
Peak MIPS utilized	516,500	8,800	58.7	60	98%

buffer amount of resource capacity may be desirable. The column "Resource Units Supplied" in Figure 7-7 shows the quantity of each resource TFS has authorized for the next period. The column labeled "Capacity Utilization" reports how close to capacity TFS expects to operate during the period.

This process used a one-period-ahead forecast to generate a resource demand model for the next period. Typically, companies that reforecast quarterly create forecasts up to five or six quarters into the future. The planning group can replicate the resource capacity planning step for each quarter's forecast: translate each quarter's forecast into a detailed sales and operating plan, update the TDABC model for expected efficiency improvements in that quarter, and run the structural TDABC model to predict resource demand for that quarter.

In this way, the company gets an advance look at where resource shortfalls may occur in future periods. It can take near-term steps to acquire and train personnel so that they become available, as needed, in future periods. The company can also start the capital acquisition process to ensure that adequate levels of physical capacity—space, servers, bandwidth, and production and distribution equipment—also come online as needed to meet future sales and operating projections.

Conversely, suppose that the TDABC had forecast that future demand for resources will be substantially lower than current levels of resource supply. The reduced demand could arise from productivity and process improvements, changes in operating policies (such as higher minimum order sizes or account balances), or anticipated declines in sales. When demand for future resources is expected to decrease, the company can start to plan ways to shed capacity so that it would not be burdened with significant excess capacity in future quarters.

This is the process by which almost all organizational costs become, as economists say, "variable in the long run." Most costs don't go away by themselves. People show up for work each day and expect to be paid, facility rent is paid each month, and idle equipment rarely walks out the door under its own power. Costs vary downward only when managers take explicit actions to reduce the supply of resources by ceasing to issue paychecks and starting to sell equipment and facilities no longer needed to support current and future operations. By acting on the information from the TDABC resource forecasting model, managers get a head start on adjusting resource supply to future needs.

As another specific example of using a TDABC model for resource capacity forecasting, consider the newly formed Private Client Group (PCG) of Global Insurance (a disguised name).[14] PCG served the insurance needs of high-net-worth clients by providing specialized risk management products and services, such as insurance for luxury automobiles, excess liability, aviation, watercraft, jewelry, art, collectibles, and kidnap and ransom. The group's offerings had been well received, and new policies written were growing at a compound annual growth rate higher than 50 percent.

A major challenge was adding professional staff to meet future service demands for functions such as underwriting, client care, claim processing, and risk management. PCG built a TDABC model that represented the demands for employee staff by skill set, by product line, and by geographic region. It then entered forecasts of product volume and mix, by region, into the TDABC model to estimate the professional staff capacity it would need—by skill set and region—if it was to realize and serve the forecast level of premium growth. Because insurance employees serving sophisticated customers require considerable education and training, the TDABC model gave PCG executives adequate time to recruit and train employees to meet anticipated demand in future periods.

Some people may worry that by tying resource capacity authorization tightly to the revenue forecast, companies might reintroduce the incentives that existed in the traditional budgeting process for managers to issue biased forecasts. We believe this should not be a major problem. If managers submit low sales forecasts to protect themselves from lower-than-expected revenue outcomes, they will face immediate pressure to cut resource capacity from current levels. Should demand come in at the expected level, which is higher than the manager forecast, inadequate resources may be available to capture that incremental demand. Conversely, if managers provide overly optimistic forecasts, so as to legitimize the spending on additional resource capacity (or to maintain existing capacity in the face of expected future declines in sales), they will bear the costs of that higher capacity in subsequent periods and will realize lower profits when actual sales are lower than their forecast. At least to a first, and perhaps second, approximation, the incentives seem to be aligned for managers to generate unbiased revenue forecasts in this process so that they can make good decisions about the quantity of resource capacities to supply into future periods.

In summary, a company, in step 3, uses its projected sales and operating plan for the upcoming period to forecast the demand for time from employees and the demand for time and space from tangible resources, such as property, plant, and equipment. The resource demand model comes from updating the historical TDABC model for known and forecast process improvements so that the resource forecast incorporates the most contemporary thinking about future sales, operations, and process efficiencies. Company planners then run their detailed sales and operating plan through the TDABC model to predict and adjust the level of supplied resources for future periods.

STEP 4: DEVELOP THE FORECAST OF OPEX AND CAPEX

Once managers have agreed on the level of resource supply for future periods, the financial implications can be calculated simply and quickly. We refer to the estimated financial spending in a future period as the budget for that period, using the word *budget* to describe an *estimate* of future expenses rather than its connotation as a fixed *performance target*.

At the end of step 3, the company has estimated the quantity of each type of resource it has agreed (or expects) to supply in a future period. The company already knows from building its TDABC model (described in the appendix for Towerton Financial) the cost of supplying each unit of resource (summarized in Figure 7-8). At Towerton Financial, each broker had a monthly cost of about $6,800, each customer service representative a cost of $4,000, and each computer server a cost of $3,200 (detailed calculations are shown in the appendix to this chapter). Before running the model, the planners should adjust the resource unit costs for any anticipated price changes. If employees will be getting raises, then the monthly cost per employee should be updated. If rent for space increases

FIGURE 7-8

Towerton Financial forecasts monthly resource costs

	Resource units supplied	Monthly resource cost per unit	Total monthly resource cost (000)
Brokers	230	$6,800	$1,561
Account managers	7	9,000	63
Financial planners	12	8,400	106
Principals	25	12,200	323
Customer service representatives	40	4,000	168
Servers	60	3,200	190

or monthly cost per server decreases, the new values should be entered into the model. In this way, the cost and spending forecasts will reflect future expectations rather than historic actuals.

Once the company has entered the most recent or forecast cost of each resource unit, it multiplies this value by the quantity of each type of resource to be supplied during the forecasting periods. This multiplication yields the forecast (budgeted) cost of supplying the quantity of each resource type, shown in the last column of Figure 7-8.

The resource costs are, in effect, the line items in the budget. But rather than the budget for line items coming from an extensive iterative and negotiated process, item by item, it arrives from a simple cross-multiplication process: multiply the quantity authorized for each resource type by the resource's cost per unit. Computers do multiplication, even of large arrays, extremely quickly, inexpensively, and accurately. The result is a budget that has been derived quickly and analytically from the sales and operating plan, rather than imposed by fiat or through power negotiations.

The process described here is exactly analogous to *material resource planning* (MRP) systems introduced for manufacturing companies in the 1980s. MRP systems took detailed forecasts of the production of each product and "exploded" them up to a total demand for materials and component parts during the production period. Purchasing and logistics people then had a sound basis for ordering and scheduling the delivery of material inputs to meet the planned production schedule.

The resource capacity planning process, described in steps 1 through 4, extends the MRP model to forecast all resource capacity demand. It explodes the detailed sales and operating plans into the total demand for all resources: employees, equipment, facilities, and distribution.

The spending to supply employees and to operate equipment and facilities is generally classified as operating expenses (OPEX). The spending to add equipment and technology capacity, and to acquire space to support growth in future operations, is considered a capital expenditure (CAPEX). Financial accountants determine whether a certain type of spending is part of OPEX, which runs through the income statement, or CAPEX, which is capitalized onto the balance sheet and depreciated over time through the income statement.

Forecasting Discretionary Spending

Before concluding the budgeting process, the company needs one additional set of estimates: the forecasts of the level of discretionary spending on items such as research, development, advertising, promotion, training, and, of course, strategic initiatives. The forecast spending on these discretionary items does not bear a tight causal relationship with sales and operating levels, and therefore it requires a parallel calculation along with the quarterly update of revenues. The spending on such discretionary items remains a judgment call by experienced executives, and not a decision that can be automated through an analytic model.

Thus, to complete the exercise of forecasting spending levels in future periods, the planner must obtain estimates, from the executive teams, of the authorized levels of discretionary spending. Financial accountants classify much of this discretionary spending as a general and administrative expense, although we argue, in Chapter 4, that spending on strategic initiatives should be classified as a new income statement line item, STRATEX.

The authorization process for spending on projects and initiatives should be revisited at least quarterly, in light of the most recent actual information and the forecast economic and competitive situation. For example, at Statoil, many projects relate to exploration for new oil and gas reserves. When Statoil operated under an annual budget, managers received an exploration budget once a year and were allowed to spend up to, but not beyond, the authorized amount. When Statoil eliminated budgets, it introduced a more flexible and dynamic authorization process. It now sets a volume target for new discoveries based on three-year averages. Frontline exploration managers can bring attractive projects forward at any time to senior management. They pressure-test the forecasts in a cross-functional meeting on a range of financial and nonfinancial parameters, including strategic fit, risk, and option values. Managers estimate the costs for approved projects at that time.

The quarterly forecasting process enables Statoil senior management to become aware of new projects earlier than before and typically well before the approval point. After exploratory drilling has occurred, the company has much better information about the potential size of the field. The amount authorized for further drilling and development will be set low if preliminary tests suggest that the field is not promising. But the authorized amount can be quite high and can be accelerated if the test findings indicate a high likelihood of a large gas field. In addition, if the quarterly forecast indicates that the company will have a lower financial capacity ahead, approval of projects can be deferred and volume targets lowered. But no budgets get "cut" anywhere in the process.

STEP 5: CALCULATE PROFITABILITY BY PRODUCT, CUSTOMER, CHANNEL, AND REGION

In addition to the total level of expected spending for the forecast period, the TDABC model supplies, essentially for free, the detailed profit-and-loss statement (P&L) for each product, customer, and region. After all, the total demand for resource supply and resource spending has been estimated by aggregating the resource demands for each product, customer, channel, and region—in fact, each transaction. By going back to the detailed sales and operating plan (Figure 7-5), the model automatically attributes the supply and cost of each resource type to the transaction, product, or customer that triggered the demand.

Towerton Financial Services' database for the forecast period already has detailed projections of the demand for resource capacity by its multiple products and customers. Thus the total spending on resources, determined in the preceding step, can be split into detailed demand for capacity resources by individual products and customers. This process provides a clear basis for attributing the cost of supplying resources to the demand by products and customers, enabling the company to produce an accurate P&L for each product, customer, channel, or any other classification scheme it chooses. Figure 7-9 shows Towerton's pro forma product-line profit-and-loss statement for the forecasted period. If Towerton is using a rolling five-quarter forecast, it can follow the five steps of this chapter to generate forecasted P&L's, like Figure 7-9, for each of the next five quarters.

FIGURE 7-9

Towerton Financial concludes its budgeting process by forecasting next period's product-line income statement

	Stock trading	Mutual fund trading	Account management	Financial planning	Total used	Unused capacity	Total supplied
Average price per transaction	$ 13.25	$ 41.45					
Sales	$ 3,644	$ 2,031	$ 113	$ 169	$ 5,956		$ 5,956
Brokers	1,290	240			1,529	32	1,561
Account managers			55		55	8	63
Financial planners				102	102	4	106
Principals	238	45	19	9	310	13	323
Customer service representatives	122	30	2	3	158	10	168
Computer server expenses	128	39	11	5	184	6	190
Total costs	**1,778**	**354**	**87**	**119**	**2,338**	**73**	**2,411**
Margin	1,866	1,677	26	50	3,618	(73)	3,545
Margin %	51%	83%	23%	30%	61%	-1%	60%
S, G & A (unallocated corporate expenses)							1,300
Operating income							2,245
Operating margin							38%

SUMMARY

Companies translate their strategic intent into detailed operating plans through a disciplined, integrated five-step process. The process starts with quarterly sales forecasts for the next several periods. Managers can generate the sales forecasts either subjectively, based on historical trends, adjusted for anticipated changes in the future, or, preferably, with the assistance of analytic driver-based planning models.

In the next step, planners translate high-level sales forecasts into detailed sales and operating plans, which specify the volume and mix of individual products and services sold, produced, and delivered, and the quantity and mix of customer-based transactions.

In a third step, the detailed sales and operating plans are converted, through a time-driven activity-based cost model, into the forecast demand for capacity of the company's primary resources. Resource capacity includes employees involved in sales, production, distribution, and customer service, as well as tangible resources for production, information processing and storage, product storage, and distribution. Based on forecast demand for resource capacity, managers determine the quantity of each type of resource that will be supplied in upcoming periods.

In step 4, planners simply and accurately translate the authorized level of resource supply into budgeted operating and capital expenses for the upcoming periods, and, in step 5, the pro forma profit-and-loss statement, in aggregate for the business unit or company and by product, service, customer, channel, and region.

This series of logical and tightly linked steps provides a mechanism for translating high-level sales growth targets into detailed plans for authorizing resource capacity and, in step 5, estimating the near-term operating profitability, by products, customers, and regions, from the strategic plan.

DEVELOPING A TIME-DRIVEN ACTIVITY-BASED COSTING MODEL

Time-driven activity-based costing (TDABC) is a new ABC variant that enables you to build powerful and flexible cost models quite simply. We illustrate the TDABC approach by building a model for the hypothetical Towerton Financial Services (TFS) company described in this chapter. TFS's financial results have been disappointing (see Figure 7A-1 for a monthly income statement). It forms a project team to build a time-driven ABC model to understand the cost and profit drivers of Towerton's operations. The model will accurately assign TFS's large costs of personnel and computing to its various product lines. TFS's resource base is shown in Figure 7-4 in the main body of the chapter. Clearly, the quantity of each type of personnel, computing resources, and space is substantial. For TFS to better manage its resource base, it must understand how the various resources are used by its various products and customers. This is exactly the role of activity-based costing.

COMPANY INFORMATION

TFS has four core products and services: stock trading, mutual funds, investment account management, and financial planning. Three classes of professional staff—brokers, investment account managers, and financial planners—deal directly with customers for these products and services.

FIGURE 7A-1

Towerton Financial Services: Monthly income statement (000)

Sales	$ 4,035
Brokers	1,561
Account managers	161
Financial planners	177
Principals	388
Customer service representatives	176
Computer server expenses	241
Total costs	2,704
Margin	1,331
Margin %	33%
SG&A (unallocated corporate expenses)	1,300
Operating Income	31
Operating margin	1%

Brokers perform stock trading and mutual fund transactions and provide advice and recommendations. TFS's brokerage customers make their own buy and sell decisions. TFS charges a flat fee per stock trade that depends on the total amount of assets a customer has on deposit with TFS. For mutual fund transactions, TFS charges 1.5 percent of the value of the mutual fund shares when purchased, and nothing when shares are later sold.

Investment account managers actively manage clients' investments, buying and selling stocks to meet client objectives. These employees meet initially with customers to learn about their investment goals, interests, and risk tolerance. Then they meet quarterly to review account performance and investment strategy. TFS charges an annual asset management fee of 1.5 percent of assets under management to each customer, regardless of the account balance.

Financial planners prepare financial life plans for customers. Financial planners help customers determine how much to save, develop a budget, and ensure that they have enough insurance. These employees serve as primary care physicians for clients' financial health. TFS charges an initial fee of $1,200 for the first financial plan and then bill their planners' time at $125 per hour for ongoing advice. Planners typically meet quarterly with clients to discuss updated plans.

TFS has several groups of support personnel. *Principals* manage and supervise brokers, investment account managers, and financial planners.

Customer service representatives handle customer requests over the telephone for sales and account services.

TFS uses two types of computer equipment. *Servers*, in centralized clusters, process customer transactions, maintain customer accounts, and perform various administrative functions. Server capacity is measured in millions of computer instructions processed (MIPS). Every employee receives a *desktop computer*, leased by TFS.

TFS rents *office space*, mainly space for individual offices for each direct labor employee and principal but also conference rooms for face-to-face meetings with customers to open accounts or service existing accounts.

Miscellaneous corporate expenses include administrative expenses for finance, human resources, audits, taxes, professional fees, and compliance.

TIME-DRIVEN ACTIVITY-BASED COST MODEL

TFS builds a time-driven ABC model using the following sequence of steps. First, it estimates the cost of supplying each type of employee resource. Figure 7A-2 illustrates the basic process for brokers: add the total compensation of the employee plus all the indirect resources that support the employee, yielding a total of $81,500 per year, or $6,800 per month. In this simplified case, the indirect resources include the cost of the space occupied by the employee and the cost of the employee's desktop computer, applications software, and IT consultant support used by each employee.

FIGURE 7A-2

Time-driven activity-based costing step 1:
Calculate the cost per unit time of supplying resource capacity

$$\text{Capacity cost rate} = \frac{\text{Cost of capacity supplied}}{\text{Practical capacity of resources supplied}}$$

Broker: Annual compensation (including fringe benefits)	$65,000
Occupies 80 sq. ft. of space @ $125/sq. ft./year	10,000
Computer consultant support	6,500
Annual cost	$81,500
Monthly cost	$6,800

Broker works 20 days per month, 7.5 hours per day.

After breaks and training, has 6.5 hours of productive time available per day.

$$\text{Cost rate} = \frac{\$6,800/\text{month}}{20 \times 6.5 = 130 \text{ hours/month}} = \$52 \text{ per hour } [\$0.87/\text{minute}]$$

In general, the total cost of an employee includes other directly traceable support resources such as human resources, supervision, and finance.

TFS then divides the total monthly cost of supplying each employee by the employee's monthly capacity. We assume that brokers work about 240 days per year (365 – 104 for weekends – 21 for holidays and vacations), or 20 days per month.[15] Brokers show up for 7.5 hours of work each day, but not all that time is available for working with customers. Some amount of time (assumed to be one hour per day for brokers) is used for breaks, training, and education. After subtracting unavailable time, each broker has a capacity of 130 hours per month (6.5 hours per day for 20 days a month).

Knowing the cost of supplying a broker ($6,800 per month) and the capacity per broker (130 hours per month), we calculate the capacity cost rate of the employee simply as $52 per hour available for work. Figure 7A-3 shows the capacity cost rate calculation for each TFS employee type.

The capacity cost rate calculations (in Figures 7A-2 and 7A-3) are straightforward for any company. The numerator of the ratio represents the monthly compensation cost of each employee type, plus all the support costs (occupancy, technology, supervision, and indirect support: human resources, information technology, finance, etc.) incurred to have that employee available for productive work. For the denominator, project team analysts estimate the number of days the employee typically shows up for work each month, calculate the down time for breaks, training, and other non-customer-related activities, and obtain the number of hours (or minutes) available for productive work each month.

FIGURE 7A-3

Towerton Financial Services' resource quantities, capacities, and cost rates

	Annual compen- sation	Monthly compen- sation	Monthly occu- pancy	Monthly IT cost	Total monthly cost	Productive hours per month	Capacity cost rate ($/hour)
Brokers (225)	$65,000	$5,417	$ 832	$539	$6,800	130	$52
Account managers (15)	91,000	7,583	832	539	9,000	130	69
Financial planners (18)	84,500	7,042	1,248	539	8,800	130	68
Principals (40)	130,000	10,833	1,560	539	12,900	130	99
Customer service repre- sentatives (50)	41,600	3,467	520	206	4,200	140	30

One complicating factor is the existence of peak or seasonal capacity, in which the company provides a resource to meet a peak demand, but the resource is less than fully utilized during the slack or nonpeak period. It is not difficult to extend the costing model to handle a peak capacity situation. We illustrate by developing the capacity costing rates for TFS's servers, which are used heavily during the eight hours of the business day, especially when the stock exchanges are open for trading, but are used much less intensively in the remaining sixteen hours of the day. We assume the usage pattern for server (computer) capacity is as shown in Figure 7A-4, where servers are used intensively during 9 a.m. to 5 p.m. and hardly at all from 5 p.m. to 9 a.m. the following morning. TFS, to meet the peak period demand, has purchased seventy-six servers, although only nineteen are busy during the evening and early morning slack period.

Each server costs $38,000 per year ($3,168 per month) in hardware, software, and maintenance and has a capacity to process 50 MIPS (millions of instructions) per hour. Servers do not take vacations and hence are available for 22 days per month, 24 hours per day, for a total of 528 hours per month.

The different demand periods require a calculation of two different cost rates. The simple calculation occurs for the slack, or off-peak, period during which nineteen servers are busy. Each of the nineteen servers costs $6 per hour to operate (obtained by dividing $3,168 per month by 528

FIGURE 7A-4

Demand for Towerton Financial Services' computer capacity peaks during business hours

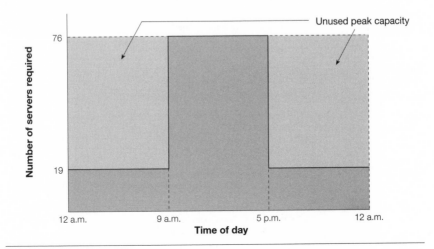

hours per month), or $0.12 per MIPS processed ($6 per hour divided by 50 MIPS per hour, its processing capacity).

For the peak period, the numerator—the cost of supplying capacity for the eight hours—includes 76 servers × $6 per hour × 8 hours. But in addition, the cost of supplying the peak capacity includes the cost of 57 idle servers (76 – 19) for 16 hours of slack (also at $6 per hour). Peak load capacity is much more expensive, because the resources are used for only one-third of their available capacity. Here is the full calculation for the cost of providing peak capacity:

$$\text{Peak Hour Rate:} \quad \frac{[(76 \times 8 \text{ hours}) + ((76 - 19) \times 16 \text{ hours})] \times \$6}{[76 \text{ servers} \times 8 \text{ hours} \times 50 \text{ MIPS/hour}]} = \$0.30/\text{MIPS}$$

We have demonstrated the calculation for only two periods of capacity utilization, but the calculation extends simply to handle complex patterns of peak and seasonal capacity usage.[16]

Now that TFS has obtained capacity cost rates for all its resources, it estimates the second parameter for its TDABC cost model: the quantity of resource capacity used by each customer transaction or interaction. Figure 7A-5 shows some sample time estimates for several of TFS's personnel types: brokers, investment account managers, financial planners, and customer service representatives. Similar estimates can be made for the server capacity required (MIPS) to process each type of transaction.

FIGURE 7A-5

Time-driven activity-based costing step 2: Use time equations to estimate resource demands by transaction and products

Broker's time =	60 minutes/new account opened + 5 minutes/trade (stock or mutual fund) + 20 minutes/meeting with existing customer
Investment account manager's time =	240 minutes/new account opened + 60 minutes/meeting with existing customer + 4 minutes/trade
Financial planner's time =	600 minutes/new account opened + 90 minutes/existing account per month
Customer service representative's time =	12 minutes (set up new stock or mutual fund account) + 18 minutes (set up new investment management or financial planning account) + 5 minutes/trading call + 7 minutes/investment management call + 10 minutes/financial planning call

Finally, the company obtains the quantity of each type of customer transaction in the most recent period (say, one month). An example of such a summary report is shown in Figure 7A-6. The model cross-multiplies the number of each type of transaction by the hours required per resource per transaction (see Figure 7A-7), obtaining the demand for resource capacity (hours of time) for each resource type by each type of product. In the final calculation, the TDABC model multiplies the hours of each resource used by each product by the capacity cost rate per hour of each resource, obtaining the cost of resources used by each product in the most recent period.

The output from the model (see Figure 7A-8) is a full-product-line P&L statement. The far-right column in Figure 7A-8 replicates TFS's summary monthly P&L from Figure 7A-1. The interior columns show that TFS's products use the company's resources in significantly different quantities. In particular, the core stock trading and mutual fund products are efficient with respect to personnel and computing usage, and they show high profit margins. The newly introduced products—investment management and financial planning—use expensive personnel resources very intensively and are operating at breakeven or loss levels.

Managers looking at the product-line P&L statement in Figure 7A-8 get an immediate message. The new investment management and financial planning services that had been introduced to grow TFS's business are either breaking even or losing money. They require substantial resources—people and computer capacity—whose costs are not being covered by the fees and transaction income from the new services.

The model revealed that TFS's traditional product lines of stock trading and mutual fund sales were quite profitable but that the newly introduced product lines were either highly unprofitable (account management services) or barely breakeven (financial planning services).

Capture monthly number of transactions from ERP system

	Stock trading	Mutual fund trading	Investment management	Financial planning
Number of transactions	305,288	26,325	5,400	6,500
Number of new accounts opened	595	255	175	130
Number of total accounts	29,750	12,750	1,200	900
Number of customer service center calls	47,600	11,475	1,320	540
Number of customer meetings	3,570	765	480	569

FIGURE 7A-7

Calculate hours of resource time utilized by each product

Time utilization (hours)	Stock trading	Mutual fund trading	Account management	Financial planning	Total	Available productive time	Capacity utilization
Brokers	27,226	2,704			29,929	29,900	100%
Account managers			2,080		2,080	2,340	89%
Financial planners				2,154	2,154	2,600	83%
Principals	2,643	262	418	130	3,453	3,900	89%
Customer service representatives	4,086	1,007	207	129	5,428	5,880	92%
MIPS—peak	465,913	30,200	96,783	11,823	604,718	668,800	
MIPS—nonpeak	99,358	105,986	72,212	11,860	289,415	334,400	

Total hours of broker usage for stock trading = 5 minutes × (number of transactions on existing accounts) + 60 × (number of accounts opened) + 20 × (number of meetings with existing customers)

= [5 × 305,288 + 60 × 595 + 20 × 3,570]/60 = **27,226 hours**

Learning of the wide disparity in product line profitability, TFS managers took several actions, including raising prices on stock trading, placing greater emphasis on increasing mutual fund sales, establishing a minimum account balance for investment management services, and repricing its financial planning services. The sales and operations forecasts (Figure 7-5) and financial projections (Figure 7-9) shown in the chapter text reflect the changes from these actions.

Towerton Financial Services' experience is not unique. Many companies adopt strategies to introduce new products, services, and channels without fully understanding the economics of their new offerings. Initially, the offerings from the new strategy are seductive. They generate new sources of income, diversification, and growth beyond the company's commoditized core products and services, and any added costs are generally hidden in overhead or indirect cost accounts. The bill for growth comes when the company must add personnel, equipment, software, and technology to produce, deliver, and service the new offerings. The TDABC model enables companies to see whether the incremental value they generate from their new offerings exceeds their incremental costs. Often, the costs of the new strategy exceed the value it creates. When this occurs, companies get a signal to reconsider their strategies.

FIGURE 7A-8

Towerton product profitability from a time-driven activity-based cost model (000 omitted)

				Cost of resources used	+	Cost of unused capacity	=	Cost of resources supplied
Sales	$2,687	$1,091	$90	$167				
Brokers	1,421	141			$4,035		(2)		$4,035
					1,563				1,561
Account managers			143		143		18		161
Financial planners			0	146	146		30		177
Principals	263	26	42	13	344		44		388
Customer service representatives	122	30	6	4	163		14		176
Computer server expenses	152	22	38	5	216		25		241
Total costs	1,958	219	229	168	2,575		129		2,704
Margin	$ 728	$ 872	$ (139)	$ (1)	$1,461		$ (129)		$1,331
Margin %	27%	80%	-154%	0%	36%		-3%		33%
SG&A (unallocated corporate expenses)									1,300
Operating income									$ 31
Operating margin									1%

Thus, as companies prepare for their monthly strategy review meetings (discussed in Chapter 8) and their annual meeting to test and adapt the strategy (discussed in Chapter 9), they need analytic studies of the causal relations among the performance measures in their existing strategy map to see whether the hypothesized linkages are being realized in practice. Among the most important causal relationships, and fortunately one of the easiest to document, are the economics of current products, services, and customers.

The as-is TDABC model described in this appendix usually reveals unprofitable products and customer relationships, inefficient processes, and excess capacity. These problems do not typically go away by themselves. Managers must take conscious, targeted actions to improve inefficient processes, reduce the supply of unused excess capacity, and transform unprofitable products and customers into profitable ones. An accurate TDABC model of current operations provides a vital input for managerial deliberations about strategic (and operational) options. Also, as illustrated in this chapter, the model can then be used with forecast sales and operating data to estimate future demand and the cost of the resource capacity required to process the demands from transactions.

NOTES

1. H. T. Johnson and R. S. Kaplan, *Relevance Lost: The Rise and Fall of Management Accounting* (Boston: Harvard Business School Press, 1987), 100–112.
2. A. Dunlap with B. Andleman, *Mean Business: How I Save Bad Companies and Make Good Companies Great* (New York: Random House, 1996); J. A. Byrne, *Chainsaw: The Notorious Career of Al Dunlap in the Era of Profit-At-Any-Price* (New York: Collins, 2003).
3. Anonymous WORLDCOM executive as quoted on Beyond Budgeting Roundtable Web site http://www.bbrt.org/beybud.htm (accessed February 17, 2008).
4. J. Hope and R. Fraser, "Who Needs Budgets?" *Harvard Business Review* (February 2003): 108–115; Hope and Fraser, *Beyond Budgeting: How Managers Can Break Free from the Annual Performance Trap* (Boston: Harvard Business School Press, 2003).
5. B. Bogsnes, "Blowing up the Budget: Statoil's Journey Beyond Budgeting," Palladium Planning and Budgeting Conference, Amsterdam (October 2006).
6. B. Jorgenson and R. S. Kaplan, "Borealis," Case 102-048 (Boston: Harvard Business School, 2001).
7. Ibid., 4.
8. Ibid.
9. Ibid., 6.
10. Ibid., 7.
11. S. G. Makridakis, S. C. Wheelwright, and R. J. Hyndman, *Forecasting: Methods and Applications* (New York: John Wiley, 1998).

12. The basic reference for time-driven ABC is R. S. Kaplan and S. R. Anderson, *Time-Driven Activity-Based Costing* (Boston: Harvard Business School Press, 2007).

13. It would also forecast the demand for another resource—space requirements for employees and conference rooms—using the same model.

14. See Kaplan and Anderson, *Time-Driven Activity-Based Costing*, 219–229.

15. Employers that are more generous with holidays and vacations may receive only 18 or 19 days per month of actual work. Employers in developing countries with long workweeks and few vacations may get as many as 22 to 24 days per month per employee.

16. See example in Kaplan and Anderson, *Time-Driven Activity-Based Costing*, 185–189.

CHAPTER EIGHT

OPERATIONAL AND STRATEGY REVIEW MEETINGS

WITH STRATEGY and operational plans in place, the enterprise embarks on executing the strategy: producing and delivering products and services to customers, implementing initiatives, and improving processes. It has been set in motion on a trajectory to achieve stretch performance targets over the next three to five years.

But like mission control after a spaceship has been launched to a distant destination, the enterprise needs to continually monitor and adjust its performance to achieve strategic objectives. Managers guide the enterprise by holding a structured set of meetings that deal with operational problems and improvement programs; their aim is to review the strategy and to adjust or transform it as needed. These meetings, portrayed on the right side (stages 5 and 6) of Figure 8-1, represent the feedback and control stages of the management system. In the language of total quality management, the various management meetings are the check and act portions (from the plan-do-check-act cycle) of the strategy implementation process.

Although the idea of separating operational review meetings from strategy review meetings seems both logical and simple to implement, many companies fail to make such a separation. A typical example is the Conner Corporation (a generic company example). After a successful IPO, Connor continued its usual practice of conducting monthly one-day meetings of the senior executives. The meeting's agenda specified that

FIGURE 8-1

The management system: Monitor and learn

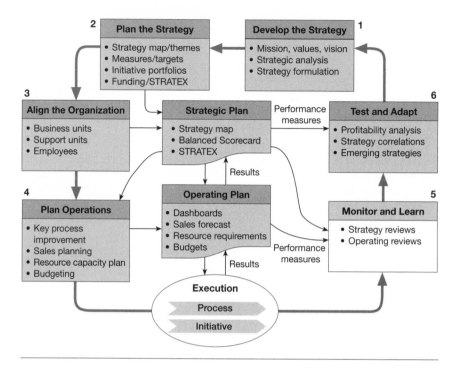

operational issues would be discussed in the morning and strategic issues during the afternoon. Unfortunately, the discussions on strategy never took place.

A typical operational meeting began with a review of actual monthly and forecast quarterly financial performance. Inevitably, revenues were lower and expenses higher than the IPO's quarterly financial targets. The rest of the day was spent discussing how to close the gaps for the quarter through pricing initiatives, capacity reductions, staff layoffs, and sales campaigns. One executive noted, "We have no time for strategy. If we miss our quarterly numbers, we might cease to exist. For us, the long term is the short term." Conner limped along, making or closely missing its numbers each quarter, but never questioning how to modify its strategy to generate better growth opportunities and break the consistent pattern of short-term financial shortfalls. Eventually, Conner was forced to sell out at a price highly discounted from its IPO.

FIGURE 8-2

Management meetings to monitor, learn, act, and adapt

Feedback and Learning Process	Objective	Barriers	Representative Activities
1. Operational Review Meetings *Are our operations in control?*	To monitor and manage short-term financial and operational performance	• KPIs and dashboards that managers review not central to the strategy	• Driver models • Variance analysis • Review of KPI dashboards • Team problem solving • Follow-up program
2. Strategy Review Meetings *Are we executing our strategy well?*	To monitor and manage the strategic initiatives and the Balanced Scorecard	• Inadequate time at management meetings for discussions about strategy implementation • Strategic, cross-business initiatives are not monitored or managed for results	• Theme monitoring • Initiative portfolio monitoring • Theme teams • Agenda management
3. Strategy Testing and Adapting Meetings *Is our strategy working?*	To periodically assess whether the results hypothesized in cause-effect diagrams are occurring as anticipated	• Data not available to review and test the hypotheses underlying the strategy • Inadequate capability in strategy analytics to test the strategy • Employees not encouraged to propose new strategic options	• Analytic studies • ABC studies of product and customer profitability • Cause-effect testing and analysis • Review of emergent strategies

To avoid problems like those experienced by Conner Corporation, companies need to clearly separate the agendas and participants at their management meetings (see Figure 8-2). *Operational review* meetings examine recent departmental, functional, and financial performance and address immediate problems that must be solved. *Strategy review* meetings examine indicators and initiatives from the unit's Balanced Scorecard to assess the progress, barriers, and risks associated with the successful implementation of the strategy. *Strategy testing and adapting* meetings discuss whether the strategy is working and whether its fundamental assumptions remain valid in light of data that have been collected on strategic measures. Participants at this meeting also assess changes in the competitive and regulatory environment and consider new ideas and opportunities that the enterprise can pursue.

The three meeting types have different frequencies, different sets of attendees, and, of course, different subject matters. Sometimes, because of travel schedules and the difficulty of blocking time on managers' schedules, two types of meetings may be held on the same day or on successive days. For example, the SprintNextel executive team meets every month in two half-day meetings; the morning is devoted to operations, and the afternoon focuses on strategic issues. We believe strongly that the meetings should be separated—with different agendas, perhaps different leaders, and distinct time schedules—to focus discussion on the specific topics best addressed at each type of meeting. Otherwise, short-term operational and tactical issues will drive out discussions of strategy implementation and adapting.

Oracle/Latin America VP of Finance Cheryl McDowell noted the importance of separating operational from strategy review meetings: "We have a very transactional, sales-driven culture. The discussion of short-term sales always squeezed out the time scheduled for strategy."[1] Oracle/Latin America solved this problem by having the subset of the executive committee most involved with sales meet monthly to review monthly financial and sales performance. Once a quarter, the executives would meet for one or one and one-half days, with an agenda focused exclusively on strategy.

As a privately held company, SAS's strategy review meetings emphasize its long-term view to gain market share. SAS's two-day management meetings in EMEA and Asia-Pacific, held three times a year, originated as operational reviews for executives and country managers to gain alignment and consistency across the organization. These have progressed, however, into strategy review meetings. "First, we replaced the yearly budget with a rolling forecast. Then we switched the business planning process to strategy-driven actions linked to our balanced scorecard and dashboards," said EVP Mikael Hagström. "Operational reviews were condensed to a monthly one-hour conference call where we review progress and action items to assess how we're executing against our strategy. We now use the management meetings to review the strategy itself, to discuss what is and what is not working, and to align our execution. An integral part of our strategy is charting where we want to be several years out and fine-tuning to stay on course." Days 1 and 2 of the strategy review meetings include break-out work sessions on pre-defined topics. At the end of Day 2, the groups present their outcomes and proposed actions. SAS management believes this structure allows them to rapidly adjust their strategy to meet the changing needs of their customers across all geographies.

In the remainder of this chapter, we discuss operational and strategy review meetings in detail. We present the details of strategy testing and adapting meetings in Chapter 9.

OPERATIONAL REVIEW MEETINGS

As mentioned earlier, operational review meetings assess short-term performance and respond to problems that have arisen recently and need immediate attention. For example, salespeople meet (often via telephone conference calls or Webcasts) to discuss the sales pipeline, recent closings, and customer opportunities and problems. Marketing personnel meet to discuss plans or results from recent advertising and promotion campaigns. Operations people review production problems, maintenance and repair schedules, equipment breakdowns or downtime, near-term scheduling and expediting issues, any supplier concerns, and distribution and delivery problems. Purchasing people discuss the lead-time, quality, and delivery performance of suppliers, along with vendor-contracting issues. Finance personnel deal with short-term cash flow issues, including collection of receivables, late payments to suppliers, treasury operations, and banking relationships.

Many management teams conduct a monthly financial review meeting. This period corresponds to the frequency with which many companies close their financial books. But most departments and functions have learned that monthly is too infrequent for their operational reviews. (We rarely encounter management teams that meet less frequently than monthly for operational reviews.) These companies schedule weekly, twice-weekly, or even daily meetings to review operating data—such as sales, bookings, and shipments—and to solve short-term issues that have just arisen: complaints from important customers, late deliveries, defective production, a machine breakdown, the extended absence of a key employee, or new sales opportunities. The operational review meetings conducted by the New York Police Department (NYPD), for example, occurred twice per week so that crime trends in New York's seventy-six police precincts could be surfaced, discussed, and acted upon rapidly.

The frequency of meetings is also influenced by how quickly new data are posted on operational dashboards. If the company has a short operations cycle, with new data posted hourly and daily, then a daily review promotes learning and rapid problem solving, as we describe in the chemical company case study later in this chapter. But for a product development group, progress against milestones and stage gates may be better evaluated monthly rather than daily. In summary, the frequency of operational review meetings should be determined by the operating cycle of the department and business and by how quickly management wants to respond to sales and operating data as well as to the myriad of other tactical issues that continually emerge.

The attendees of most operational review meetings come from a single department, function, or process. Team members from the same discipline or function can apply their shared expertise, experience, and culture to analyze and solve operational problems. Issues that require cross-functional and interdepartmental solutions are typically addressed at the less-frequent strategy review meetings described later in this chapter.

Operational meetings should be short, highly focused, and action oriented. One company holds its operational review meetings in a chairless room whose walls are covered with whiteboards and flip charts. Attendees post agenda topics in advance. The meeting is only as long as needed to discuss each issue, develop an action plan, and assign responsibility for carrying it out. Forcing everyone to stand signals that the meeting's purpose is not for attendees to spend time together, passively listening. Instead, they engage in active and brisk problem-solving discussions on the most pressing issues of the day.

Many companies' operational review meetings devote too much time to distributing and presenting data. Such an agenda is a legacy of the pre-computer or even the centralized computer age, when finance and data processing departments had a monopoly on collecting, aggregating, and reporting operating data. In the Web-enabled, distributed computing environment, managers should not use their scarce, valuable time together to read or listen to data presentations. Best-practice organizations distribute reports in advance or make the underlying data accessible through Web-enabled information technology.

Online dashboards that are used to inform day-to-day operations and process improvement projects provide excellent inputs to operational review meetings (we discuss the development of operational dashboards in Chapter 6). Among the information to be reviewed are data on the revenue drivers, as discussed in Chapter 7. Marketing and sales managers can use these data to assess the likelihood of achieving the revenue forecasts in the sales plan and to propose actions to influence these drivers. The attendees of all operational review meetings review the reports and data in advance so that they can spend their time together on analysis, problem solving, and decisions.

For the meetings to be most effective, all the operational team members should attend. When Jack Maple was NYPD deputy commissioner, he initiated 8 a.m., twice-weekly meetings of precinct commanders. He soon learned that many could not attend because of prior commitments, such as breakfast meetings with community groups or the difficulty of getting to police headquarters through New York's notorious rush hour traffic. Maple rescheduled his review meetings to start at 7 a.m. If anyone had a scheduling conflict with that time, he offered to start the meetings even earlier. Soon all conflicts with the 7 a.m. meetings disappeared. Maple's experience at the NYPD provides an interesting case study on the power of frequent, well-structured and data-rich operational meetings.

Case Study: NYPD CompStat Meetings

Rudolph Giuliani was elected mayor of New York City in November 1993. Giuliani, a former U. S. attorney, had a reputation as a tough fighter against corruption and organized crime. He campaigned and won election on a commitment to reduce crime in the city. Giuliani appointed William Bratton, police commissioner of Boston, to become commissioner of the NYPD.[2] During his interview, Bratton promised to reduce violent crime in New York by 40 percent in three years, more than triple the drop in crime (12 percent) in the previous three years. Bratton hired Jack Maple, an associate from Boston, to be his deputy commissioner for crime control strategies.

Bratton, Maple, and other senior NYPD officials launched several new policing initiatives that addressed quality-of-life offenses, such as public drinking, graffiti writing, and harassing motorists idled in traffic. They introduced more assertive policing, devolving authority to local precinct commanders, and boosted police morale and support. But they did not have data about the effectiveness of their new crime-fighting initiatives. The new senior NYPD executives learned, to their astonishment, that NYPD had virtually no current data on crimes committed or prosecuted. NYPD compiled crime statistics only quarterly, in conformance with FBI requirements.

Believing that he could not improve a process that had no measurements, Maple launched an effort to collect weekly crime data from each of the seventy-six precincts for the major FBI crime categories: homicides, rapes, robberies, burglaries, felonious assaults, grand larcenies, and auto thefts. Initially, the precincts sent the data manually; the data then had to be transcribed onto a central map of the city. The manual reporting and posting of data proved tedious and inhibited timely reporting and analysis.

During 1994, the department developed an automated system to display computer-generated maps of crime incidents throughout the city. The system came to be called CompStat, for "computerized comparison crime statistics." CompStat became the dashboard for the NYPD's twice-weekly operational reviews.

Each precinct recorded, using an online complaint system (OLCS), the exact time and location of each crime and local enforcement activity. Weekly, it sent the information to a citywide database managed at a central office. The data could be displayed for the most recent week, week-to-date, month-to-date, year-to-date, and prior-year comparison. CompStat ranked all seventy-six precincts in each crime and arrest category.

The CompStat data, though unprecedented and valuable in its own right, became even more valuable through the mechanism of Maple's operational review meetings. Maple hosted twice-weekly meetings for all precinct commanders to discuss the incidence of crimes and the tactics that were working or failing to work to combat various types and intensities of crimes. Maple notified an individual commander thirty-six hours in advance that his or her precinct's experience would be discussed at the next meeting.

As the precinct commander strode to the elevated podium, the CompStat data for the precinct was displayed on a large screen at the front of the large meeting room. Maple and other senior NYPD officials sat, with microphones, in the front row and asked questions. The sessions were not about blaming the commander or attempting to assign responsibility for upward blips in crime rates of a particular type. Maple would ask, "What are we doing about the shootings in the housing projects? How are we doing with buy-and-busts? Why are car thefts down 20 percent citywide, but up 10 percent in your area? Why are assaults, which have been trending down for six months, starting to rise? Are you doing any quality-of-life enforcements?"

Maple used his questions to understand how the precinct commander was responding to the crime data: what countermeasures were being attempted, what worked, what didn't, what the precinct commander expected to occur next week if a particular action were taken. The goal was to discover innovative and successful tactics—information that was shared with the other seventy-five precinct commanders in the audience. Precinct commanders were not punished for trying something that didn't work; they got into trouble for not being aware of problems that needed attention and for not implementing proven or innovative countermeasures.

In responding to Maple's questioning, precinct commanders began coming to the meeting with representatives from other departments, such as detectives. In this way, the meetings helped to break down barriers between departments and encouraged interdepartmental problem solving and, through compulsory attendance at the meeting, interprecinct task forces and cooperation.

The system rapidly exposed precinct commanders who were not tracking the incidence and causes of crime in their neighborhoods, did not understand the drivers of changes in their crime statistics, and were not generating effective, creative, or innovative countermeasures. It also revealed those officers who monitored operations closely and who developed effective new approaches for reducing and preventing crimes. Within a year, about two-thirds of the precinct commanders had been shifted out of their positions and replaced by officers who had demonstrated their leadership capabilities.

In 1994, the major crimes reported in the CompStat system declined 12 percent; comparable crimes in the rest of the country declined 1.1 percent. In the first half of 1995, New York City accounted for 61 percent of the total reduction in serious crimes for the entire United States. The pattern continued through Giuliani's two terms, with murders and other major crimes down by 65 percent from the levels eight years earlier. In 2001, homicide rates were rising in many U.S. cities, including Boston, St. Louis, Atlanta, Los Angeles, and Chicago. New York City's rates continued to decline and were at a level lower than that of San Diego.

Some people expressed concern that New York City's drop in crime rates was associated with police misconduct and excessive force. Indicators of officer misconduct had been added to the CompStat system so that they could be tracked and reduced in the same manner as crime rates. In the year before Giuliani became mayor, eighty-one people had been shot by New York police, twenty-five fatally. In 2001, twenty-six people were shot, ten fatally. The incidence of fatal police shootings in New York was one-third that of Philadelphia, 18 percent that of Detroit, and 15 percent that of Los Angeles.[3]

The success of the NYPD's use of operational dashboards (CompStat) and frequent operational review meetings led Mayor Giuliani to extend the concept to many other city services, including the Department of Corrections, the Human Resources Agency (finding employment for welfare recipients [JobStat]), and twenty other city agencies.[4]

Maple reflected on the critical ingredients that made his intense CompStat operational review meetings effective.[5] First was having accurate and timely data. Managers had to know the facts about what was happening under their responsibility and control. Second, NYPD had to respond quickly and decisively once a crime pattern (an operations problem) had been revealed. The twice-weekly meetings enabled police to respond rapidly to an outbreak of problems by taking actions based on tactics that had already been proven effective for similar problems.

Finally, senior management had to follow up and assess the efficacy of the tactics deployed. Before initiation of the CompStat meetings, crime statistics were a way of keeping score at the end of the year, and not a way to manage for results.

The lessons from NYPD's CompStat meetings are generalizable to private-sector operational review meetings. First, the meetings should be based on valid operational data. NYPD created an internal audit team to ensure that the numbers reported to the CompStat system were not being manipulated. Second, managers are not blamed for problems, a pathology that leads some managers, after being grilled mercilessly for failing to reach a predetermined target, to declare, "I'd rather be dead than red." Managers get into difficulty only when they are unaware of problems and have not attempted to devise solutions. One military officer recalled a sign on his general's desk: "The only thing worse than bad news is bad news *late*."

Third, the meetings focus on near-term operational issues and generate actions that can be taken immediately to address the problems. Accountability is clearly assigned for follow-up and to document the consequences of the actions. These lessons seem to be a good recipe for conducting all operational review meetings.

Case Study: 3B Chemical Plant

A private-sector example of innovative operational review meetings occurred in department 3B, a hydrocarbon cracking unit of Texas Eastman, a large chemical company.[6] The company had made a deep commitment to a total quality approach built on a three-pronged system: teamwork, performance management, and statistical quality control. Implementing the performance management component had identified key result areas for driving improvement and had developed measures for each key result area to assess how well the employee work team was performing its mission. The intense focus on measurement and statistical quality control had led to a major investment in information technology. Every two to four hours, the dashboards of department managers displayed thousands, often tens of thousands, of observations about physical operating parameters, throughput, and quality.

In this environment, a chemical-engineer department manager had developed, on his own, a daily income statement for the operators in his department, the 3B cracking unit. A typical first reaction to such a development is virulent skepticism. After all, U.S. managers have been extensively criticized for their short-term orientation when using a quarterly income statement. How could a daily income statement motivate employees to engage in long-term process improvement? A second reaction reflects the enormous quantity of computer-accessible information that operators were already receiving about the processes under their control. What incremental benefit could an aggregate financial measure, such as daily profit, add to this information set?

The construction of the daily income statement was elegantly simple (see the sample report in Figure 8-3). The existing system already measured, on a continual basis, the quantities of inputs used (hydrocarbon feedstock, energy, cooling water, and machinery) and the quantities of outputs produced (ethylene, propylene, and several by-products). It also measured the quality of the outputs produced, defined as the incidence of impurities in the intermediate products made by the cracking unit.

The department manager created the daily income statement by estimating the cost of each input and the approximate value of each output. The main output products could be purchased or sold in external markets, so it was easy to estimate output price values. The manager even included the cost of capital by estimating the daily mortgage payment (calculated using an estimate of the replacement value of the assets employed, the division's cost of capital, and the expected useful life) required to pay back the company for use of the asset. The operators may have found depreciation an obscure concept, but all of them were familiar with repaying loans for assets like cars, trucks, homes, and family farms.

In a clever innovation, the department manager assigned a penalty for poor-quality production. The employees earned the full revenue from production of output products only if the output was within statistical control limits ($\pm 3\sigma$). The price of output that was outside the control limits, but still within rated specifications (it was still usable), was discounted at 50 percent of the standard price (a 50 percent penalty). Output that was unusable received a 100 percent penalty; the income statement recorded no revenue for output that had critical parameters outside rated specifications.

As a final motivator, the manager issued "stock certificates" to the operators, showing them to be the virtual owners of department 3B. As owners, they were entitled to receive an income statement describing how well their company did each day. The manager launched the program by promising the employees a new kitchen in their control unit if they achieved a stretch profit target for ninety days.

The daily income statement proved a big hit. Every morning, the employees had an operational review meeting to examine the preceding day's

FIGURE 8-3

The 3B daily income statement

SALES			$/dy	
Steam	+ 600 #	87,938 lb/hr	8,416	
	+ 160 #	11,972 lb/hr	1,068	
	– pyro	24,516 lb/hr	2,368	
	– 30 #	11,624 lb/hr	1,037	
	Net	63,770	$6,079	
Ethylene:	High Grade	776,042 lb/day	124,167	
	Low Grade	0 lb/day	0	0 % out
	Waste	0 lb/day	0	
	Total	776,042	$124,167	
Propylene:	High Grade	358,280 lb/day	68,073	
	Low Grade	32,429 lb/day	3,081	8.3 % out
	Waste lb/day	0 lb/day		
	Total	390,708	$71,154	
Hydrogen, capacity		7 lines	$57,708	
Methane, capacity		9 lines	$5,058	
Heavies		(fixed for now)	$ 1,732	
TOTAL SALES			$265,898	
COSTS				
Feedstock:	Ethane	227,865 lb	6,471	
	Propane	1,595,066 lb	108,305	
	Total	1,822,930 lb	$114,776	
Maintenence and repair		(1987 Average)	$4,168	
Utilities:				
	Electricity	1,234 amps	$8,359	
	Cooling water	4.8 lines	$4,109	
	Natural gas	3.1 lines	$3,442	
	Other (typical)		$607	
		Total utilities ____	$16,517	
Other costs			$45,714	
Total cost of goods sold ____			$181,175	
Loan repayment			0	
Mortgage			$ 54,946	
Total costs ____			$236,122	
Gross profit			$29,776	
Less taxes @ 35%			$10,422	
NET PROFIT			$19,354 /day	

(equivalent to $541,923/period profit)

Source: "Texas Eastman Case" Case #190-039 (Boston: Harvard Business School), Exhibit 10, page 22.

income statement. The employees identified the causes of production limits or substandard quality, and they instituted small changes in procedures and operating conditions to cure the problem. The team soon set records for throughput and quality and earned its new kitchen in the first ninety days of operations with the new report.

As with NYPD, the frequent operational review meetings at the Texas Eastman 3B plant relied on data about existing operations, were focused on issues within the department's responsibility, and led directly to actions to eliminate defects and improve processes. The meetings helped employees understand the root causes of defects, identify the factors that constrained output, perform joint problem solving, and develop action plans to correct problems and enhance performance.

These are the characteristics of excellent operational review meetings. They should be short, frequent, and data-driven. They should focus on departmental and process performance and provide opportunities for feedback, problem solving, and learning. These meetings do not review or question the strategy. That is the agenda for the next set of management meetings.

STRATEGY REVIEW MEETINGS

In strategy review meetings, the members of a business unit's leadership team come together to monitor and discuss the progress of the unit's strategy. Operational issues, unless they are particularly significant and cross functional, should not be discussed at these meetings, because they would normally be the subject of the more frequent and functional operational review meetings described in the preceding section.

Attendees at a strategy review meeting typically do not question the validity of the strategy. Instead, the discussion focuses on whether strategy execution is on track, identifies the risks of successful strategy execution, detects where problems are occurring in the implementation, attempts to determine why the problems are occurring, takes actions to correct the cause, and assigns responsibility for achieving the targeted results.

Strategy review meetings require mandatory attendance and a commitment to start and end meetings on time. Bill Catucci, as president of AT&T Canada in the late 1990s, scheduled his strategy review meetings one year in advance and made attendance compulsory for himself and his eight business unit heads.

Frequency of Strategy Review Meetings

Most strategy review meetings are scheduled every month, but no consensus has emerged that this is the optimal frequency. As noted earlier in the chapter, Oracle/Latin America meets quarterly, SAS/Europe meets bimonthly, and SprintNextel meets monthly. Monthly meetings work well for management team members in close proximity to each other. But because strategy is a long-term commitment, quarterly meetings may be adequate for reviewing the progress of the strategy.

Typical strategic issues—such as developing new workforce competencies, redefining the brand, developing new products and customer relationships, and reengineering a key business process—take more than a month to yield measurable results. Quarterly meetings conserve travel time for dispersed executive teams, although it will then likely require at least an entire day to conduct an active discussion of the issues of every strategic objective and theme on the strategy map.

One concern with quarterly meetings is that for most of the remaining eighty-nine days the strategy could be out of sight and therefore out of mind. Given that the management culture is already dominated by short-term thinking, companies should strive to regularly set aside some of the time of busy executives for thinking about long-term strategy management issues. A monthly strategy review meeting helps establish a new longer-term culture.

Attendees of Strategy Review Meetings

Obviously, the attendees of the strategy review meeting should include members of the organization's *executive committee* (EC), consisting of the senior leaders responsible for overall management of the company. This group represents all constituencies within the organization and has the power to make important decisions.

Consider the experience of Canadian Blood Services (CBS), as summarized in Figure 8-4. According to Sophie de Villers, strategy management officer, "We tried several approaches and are still experimenting."[7] Initially, the ten-member executive committee met monthly to discuss the information on the newly introduced Balanced Scorecard. The discussions and team building were excellent at this meeting, but participants recognized that they seldom had the subject matter expertise to resolve many of the issues they faced.

The second-generation committee supplemented the EC by adding twenty new people representing all parts of the organization. The EC believed that this broader representation at strategy review meetings would close the knowledge gap. Yet the exact opposite happened. "Everybody clammed up," said de Villers. It appeared that the senior EC members were embarrassed to reveal their knowledge gaps, and the new members, uncertain of the political climate at the meeting, were reluctant to offer opinions and advice. The third, and most successful, try included the EC and members of the three strategic theme teams.

FIGURE 8-4

Evolution of the strategy council at Canadian Blood Services (CBS)

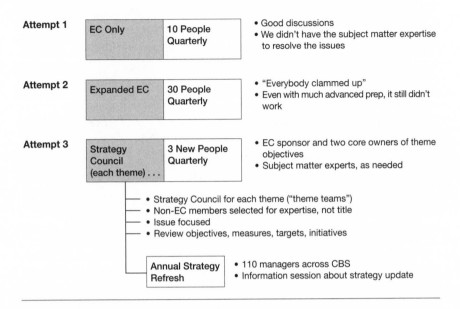

Porcher Industries, a European manufacturer specializing in high-tech materials for products such as air bags and sports equipment, designed its executive committee specifically to provide strategy oversight. The fifteen-member EC consists of the CEO, five business unit managers, four support unit managers, and the five strategic theme owners.

BMW Group Financial Services has a nine-member EC that is responsible for overall strategy execution. The EC invites subject matter experts to attend its quarterly strategy review meetings, as required by the agenda.

Our view supports the approach used by Porcher and BMW Group Financial Services. Executive committee members should be core participants in the strategy review meetings, with people added over time who have either a comprehensive strategic perspective or in-depth knowledge of an important function. Assigning responsibility for individual strategic themes to new committee members is an excellent way to give them legitimacy comparable to that of the traditional members, who have an existing power base. Through leading and managing their strategic themes, the new members provide a depth of knowledge and a cross-business perspective that complements the traditional structure. To differentiate the focus of this new body, we refer to it as the *strategy council*.

Agenda for Strategy Review Meetings

As with operational review meetings, the strategy council's time should not be spent listening to report presentations. Instead, strategy council members should discuss issues, solve problems, and propose action plans. Figure 8-5 shows the shift in distribution of meeting content that can occur if you make Balanced Scorecard reports accessible in advance of the meeting. The BSC provides a framework to cut the clutter from reports. It enables strategy implementation issues to surface clearly, and it allows managers to drill down to detailed operating data, in advance of the meeting, to understand potential causes of underperformance. Managers come to the strategy review meeting already familiar with the data to be discussed, thinking about explanations for recent performance, identifying the risks to successful implementation of the strategy, and formulating options they can recommend to correct problems that have been revealed.

In the early years of Balanced Scorecard implementations, we encouraged a full discussion of BSC measures at each strategy review meeting. It soon became apparent that the normal time allowed for a monthly management meeting—say, two to four hours—did not permit a full discussion of all the objectives, measures, and initiatives on the business unit's strategy map and scorecard. One current best practice is for the agenda to include a quick overview of the entire scorecard. In this way, the executive leadership team can identify any strategic issue requiring its immediate at-

FIGURE 8-5

The new strategy review meeting

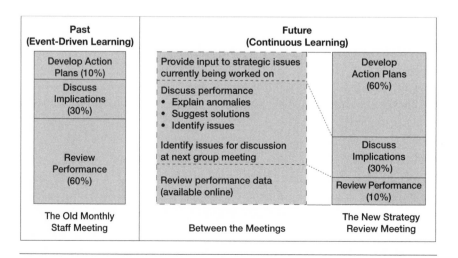

tention, devote some time to discussion of monthly financial performance, and spend the bulk of the time in a focused deep dive into one of
the other three Balanced Scorecard perspectives or a single strategic theme.

We first became aware of the power of deep, focused dives by reflecting on Bill Catucci's experience as president of AT&T Canada (see Figure
8-6). Catucci, an outside appointment to the presidency, initially had one-
on-one monthly meetings with each member of his executive committee:
the business unit heads (commercial, retail, and local services) and functional heads (network operations, finance, strategic planning, legal, and
human resources), as shown at the bottom of Figure 8-6.

Catucci soon became frustrated with trying to execute a new business
strategy through individual meetings with the EC members. The business and
functional heads focused on the demands and performance of their own
departments, to the exclusion of all others. Catucci wanted to discuss the
major strategic issues with his entire management team. He believed that
no one business unit or function could solve the tough issues by itself. So
Catucci disbanded the executive committee and replaced it with four
strategy councils, one for each of four new strategic themes:

FIGURE 8-6

AT&T Canada executive team manages cross-functional themes

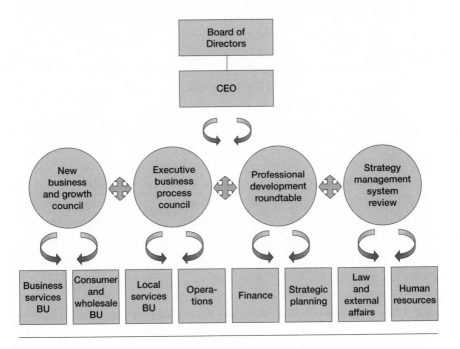

- New business and growth
- Business process and productivity
- Professional development
- Strategy management

In addition to the business and functional heads, Catucci expanded the membership of each council to include individuals who had knowledge relevant to each strategic theme. The agenda of the councils dealt with cross-business strategic behavior. He rotated the agenda for the management meeting among the four strategic themes: growth (the customer perspective), business process (the process perspective), human resources (the learning and growth perspective), and the overall strategy. Catucci emphasized the importance of using the cross-functional strategy review meetings for learning and not for blaming:

How you conduct the meeting, how you react to the reported numbers, is tremendously important. In the past, the person reporting an unfavorable number was lonely and isolated. Now, I want people to admit to short-falls and have everyone else respond, "How can we help?" Nothing that happens in this company is the sole responsibility of a single business unit head. If an indicator is in the red (unfavorable) zone, we identify the people who can influence that indicator and ask them to come to the next meeting with an action plan. This is an entirely new management model for the company. We're sharing information and working together as a team to improve operations and fix problems.

The review meetings became so interesting, people started to ask me if they could attend. Soon it was standing-room only and I could have sold tickets to attend it.[8]

Catucci's new approach for management meetings led to dramatic performance improvements, even in an environment where the price of a long-distance call dropped by more than 90 percent.

The City of Charlotte (North Carolina) evolved a similar approach. The city government consisted of several highly specialized departments (such as police, fire, transportation, waste, and utilities) and functional support units (planning, finance, and human resources). At an operational level, the departments had little in common and apparently less need for interaction. City Manager Pam Syfert articulated a vision for the city ("to be a world class city in which to live, work and play") and a new strategic agenda.[9] She advocated a new organizational approach to execute this strategy. In a system similar to that used at AT&T Canada, she formed five management councils corresponding to the five strategic themes on the city's strategy map. Each council's membership represented a mix of the business units and functions, an arrangement that facilitated cross-organization teamwork and action related to the strategic theme.

The innovations at AT&T Canada and the City of Charlotte have been adopted by many organizations as they structure their strategy review meetings according to their strategic themes. HSBC Rail, described next, provides a best-practice case study of organizing strategy review meetings by strategic themes.

Case Study: HSBC Rail

HSBC Rail, an operating unit of the HSBC Group, purchases, leases, and maintains the locomotives and cars for the U.K. and other nations' railroad systems. In 2007, HSBC Rail leased equipment to the U.K. system's twenty-six passenger railroad operating companies and five freight railroads. Figure 8-7 shows the HSBC Rail strategy map, which is organized by four strategic themes: capital efficiency, customer relationship management, operational excellence, and learning and growth. At first glance, these themes seem to be alternative ways of naming the four Balanced Scorecard perspectives, but Figure 8-7 shows that the customer relationship management and operational excellence themes have objectives in the financial, customer, and process perspectives, and the capital efficiency theme has objectives in the financial and process perspectives.

The HSBC Rail strategy council meets for two and a half hours each month. The council consists of the CEO (Peter), the head of finance (Dave), the head of customer relationship management (Robert), the head of operational excellence (William), the head of learning and development (Nick), and the strategy management officer (SMO) (Paul), who comes from the finance organization.

The SMO coordinates the data collection and reporting on the objectives, measures, and initiatives for each strategic theme in advance of the meeting. The data go into a monthly report that has a section for each strategic theme. The section contains the theme's strategy map, objectives, targets, and initiatives, with each component color-coded:

- *Green:* The objective is being achieved. This does not mean that the objective is merely "on track." The theme owner needs a strong justification to have an objective with a green assessment.

FIGURE 8-7

HSBC Rail strategy map

HSBC Rail strategic destination by 2010: Transition from being capital-intensive to making more efficient use of capital (color evaluations for illustrative purposes only).

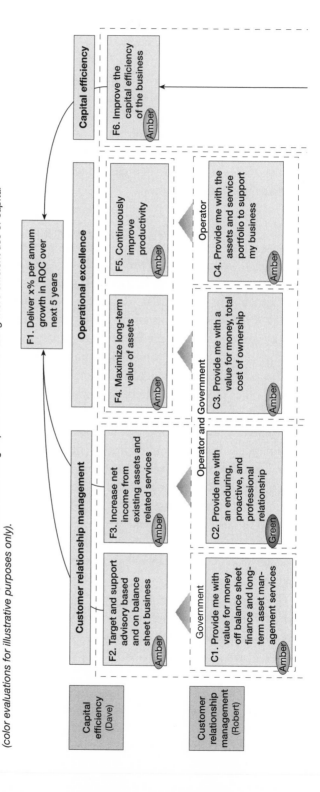

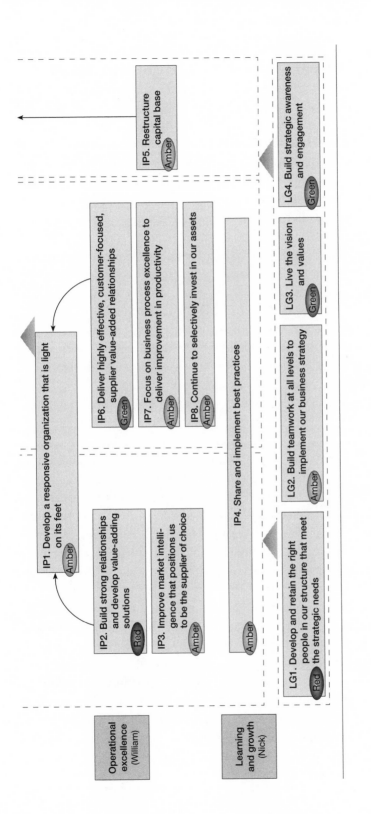

- *Amber:* Everything is OK or under control. This could include an objective that is on track but whose target has not yet been achieved. Alternatively, it could be an objective that is off track but that is not yet critical and does not require management attention at this review.
- *Red:* The company is off track on this objective, *and* it requires management attention because of critical issues relating to this objective. The strategy council should spend time during the strategy review meeting understanding the issue and ways to resolve it.
- *Gray:* This objective has not been assessed.

Each theme's section also contains evaluations and commentary from the theme owner about any performance gaps, along with proposed actions for addressing them.

The monthly meeting consists of a high-level overview of the business, a summary discussion of the status of each strategic theme, and an in-depth discussion of one strategic theme. (At one monthly meeting each quarter, the strategy council covers two strategic themes in depth, enabling each theme to be covered each quarter.)

Figure 8-8 shows the agenda for the meeting that featured the discussion of the capital efficiency strategic theme. The strategy management officer started the meeting by discussing a one-page update of the action log from the preceding meeting, indicating those actions that had been accomplished and those still under way. The CEO then did a quick review of the color-coded strategy map and gave his perspective on the business.

After completing his strategy map review, the CEO asked the other members, "Is this the way you see the business?" The executives commented from their perspectives and identified key issues for subsequent discussion. The CEO then turned to the CFO, the strategic theme owner, to lead the in-depth discussion of the capital efficiency theme.

During the discussion of the capital efficiency strategic theme, the CEO introduced a challenge by interjecting, "This objective is critical; what do we need to track and do to ensure we can deliver the results?" The council executives generated suggestions and solutions to develop an action plan, which the SMO noted for follow-up and implementation.

The CEO continually moved the discussion along, allowing adequate time for presenting issues related to each strategic objective in the theme. The council decided to expand the resources and priorities for one of the strategic initiatives, at which point the CEO asked, "Will this put any other important initiative at risk?"

FIGURE 8-8

Agenda for strategy review meeting

Time	Item	Detail	Duration	Responsibility
10:10	Action log	Review status	5 mins	Paul
10:15	Overview	Review strategy map	10 mins	Peter
		Highlight key issues		
		Review initiatives		
		Review measures		
10:25	Theme assessment	Capital efficiency	60 mins	Dave
11:20	Break		10 mins	
11:30	Theme summary	Learning and growth	5 mins	Nick
11:35	Theme summary	Customer relationship management	5 mins	Robert
11:40	Theme summary	Operational excellence	5 mins	William
11:45	Hot topic	Resourcing challenge	30 mins	Peter
12:15	Meeting review	Communication summary	10 mins	Peter
12:25	Meeting review	Feedback	5 mins	Peter
12:30	Action log	Review of new items	5 mins	Paul
12:35	AOB and meeting close			
	Next meeting	Theme assessment: CRM		

For some issues, the theme owner described operational measures that indicated progress was being made but that the Balanced Scorecard measures had yet to reflect the gains. The members discussed why local improvement measures were not translating into higher performance on the scorecard; they suggested the need to look at either the local dashboard measures or the corresponding scorecard measure to improve the linkages. At the end of the sixty-minute discussion, just before going to the break, the CEO noted some issues that he wanted discussed by the finance operational review team at its next meeting.

After the break, the three other theme owners gave five-minute high-level summaries of the status of their strategic themes, indicating why some of the objectives were red and what they were doing about it, and brief discussion of objectives that had been coded amber. The discussion of the three strategic themes took only fifteen minutes.

The strategy council next turned to an extended discussion of the meeting's *hot topic*—an emerging issue, identified in advance, that the council wanted to discuss in-depth at the meeting. For this meeting, the hot topic was a major change to the company's market environment. On the whiteboard, the CEO diagrammed some key issues that he saw the company facing. The council members engaged in an active discussion to decide what needed to be done and where to obtain the financial and personnel resources to carry out the resource restructuring plan. The hot topic agenda item provided an opportunity for the company's senior management team to respond to important changes in the regulatory and competitive environment on a timely basis.

The meeting concluded with several short items. The council discussed what and how to communicate to employees the results, action plans, and new initiatives discussed or decided at the meeting. This agenda item ensured that strategy results and updates would be continually communicated to employees.

The CEO then asked for feedback from the council members on their perception of the meeting. What worked well? What didn't they like? How could the meeting be improved? In this way, the CEO, in addition to getting valuable feedback, acknowledged that leading the new strategy review meeting was a learning experience for him. The council members concurred that the structure and conduct of the monthly meeting had evolved a great deal in the past twelve months. Previously, the CEO had dominated discussion at the meeting, with the remaining executives listening and acknowledging. Now each had as much or more airtime at the meeting as the CEO. The executives commented, "Very good meeting to reflect on where we are and what still needs to be done"; "Very action-oriented, disciplined, and forward-looking"; "We are no longer just running down operational details. We have a chance to review the external environment and respond to new challenges." To conclude the meeting, the strategy management officer summarized the new action items, and the meeting adjourned—on time.

Observations on the HSBC Rail Strategy Review Meeting

Although the subject matter was different from the NYPD operational review meetings, the conduct and objectives of the HSBC Rail strategy review meeting were quite similar. Skilled executives led both meetings. At HSBC Rail, CEO Peter Aldridge probed participants about why certain results were occurring, what could be done to deal with emerging problems and issues, who would be responsible for implementing the recommended actions, and how soon results could be expected.

The meeting participants came to the meeting already familiar with the data and prepared to discuss the implications and propose action plans. The members had gained trust and confidence in each other, and now they listened respectfully and built constructively on the discussions and proposals that were on the table. Aldridge questioned and probed, kept the meeting focused on the key issues, encouraged dialogue and debate, and ensured that the meeting stayed on schedule so that all items received attention without extending the scheduled meeting time. The strategy management officer recorded all action items so that he could follow up after the meeting with the designated accountable person to ensure that the actions would be taken.

The in-depth review of each strategic theme is repeated each quarter, thus ensuring a comprehensive review of the strategy each quarter while reinforcing the new culture of strategy execution through monthly meetings. In summary, HSBC Rail's strategy review meeting was focused, productive, and action oriented. It promoted learning and problem-solving opportunities. And it started and ended on time.

HSBC Rail earned an execution premium described in the insert:

HSBC RAIL'S EXECUTION PREMIUM

- Assets weighted for risk decreased substantially in 2007–2008. This decrease led to a substantial increase in return on equity (ROE) in two years for this capital-intensive, asset-driven business.
- The net present value of secured future cash flows increased through implementing strategic initiatives. Such initiatives increased near-term revenue and ROE, and significantly reduced the need for additional investment capital in 2008 and beyond.
- Adoption of the BSC was cited by ISO 9001:2000 auditors as one reason for recertification in 2006.

Case Study: Ricoh's Meeting Structure

Ricoh provides another good example of well-structured strategy review meetings. Ricoh holds a series of monthly and quarterly strategy review meetings at corporate and business unit levels (see Figure 8-9). Ricoh uses its meetings for strategy review, exploration, inquiry, and decision making. They are cross functional, with focus on performance, assessment, gap analysis, and consideration of root causes. The Strategy and Planning Office (SPO) prepares and facilitates the meetings.

Monthly, the CEO and the head of the SPO meet with each business unit, for about two hours, to review progress on the unit's most important key performance indicators (KPIs). In the past, business unit meetings focused only on shortfalls in financial metrics. Now the review meetings

FIGURE 8-9

Corporate strategy management review meeting at Ricoh Corporation

Review Meeting		Frequency	Purpose
Chairman's Leadership Forum		Twice per year	Strategy deployment
President's Meeting		Once/3 months	Share and discuss important issues among management
Business Unit Review Meeting		Every month	KPI status; risk/opportunity against plan; clarification of action plan
Cross-Functional Team Review Meeting	Theme 1	Every month	KPI status; risk/opportunity against plan; clarification of action plan
	Theme 2	Every month	KPI status; risk/opportunity against plan; clarification of action plan
	Theme 3	Every month	KPI status; risk/opportunity against plan; clarification of action plan
Solution Marketing Review Meeting		Every month	KPI status; clarification of action plan
		For investment	ROI plan and decision making
Strategy Fund and Review Meeting		Once/3 months	KPI status; risk/opportunity against plan; clarification of action plan
Product Launch Meeting (for strategic product)		As required	Share of positioning; specification; competitiveness; P&L impact; and clarification of action plan

In addition, corporate functions such as HR, IT, SCM, and Finance hold review meetings on a regular basis.

also examine leading indicators and nonfinancial outcome measures. Ricoh expects business unit heads to use the plan-do-check-act cycle to show the root causes of shortfalls in KPIs and the countermeasures they have taken or planned. The new process has been in use for more than a year, and business unit leaders are beginning to use the same approach when reviewing their direct reports' progress. In addition to these short business unit review meetings, the CEO and SPO attend one full-day business unit meeting each month to participate, with the unit's management team, in a detailed examination of the unit's KPI performance.

Quarterly, the CEO hosts an informal meeting, attended by the vice president of marketing and all business unit heads, to discuss the short- and long-term strategy. Participants review the current and past performance of the strategy, discuss the cause-and-effect relationships among strategy map objectives, and determine the corrective actions needed to ensure achievement of strategic goals. Quarterly, the CEO and the SPO meet with each business unit for full BSC reviews.

In addition, the CEO and the SPO meet quarterly with each owner of a funded strategic initiative. Every three years, as part of its three-year planning cycle, Ricoh establishes four cross-functional strategic theme teams. The theme teams initially develop comprehensive action plans for their themes. During the remainder of their three-year life, they met bimonthly to review progress and update action plans.

Each business unit conducts semiannual meetings with all employees to discuss the state of the business. The unit head communicates business results using the unit's BSC. The meetings are interactive, motivating all employees to make strategy everyone's job.

Before Ricoh implemented the BSC, management meetings covered only progress against the financial targets. Little discussion or questioning occurred, whether the targets were made, exceeded, or missed. Now the management meetings have changed from strictly financial to a more holistic strategy review. The concept of root cause analysis of shortfalls was initially foreign but is now practiced regularly. Probing deeply into the reasons for results leads to the discovery of very different causes and different solutions. It also leads to inquiry concerning the implementation of the strategy.

For example, one review meeting considered the below target performance of dealer recruitment, an important objective on the Ricoh Balanced Scorecard. Attempting to identify the root causes for the shortfall stimulated a discussion and revealed the need for additional data collection. Inquiry and discussion led to a series of countermeasures that were then reviewed regularly at subsequent meetings, with discussion about needed course corrections. By year-end, the dealer recruitment target had been exceeded.

Ricoh's management formerly reviewed strategy only once a year or once every three years. The meeting consisted of only one or two people and generated a document that was never looked at again. Now, senior executives, business unit heads, and employees at each business unit meet frequently for strategy reviews of financial and nonfinancial KPIs.

SUMMARY

Operational and strategy review meetings help keep organizations on a strategic trajectory for breakthrough performance. The meetings serve different functions, occur at different frequencies, typically have different attendees, and have different agendas. Operational review meetings are typically departmental, functional, or process-based and are attended by people who are expert and experienced in the issues to be discussed. These meetings are frequent—corresponding to the time scale of work accomplished by the unit or process—and are informed by operational dashboards summarizing recent performance. The goals of the meeting are to solve problems that have recently emerged and to learn from the operational data that have been accumulated.

Strategy review meetings are held monthly or quarterly to assess recent performance of the strategy and guide its future implementation. The meetings are cross functional, involving members of the senior executive committee, owners of the strategic themes, and managers having specific functional or business expertise that can add to the meeting's discussion. Attendees conduct a high-level overview of the strategy implementation and its risks, as well as a deep dive into one or two strategic themes or a single strategy map perspective.

Despite differences in meeting frequency, attendees, and agenda, operational and strategy review meetings share important characteristics. Meetings start and end on time. Attendance is mandatory so that the members build confidence and trust in each other and understand that each person attends the meeting because he or she has important knowledge and experience to contribute. The meetings are data driven, with participants having studied the relevant data in advance. They spend their time at the meeting problem solving, learning, and formulating actions, not listening passively to reports. The meetings encourage frank discussions among all participants, regardless of rank. The leader stresses the importance of deciding "what is right" and not "who is right."

Participants in operational and strategy review meetings share the same assumptions about the strategy that all of them are attempting to implement. Periodically, senior executives and managers need to sit back to assess whether the agreed-upon strategy remains valid in light of new knowledge, information, opportunities, and changes in the competitive, technological, economic, and regulatory environment. Such an assessment of the strategy is the subject of the strategy testing and adapting meeting, to be discussed next in Chapter 9.

NOTES

1. Remarks at "Office of Strategy Management Workshop," The Balanced Scorecard Collaborative, November 2006.
2. Material for this section was drawn from J. Heskett, "NYPD New," Case 396-293 (Boston: Harvard Business School, June 22, 1999), and J. Buntin, "Assertive Policing, Plummeting Crime: The NYPD Takes on Crime in New York City," Case C16-99-1530.0 (Boston: Harvard University Kennedy School of Government, 1999).
3. Data from R. Giuliani, *Leadership* (New York: Hyperion, 2002), 79–80.
4. Ibid., 82–91.
5. Heskett, "NYPD New."

6. R. Kaplan, "Texas Eastman Company," Case 9-190-039 (Boston: Harvard Business School Press, 1989).

7. "Conducting Strategy Reviews," Office of Strategy Management Working Group workshop, Balanced Scorecard Collaborative, March 28, 2006.

8. W. Catucci, "Making Strategy Execution a Core Competence," Balanced Scorecard Collaborative Conference (Bal Harbour, FL, December 2003).

9. R. Kaplan, "City of Charlotte (A)," Case 9-199-036 (Boston: Harvard Business School Press, 1998).

CHAPTER NINE

MEETINGS TO TEST AND ADAPT THE STRATEGY

Not all long-term strategies are profitable strategies.

A STRATEGY MAP and Balanced Scorecard make explicit the linked hypotheses underlying an organization's strategy. But even with a good map and scorecard, success from the strategy remains uncertain. Apart from a company's ability to execute its strategy, it cannot be certain that the assumptions and hypotheses underlying the strategy are valid.

As discussed in Chapter 2, the executive team formulates a strategy using its best assessment available of the external and competitive environment, market segments, customer preferences, and the cause-and-effect relationships required for the strategy to succeed. But strategy formulation remains an art, and not yet a science. A principal benefit of implementing a strategy with a Balanced Scorecard is that a company can use the scorecard data to periodically assess whether its strategic hypotheses are valid.

This assessment is distinct from reviews of operations and strategy implementation, which are discussed in Chapter 8. *Strategy testing and adapting meetings* are designed for the executive team to learn about the validity of the strategy—not only its execution—and to modify and adapt the strategy over time. This is the sixth stage in the closed-loop strategy management system we have described (see Figure 9-1).

The chain of linked hypotheses in a well-formulated strategy map and Balanced Scorecard typically starts with the learning and growth perspective.

FIGURE 9-1

The management system: test and adapt

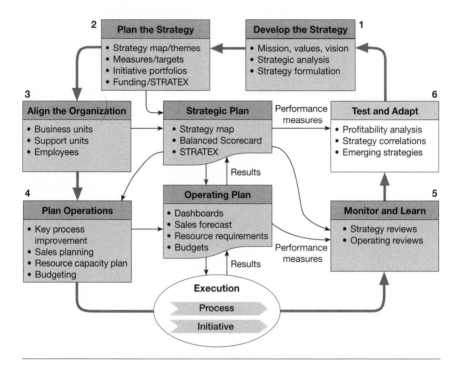

The company assumes that achieving the strategic objectives for human, information, and organizational capital will drive improvement in critical strategic processes.[1] The strategy's next two assumptions are that being excellent at performing these strategic processes will (1) create and deliver a desired value proposition to targeted customers and will (2) drive productivity improvements, a strategic financial objective. The strategy then assumes that delivering the desired customer value proposition will create highly satisfied and loyal customers, who, in turn, will increase the volume and margin of business they do with the company. Finally, increased customer satisfaction and loyalty are assumed to deliver the financial objectives of revenue growth and increased profitability. Thus, a well-formulated strategy map, with its accompanying Balanced Scorecard, represents a linked and comprehensive set of assumptions about how the strategy will create and sustain long-term shareholder value.

The strategy map and scorecard inform and focus a broad range of strategy execution processes: initiative selection and rationalization, resource allocation, communication, alignment, individual performance management, reporting, accountability, and operational and strategy review meetings. But suppose the assumptions used to create a company's strategy map and scorecard are invalid or obsolete. In this case, the company has been operating with a poor strategy, especially when significant changes in the company's macroeconomic, competitive, regulatory, and technological environment have occurred since the strategy was last reviewed. Effectively executing a strategy with flawed assumptions will enable a company to fail that much faster.

Thus, every company should, at least annually—and perhaps as often as quarterly (depending on the speed of competitive, technological, and consumer dynamics in the industry)—conduct a separate meeting to assess the performance of its strategy and consider the consequences of recent changes in its external environment. This meeting can and should be the same meeting described in Chapter 2 for developing a new strategy. Once the strategy has been formulated and implemented using the approaches described in Chapters 3 through 8, the company must periodically cycle back to review new information that has become available about the external environment and the performance of the strategy. This meeting completes the strategy planning, execution, and control loop by providing the executive team with a formal opportunity to assess the performance of its strategy in light of the new information acquired since the previous meeting that reviewed and updated the strategy.

The output of the strategy testing and adapting meeting can be to reaffirm the existing strategy, in which case the executive team updates targets, reprioritizes strategic initiatives, and transmits new expectations to business units and functions. Or participants at this meeting might make incremental changes to the strategy by changing one or more strategic objectives, replacing some measures with new ones, and recalibrating the strategy's targets and initiatives. Occasionally, the company may learn that its strategy has significant flaws or has become obsolete because of changes in the external, competitive, regulatory, or technological environment. In this case, the company reverts to the strategy development process described in Chapter 2 to develop a new transformational strategy. The strategy testing and adapting meeting allows a company's leadership team to meet at least once a year to decide which of these three strategy update options to adopt.

Discussions at the strategy testing and adapting meeting will benefit from economic and statistical models that provide quantitative feedback on the assumptions underlying the current strategy. These models provide empirical estimates of the correlations between the strategic drivers (the metrics in the process perspective and the learning and growth perspective) and the strategic outcomes in the customer and financial perspectives. The empirical estimates help managers set priorities and establish the rationale for initiatives designed to improve the performance of the strategic drivers.

Occasionally, the analytics inform companies that their strategy is not working as intended. Using formal economic and statistical models, managers can distinguish when disappointing outcomes in the financial and customer perspectives arise from flawed execution or from executing a flawed strategy. In this chapter, we provide a detailed study of how a statistical analysis of one company's data revealed flaws in the strategy even before managers became aware of the problems. The statistical data also suggested a contingency between employee competencies and strategy execution that had eluded company management.

Of course, when testing and evaluating the company's current strategy, meeting participants must also consider changes in external conditions. The executive team needs to assess whether such changes require abandoning or modifying the strategy in some significant way. Also, the executive team should explicitly think about recent competitor actions and attempt to consider the consequences of future possible scenarios and competitive dynamics.

Finally, the strategy testing and adapting meeting provides an ideal time for the executive team to consider ideas about strategy revisions and initiatives that have emerged from within the organization. Many ideas for new strategic options can arise from employees closest to customers and processes. Companies should actively solicit and assess ideas for new strategic options so that they can benefit from the awareness of the strategy by all employees in the enterprise and their motivation to help it succeed.

OPERATIONAL FEEDBACK THAT TESTS THE STRATEGY

In Chapter 2 we discuss how companies examine external data and information during their strategy development meetings. The strategic planning department conducts a PESTEL analysis to bring together data on political, economic, social, technological, environmental, and legal conditions. All these data need to be updated to reflect changes that have occurred since the last strategy update meeting in political and external macroeconomic conditions, such as interest rates, currency exchange rates, inflation rates, commodity prices (including energy), regulations, and country- and region-specific growth rates. The planning department also updates the information on industry trends, market shares, competitor behavior, technological changes, growth rates by market segment, and any changes in customer preferences.

Such external data are a vital input for strategy testing and adapting meetings. But the executive team also needs detailed data on the company's current performance. Executives cannot assess the quality of the strategy by using only the highly aggregated financial data in income statements, balance sheets, and cash flow statements. Financial statement data show total or average performance but do not reveal performance by market segment or by product line, and certainly not by individual products, customers, and facilities. Granular P&L data give companies much more visibility into the strengths and weaknesses of their current performance. The detailed data also provide the executive team with feedback on the linkages between the companies' leading indicators—the metrics on the performance of people, information, processes, and the customer value proposition—and the lagging outcome indicators of customer and financial performance.

Companies can enhance their strategy review process by examining the existing microeconomics of their individual products and customers, along with the statistical correlations between the assumed drivers of their strategies and the outcomes they are experiencing. Such detailed examinations reveal gaps or even flaws in the existing strategy that managers can act to correct in future periods.

We have identified two principal analytic tools that provide valuable inputs to strategy review processes. Activity-based cost and profitability models produce an economic map of the enterprise, displaying where the company makes and loses money. Statistical models estimate the strengths of the linkages among the strategic variables in a company's Balanced Scorecard. We discuss both analytic approaches in the next two sections.

TIME-DRIVEN ABC MODELS OF PRODUCT AND CUSTOMER PROFITABILITY

In Chapter 7, we introduce time-driven activity-based costing (TDABC) as a simple and powerful analytic tool for planning the resource capacities required to implement the strategy. The heart of the resource planning model is a TDABC model that calculates the profitability of each of the companies' products and customers. For example, Towerton Financial Services, a hypothetical company described in Chapter 7, learned that a newly introduced service line—customer investment management—was operating only at breakeven levels, and another new product—financial planning and advice—was losing substantial amounts of money each period. Clearly, losing money on new service offerings was not what Towerton's strategy planners had in mind.

A large New York City bank had a profitable product line of demand and time deposits. It launched a major client retention initiative to retain all clients with deposit balances that exceeded $25,000. As shown in Figure 9-2, its existing, somewhat aggregate profitability measurement system showed that every balance tier greater than $25,000 was profitable.

The bank then conducted a more detailed ABC study to calculate the cost to serve and the profitability of every customer account in the high-deposit segment (see Figure 9-3). It learned that 35 percent of all the households targeted for retention were unprofitable, with cumulative losses totaling more than $2 million. Unprofitable customers could be found in every balance tier up to $1 million.

Managers at first could not believe that high-deposit individuals could be unprofitable. Further analysis revealed that the unprofitable customers conducted a large number of transactions in the branches, the most expensive banking service channel, and kept most of their deposits in accounts that yielded low margins to the bank. Fortunately, the bank discovered this error in its strategy before launching major initiatives to retain unprofitable customers.[2]

FIGURE 9-2

Bank profile of customers with balances > $25,000

Balance Tier ($000s)	Number of Households	Earnings before Taxes	Total Balances
25–50	116,835	$2,419,918	$4,157,734,498
50–75	57,470	$2,023,068	$3,509,623,133
75–100	34,588	$1,874,109	$2,999,458,338
100–200	34,680	$3,379,299	$4,522,312,875
200–300	5,467	$1,221,739	$1,300,445,137
300–400	1,613	$579,844	$550,756,999
400–500	642	$3,047,482	$284,588,268
500–1,000	758	$552,239	$489,149,727
1,000–1,500	126	$171,737	$150,248,037
1,500–2,000	40	$80,980	$69,196,207
>2,000	47	$475,642	$235,241,062
TOTAL	252,266	$15,826,057	$18,268,754,281

FIGURE 9-3

Thirty-five percent of customers with balances > $25,000 were unprofitable

Households with balances >$25,000 that have negative net earnings before taxes (NEBT)

Balance Tier ($000s)	Number of Households	NEBT	Total Balances
25–50	47,555	($1,163,707)	$1,697,728,391
50–75	22,742	($553,457)	$1,378,703,079
75–100	9,813	($272,351)	$844,449,799
100–200	6,808	($269,338)	$860,603,493
200–300	484	($37,549)	$112,654,354
300–400	70	($11,155)	$23,438,342
400–500	30	($7,436)	$12,987,906
500–1,000	17	($10,050)	$9,979,015
1,000–1,500	1	($69)	$1,000,000
1,500–2,000	0	$0	$0
>2,000	0	$0	$0
TOTAL	**87,520**	**($2,325,112)**	**$4,941,544,379**

Similarly, a large medical distribution company was incurring high costs to meet customers' special requests for frequent deliveries of small orders and for expedited overnight delivery. The customers greatly appreciated the company's willingness to deliver numerous small orders directly to their point of use, bypassing the use of the customers' receiving, inspection, and stocking departments. Customer satisfaction and loyalty were at all-time highs, but the distribution company learned, after building an ABC model of its costs to serve, that it was losing substantial money by providing such customized services, especially to some of its largest customers.

Kemps, a leading Midwestern U.S. dairy company, learned from its time-driven ABC model the adverse consequences of its existing strategy.[3] The company had developed long-term relationships with retail and wholesale customers by delivering the right products in the right quantities at the right time, as defined by customers. This strategy had led to massive complexity in production, packaging, warehousing, and distribution. Kemps's TDABC model accurately measured the costs of producing, storing, delivering, and invoicing each order for each customer. The model revealed the drivers of high costs in many processes and the existence of unprofitable customers. The analysis convinced the Kemps CEO,

Jim Green, that the company could no longer follow a strategy "to be all things to all people."

These experiences are not isolated or unusual. In applying activity-based costing to many companies in many industries, we have learned that the 20-80 rule does not apply to the profitability of products and customers.[4] It may be true that 20 percent of the products and 20 percent of the customers generate 80 percent of sales, but profits, which are calculated as the residual remaining after subtracting one large quantity (expenses) from another (revenues), do not follow the same rule. The most profitable 20 percent of products and customers generally produce between 150 and 300 percent of total profits (see Figure 9-4). For example, a large sample study of retail banks showed that 140 to 170 percent of a typical bank's profits came from 20 percent of customers, and 80 percent of losses could be attributed to 20 percent of the customers.

Whenever a company meets to review its strategy, it should first understand the economics of its existing strategy. As Harvard philosopher George Santayana observed, "Those who cannot remember the past are condemned to repeat it." A company that forgets, or never realizes, that it has unprofitable products and customers in the current period will almost surely continue to incur losses in unprofitable products and customers in future periods. Having a clear picture about where the company is making money and losing money should be a vital input to any strategy review.

FIGURE 9-4

Cumulative profits versus customers: The 20-180 rule

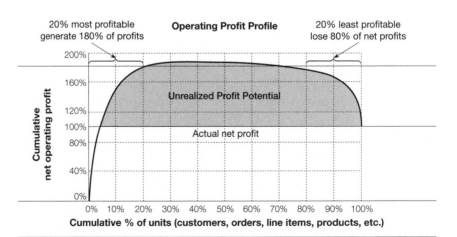

The origins of activity-based costing can be traced to the practices of strategy consulting firms in the 1970s. The strategy consultants understood well that their client companies' cost accounting systems produced huge distortions in product and customer profitability. The consultants, through interviews of personnel in operations, warehousing, distribution, and marketing and sales, made an approximate but far more accurate assignment of costs to products and customers. The consultants then matched each product's and customer's costs to the revenues it produced to learn which product lines and customer segments were highly profitable and which were generating losses. With this information, the consultants' strategy recommendations were now obvious, and reaching them didn't really require an MBA: do more of the former (that is, make more of the profitable products and sell them to profitable customers) and less of the latter (make fewer unprofitable products and reduce sales to unprofitable customers). The near-term profit improvements from the new strategy usually repaid the high consulting fees many times over.

Activity-based cost models formalize the process used by the strategy consulting firms and enable companies to routinely produce accurate economic profit-and-loss maps of their operations and sales. Companies don't need to hire consultants to figure out how to modify their strategies to enhance profitability. They can take operational actions that target specific process improvements in high-cost processes, as discussed in Chapter 6. And they can introduce dramatically different pricing strategies, change the way they work with currently unprofitable customers or customer segments, and even abandon segments and channels where profit turnarounds seem unlikely, time-consuming, or costly.[5] Companies can also discover small, but highly profitable, product niches and customer segments where they can focus more resources to grow them into major profit contributors.

Figure 9-5 summarizes the various operational and strategic actions taken by Kemps to improve its profitability. CEO Jim Green commented on the success of its new strategy: "ABC enabled us to reduce complexity across all our operations, especially complexity that customers did not want to pay for. Today, we do not do any new contract without first going through an ABC analysis."[6]

The medical distributor discussed earlier illustrates the power of introducing an entirely new pricing strategy. It replaced its traditional pricing scheme, based on an average markup over purchasing cost, with menu-based pricing, in which customers paid for each individual special service they requested, such as expedited delivery, breakpack orders, and direct delivery. Customers who ordered standard products in standard

FIGURE 9-5

Kemps took operational and strategic actions to generate substantial near-term profitability improvements

Process Improvements	Product and Pricing Decisions	Redefinition of Customer Relationships
Accumulated customer orders weekly leading to fewer production runs/product:	Formed senior executive SKU rationalization team, which met monthly:	Consolidated labeling across three store chains; fewer deliveries of larger quantities:
Saved 2 hours per product per month plus reduced materials loss at start and stop of each run	*Repriced or dropped unprofitable products, increased production volumes of remaining products*	*Lowered price to customer and retained business without competitive bidding*
Standardized ingredients, such as label to reduce changeovers:	Shut down one plant by consolidating production into headquarters plant	Cross-docked orders with large sophisticated customers (SuperValu):
Reduced overtime and eliminated 1 shift/week		*Enhanced value-creation with strategic supply-chain partners*

quantities using standard delivery enjoyed a discounted price; customers who valued special features got those services, though at a price that reflected the incremental costs (plus potential pricing premiums) associated with each feature. Most customers migrated voluntarily to the more transparent pricing model. The distributor's profits and market share increased, and soon the strategy evolved further, with the company integrating forward into its customers' value chain by managing an integrated procurement and distribution process for its customers.

In summary, the ultimate test of any strategy is whether it makes more money for the company. But rather than work only with a highly aggregated income statement to determine whether it is making money, the company should calculate individual product, customer, segment, channel, and regional P&L statements. Computer-based TDABC models deliver individual P&Ls accurately and at low cost, facilitating such strategy reviews. These data enable a company to follow a rifle approach for strategy modification rather than a shotgun one. It targets those areas where profit enhancements are most needed and are most likely to be realized.

STATISTICAL TESTING OF OPERATIONAL LINKAGES

Measuring whether the company's value proposition and cost structure have produced profitable customer relationships is one powerful test of a strategy. Another test, complementary to the ABC test, is to examine statistically the linkages among improvements in the Balanced Scorecard metrics. The strategy map hypothesizes that improvements in learning and growth metrics should lead to improvements in process metrics, which, in turn, should lead to improvements in customer and financial metrics. Several organizations have conducted formal statistical tests of the linkages hypothesized in their scorecards.

Case Study: The Sears Employee-Customer-Profit Chain

In the mid-1990s, Sears adopted a new employee- and customer-centered strategy. The strategy was based on the service management profit chain, a causal modeling methodology introduced at Harvard Business School at about the same time as the Balanced Scorecard.[7] The *service management profit chain* theory states that increasing employees' satisfaction and commitment leads to increased customer satisfaction, and that, in turn, drives increases in profits. Sears, in implementing the employee-customer-profit model, invested heavily in developing relevant indicators and collecting data on employee and customer satisfaction. This investment enabled an internal analytic team to perform statistical analyses that validated and estimated the strength of the linkages between employee attitudes, customer satisfaction, and changes in company profits. A classic *Harvard Business Review* article described how the new approach was implemented at Sears.[8]

Arthur Martinez, who joined Sears in 1992 as head of the merchandising group and became CEO in 1995, led the turnaround strategy based on making Sears "a compelling place to work, to shop, and to invest."[9] Although the vision was inspiring, it lacked specificity to drive action at local levels. Several task forces worked to translate the vision into tangible, action-oriented objectives, resulting in the objectives and metrics shown in Figure 9-6.

The Sears project team performed detailed statistical testing of the interrelationships among the employee, customer, and financial metrics. The team set a goal to construct a model that showed the pathways from improvement in employee attitudes to improvement in profits. By understanding the relationship between, say, a given increment in employee product knowledge and increased customer loyalty and, subsequently, higher revenues and margins, Sears could answer a question such as, "How much should be spent to increase employees' knowledge of products?" The project team collected data from eight hundred stores for two calendar quarters and processed the data through cluster and factor

FIGURE 9-6

Sears initial model: objectives and measures

	A Compelling Place to Work	A Compelling Place to Shop	A Compelling Place to Invest
Objectives	• Environment for personal growth and development • Support for ideas and innovation • Empowered and involved teams and individuals	• Great merchandise at great values • Excellent customer service from the best people • Fun place to shop • Customer loyalty	• Revenue growth • Superior operating income growth • Efficient asset management • Productivity gains
Measures	• Personal growth and development • Empowered teams	• Customer needs met • Customer satisfaction • Customer retention	• Revenue growth • Sales per square foot • Inventory turnover • Operating income margin • Return on assets

analysis: statistical routines to identify those employee measures that had the highest correlations with customer and financial outcomes.

The team found that two dimensions of employee satisfaction—attitudes about the job and about the company—had the greatest effect on employee loyalty and employees' behavior toward customers (see Figure 9-7). Ten questions on the seventy-item employee survey measured these two employee attitudes. The team recommended discontinuing questions that measured personal growth and development and empowered teams (as initially hypothesized), because the responses to these questions showed no correlation with customer satisfaction or loyalty. The team retained those questions of the remaining sixty that helped to predict or drive employee responses on the ten attitude questions. These items gave local store managers insights about the levers they could control on a daily basis to improve their employees' attitudes about their jobs, the customers they served, and the company they worked for.

Over eighteen months, the project team performed several iterations on the model, refining measures and making new estimates of relationships using multiple regression and causal pathway analysis. It ended up with the model shown in Figure 9-8.

One of the estimated pathways in this model indicated that improving employee attitudes by 5 points would drive a 1.3-point improvement in customer satisfaction, which, in turn, would drive a 0.5 percent (50 basis points) improvement in revenue growth. For example, if one Sears store could increase its aggregate employee attitude score by 5 points, and if the

FIGURE 9-7

Sears identified the 10 key questions about being a "compelling place to work"

Responses to these 10 questions on the 70-question employee survey had the highest impact on employee behavior (and therefore on customer satisfaction).

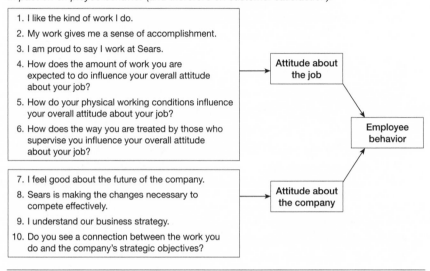

1. I like the kind of work I do.
2. My work gives me a sense of accomplishment.
3. I am proud to say I work at Sears.
4. How does the amount of work you are expected to do influence your overall attitude about your job?
5. How do your physical working conditions influence your overall attitude about your job?
6. How does the way you are treated by those who supervise you influence your overall attitude about your job?

7. I feel good about the future of the company.
8. Sears is making the changes necessary to compete effectively.
9. I understand our business strategy.
10. Do you see a connection between the work you do and the company's strategic objectives?

FIGURE 9-8

Sears revised employee–customer-profit chain model

The rectangles represent survey information; the ovals, hard data. The measurements in gray are collected and distributed in the form of the Sears Total Performance Indicators.

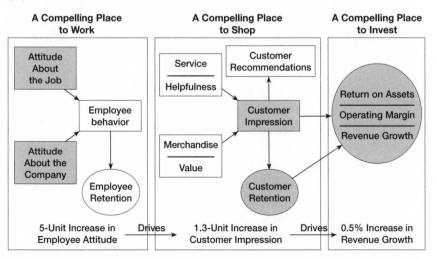

store was in a region that had, say, 6 percent revenue growth, that store could be expected to have a sales increase of 6.5 percent, or nearly 10 percent higher than the average for the region.

At the time, Sears had annual sales of about $50 billion and an average same-store sales growth rate of about 4 to 5 percent. If Sears, by improving employee involvement and commitment, could generate an additional 0.5 percent growth rate in sales, it would add $250 million in revenues per year. Given normal gross margins and the market's existing earnings capitalization rate, the revenue increase could translate into an increase in market value of several billion dollars.

The statistical analysis also revealed that most of the financial gains occurred with a two-quarter lag from the measured improvement in employee attitude scores. So the tool enabled better sales forecasting based on measured changes in current employee metrics.

The best measure of customer satisfaction and loyalty turned out to be the percentage of customers at the store who scored their buying experience as a 10 (scaled as "definitely would recommend") on a 1 to 10 scale. Previously, customer satisfaction had been measured by the average score of all surveyed store customers on the 1 to 10 scale. The statistical analysis showed a sharp drop-off in repeat purchases and revenue growth for customers who scored the buying experience as a 9 compared with those who scored it a 10.[10] This finding had a large impact on behavior, because moving an already satisfied customer to extremely satisfied was considerably more challenging than transforming a neutral customer to satisfied.

In addition to the pathway from employee attitudes to customer loyalty, the statistical model identified the contributions from the quality and availability of product and its position and merchandising within the store. Sears now had a quantitative model that connected three marketing P's—people, product, and place—to customer satisfaction and loyalty.

The team further learned that the responses to improvements in employee attitudes and to customer loyalty varied by product line. For example, a 1-point improvement in percentage of customers scoring the buying experience as a 10 led to a 7.4 percent sales gain for women's ready-to-wear intimate apparel, but a 14.2 percent sales gain in men's and children's apparel.[11] In general, each Sears line of business (e.g., apparel, appliances, automotive, and hardware) had a different weight and even a somewhat different predictive model on its employee-customer-profit causal chain model. At a Sears hardware store, customers expected knowledgeable employees who understood the technical requirements of the job for which the customer was purchasing hardware. In department stores, customers valued responsiveness, friendliness, and speed, not technical knowledge.

The knowledge of product-specific relationships informed actions—such as communication, training, merchandising, and incentives, to be tailored to each line of business—based on proven relationships between employee attitudes and customer loyalty and to the correlations of these two variables to the financial metrics of revenue growth, operating income, and return on assets.

The statistical testing done at Sears (and that done at TD Canada Trust, as described in Chapter 6) affirmed the company's strategy. The relationships between employee attitudes, customer satisfaction, and financial performance all moved in the hypothesized directions. The statistical analysis added quantitative information about the magnitude of the correlations between the strategic variables as well as estimates of the time delays between improvement in a leading indicator and the reaction in a lagging or outcome indicator.

We now turn to statistical analysis that tests whether the company's underlying strategy is valid. This analysis allows the strategic hypotheses to be disconfirmed, providing a highly valuable signal of the need to change the strategy or its implementation.

STRATEGY TESTING AND ADAPTING

Strategies, especially newly introduced ones, are hypotheses about value creation. With data collected from the strategy's Balanced Scorecard, statistical analysis can test whether a variable, assumed to have a strong positive connection to a customer or financial outcome, actually has zero or a negative correlation with these strategy outcome indicators. Such a finding would signal to the executive team that some of the assumed logic in its strategy may be invalid. In this case, the team would need to collect more data to validate and understand, at a deeper level, why the causal connection was not working as intended. The analysis prepares executives to abandon some aspect of the strategy and replace it with a new value proposition in which the links from driver variables to desired customer and financial outcomes are more likely to be valid.

For example, a money center bank learned, after a large merger with a local competitor, that one of its original BSC customer objectives—to retain as many customer accounts as possible—was leading to retention of many unprofitable customers. In a subsequent merger with another local bank, the executive team modified the customer objective to retain only large and profitable accounts, allowing small, unprofitable accounts to close. The chief administrative officer commented about the benefits of the modified strategy: "It saved us several billion dollars of balances and added somewhere between 20 and 30 million dollars per year to earnings." Companies can conduct formal statistical analysis to detect when their strategies are not delivering the expected results, as we discuss in the next case study.

Case Study: Store 24

Store 24, one of New England's largest convenience store chains, implemented a new customer intimacy strategy in May 1998, which it referred to as "Ban Boredom."[12] Store 24 CEO Bob Gordon believed that providing an entertaining shopping atmosphere, including frequent themes and promotions, would differentiate the shopping experience at the chain from its competitors. Gordon hoped to create loyalty to Store 24 among its targeted customer base of young, urban adults between the ages of fourteen and twenty-nine. A Store 24 manager noted that marketing research revealed that this group "gets bored easily and needs to be stimulated. We wanted this group to always see new and different things in the store."[13]

Store 24 actively promoted its Ban Boredom strategy on billboards, buses, and trolleys. Its retail outlets placed a large display case at the head of the center aisle to feature the promotional items for the current theme, such as life-sized cutouts of movie stars and discounted videos for an "old movie" theme.

Store 24 created a strategy map and Balanced Scorecard (see Figure 9-9) to communicate and help implement the new strategy. Store managers had discretion in how they executed the strategy. Some managers dressed up in costumes consistent with a current store theme to recognize an upcoming holiday. Others, however, ignored the strategy and kept traditional convenience store items, such as chips, on the end-aisle displays, rather than the higher-margin promotional items.

Within two years Store 24 learned that its strategy was not working. Gordon commented, "Overall, same-store sales were fine. However, we were getting strong negative feedback about the Ban Boredom strategy from in-store comment cards . . . Our telephone surveys also showed that customers simply were not identifying with the fun, entertaining atmosphere we were trying to create in our stores. Finally, focus groups with our customers suggested overwhelmingly that they valued our traditional strengths of good product selection, quick service, and clean surroundings, and they did not at all value the Ban Boredom experience we were trying to create."[14]

The feedback from individual customers and focus groups led Store 24 to abandon its innovative Ban Boredom strategy after two years, in

FIGURE 9-9

Strategy map and scorecard for Store 24's new Ban Boredom strategy

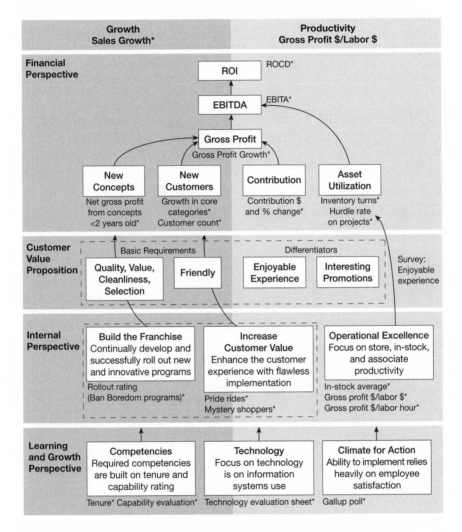

*Measures basic requirements.

April 2000, and replace it with an updated version of its previous strategy, which featured fast and efficient service. Figure 9-10 shows the strategy map and scorecard for the updated strategy, branded as "'Cause You Just Can't Wait."

Store 24 did not have the internal analytic capabilities of Sears to test the causal relationships in its Ban Boredom strategy map. It relied on

FIGURE 9-10

Store 24's updated strategy: "'Cause you just can't wait"

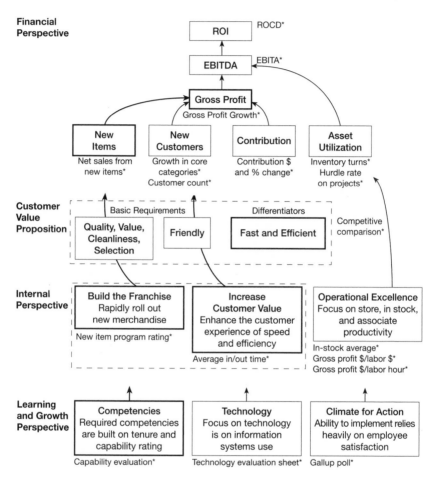

*Measures basic requirements.

customer feedback to eventually learn that the strategy's value proposition of providing a "fun and exciting shopping experience" was not working. In fact, the value proposition was actually creating some dissatisfied customers, who were distracted by the ever-changing featured displays and promotions and unhappy about inattentive store employees dressed in costumes.

A Harvard Business School faculty team gained access to the monthly data from Store 24's eighty-five retail outlets and performed statistical analysis to see whether the flaws in the Ban Boredom strategy could have been visible to the company's executive team earlier.[15] The team gathered data on quarterly performance for sixty-five stores from May 1, 1998, through April 30, 2000, when the Ban Boredom strategy was terminated. The initial look at the data suggested that Store 24's strategy worked fine in the initial implementation year. Same-store sales grew by the industry average of 6 percent.

Before performing a more comprehensive cross-sectional analysis to explain variation in store profitability, the research team adjusted for structural characteristics unique to each store—including the targeted population, income, and number of competitors within each store's half-mile radius—and store operating characteristics, such as size and hours open per day.

Store 24 had obtained customer satisfaction data from a third-party research firm, which it hired to conduct in-store interviews with customers. It aggregated these interviews into a customer perception metric on the percentage of customers who ranked the store as "an entertaining place to shop." Store 24 also did an on-site assessment, twice each quarter, of each store's compliance with Ban Boredom operating standards. This assessment is the "Rollout rating (Ban Boredom programs)" in the Balanced Scorecard shown earlier in Figure 9-9.

The study found a slightly negative average relationship between quarterly normalized store operating profits and the Ban Boredom rating (see Figure 9-11). Apparently, better implementation of the Ban Boredom program had zero or a slightly negative effect on store performance. Profit variation across stores was explained by variables not related to the strategy, including store manager skills, local population, and degree of local competition.

The statistical analysis also revealed that store-level implementation of the Ban Boredom strategy was associated with higher store inventory levels, suggesting that the differentiating strategy adversely affected inventory management. These relationships were apparent from data collected one year earlier than termination of the Ban Boredom strategy. Working only from these (and several other) simple correlations, Store 24 management could have learned at the end of its first year of strategy implementation that the Ban Boredom strategy was not working as intended.

The study found, however, that customer satisfaction (as measured by the third-party research firm) was positively influenced by the quality of the Ban Boredom implementation. Thus, customers noticed differences in the quality of the strategy implementation, but measured customer satisfaction

FIGURE 9-11

A negative relationship existed between Ban Boredom execution scores and store profits

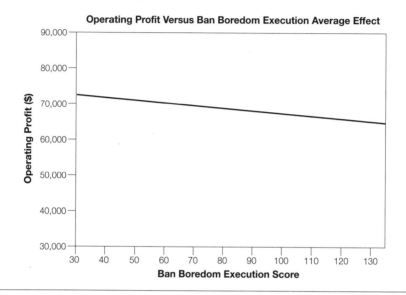

did not apparently translate into higher profits, suggesting that the strategy itself might be flawed.

A more detailed analysis revealed that the average relationship shown in Figure 9-11 masked a more complex relationship among the Balanced Scorecard variables. The research team added an interaction term reflecting both quality of strategy implementation and crew skill level at each store (labeled "Capability evaluation" in Figure 9-9). Adding this interaction term to the regression equation led to the findings shown in Figure 9-12. Stores with high crew skills that implemented the Ban Boredom strategy effectively had considerably higher profits than stores with comparably skilled crews but that were less effective in implementing the strategy. Conversely, stores with low- or average-skilled crews that faithfully implemented the Ban Boredom strategy were much less profitable than other stores with low- and average-skilled crews that focused on operating efficiency and did not implement the Ban Boredom strategy.

Thus the success of the strategy was critically dependent on the skills of the employees in the store. Inexperienced personnel who followed the Ban Boredom rules did not serve customers well and introduced inefficiencies in operations, and that led to lower store profits. Experienced crews, in con-

FIGURE 9-12

The negative relationship existed between Ban Boredom score and store performance was due to low-skilled employees

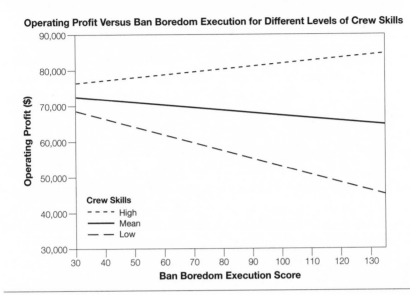

Operating Profit Versus Ban Boredom Execution for Different Levels of Crew Skills

trast, maintained operating efficiency and customer satisfaction while creating the differentiating buying experience of the Ban Boredom strategy.

The formal statistical analysis, had it been done in time to inform Store 24's meeting one year into the Ban Boredom strategy, would have raised several interesting questions for discussion. Managers could have seen that the strategy would be successful only if the crew skills of all stores could be increased to high levels. The management team might have judged that upgrading and maintaining high crew skill levels at every store was not possible given the high personnel turnover rate in retail stores (typically more than 200 percent per year). In this case, the management team might have concluded that the Ban Boredom strategy should be abandoned, making this decision one year earlier than it actually was.

Alternatively, understanding now the critical link between local store crew skills and successful strategy implementation, the company could have launched major human resource initiatives to increase employee retention rates and to upgrade the skill levels of all store crews to those of its best stores. Also, it could have spent more time (and money) in the training and orientation of newly hired crew members so that they would be better skilled to execute the Ban Boredom strategy effectively even in their early months of employment. In this case, the company would have continued with its differentiating strategy and would have enjoyed the profit improvements that currently only its best-performing stores (with high quality of strategy implementation and high crew skills) were realizing.

The Store 24 experience shows the benefits of using the data from a well-functioning Balanced Scorecard system to obtain feedback on a company's strategy. The data enables tests of whether the strategy is being implemented effectively. Effective strategy implementation would be measured, in the Store 24 case, by store-specific scores on complying with the Ban Boredom standards as well as the correlation between the Ban Boredom scores and customer recognition of the "fun and exciting shopping experience" at the outlet. But the data also permits a test of whether the strategy is effective. In the Store 24 case, average store profits did not increase with increases in the Ban Boredom implementation score. Further analysis revealed a contingency, previously hidden, that the strategy implementation was effective only when done at stores with high crew skills. The skilled employees balanced the demands of the new strategy with the requirement to operate efficiently, including rapid checkout times, good merchandising, and effective inventory management.

Requirements for Formal Statistical Testing

The case studies of Sears and Store 24 indicate the features that facilitate formal strategy estimation and testing. First, the companies had multiple observations per time period. Sears had monthly data on eight hundred stores and Store 24 had quarterly data on sixty-five to seventy-five retail store outlets. Effective and informative statistical analysis on cross-sectional data can be done when companies have a large number of homogeneous units (either sites or customers), each generating a full scorecard of data each month (or reporting period). If a company gets only one set of observations per month, at least two years will pass before it has enough data (say, twenty-four observations) to conduct even a simple statistical analysis.

Second, the companies had disciplined processes for collecting data from each site about customer satisfaction and loyalty, process characteristics, and employee attitudes and skills. Getting valid data is necessary for statistical testing and estimation. When companies use the Balanced Scorecard or the similar employee-customer-profit chain model as their main management system, the data collection comes as an essential part of the company's strategy management system. The data then become available for feedback, testing, and learning about the company's strategy. ERP and business intelligence (BI) software gathers data from underlying transactions, stores the data in a convenient form, enables ready access to the data, and, in many cases, incorporates sophisticated statistical analysis and reporting capabilities.

The final requirement is a capability to perform the statistical analysis in a valid and credible manner. It is easy to misuse and misinterpret statistics. Companies that want to use their Balanced Scorecard data to test strategic hypotheses should have an internal group or external consultants who are well trained and experienced in designing, estimating, and testing statistical models.

INCORPORATING EXTERNAL DATA
AND COMPETITIVE INFORMATION

The examples presented so far in this chapter have discussed the use of internal data—activity-based cost and profitability reports on products and customers, and Balanced Scorecard data—to review, test, and adapt the strategy. In addition, companies need to bring external data into their strategy discussions.

LG Philips LCD (LPL), a South Korean joint venture between LG and Philips, designs and produces high-technology liquid crystal display (LCD) screens for application in television, information technology, and special displays. LPL hosts a quarterly BSC "war game" meeting to assess and adjust its strategic hypotheses. Executives and team leaders of planning departments from each function attend this meeting, where they address six key questions:

1. Is our strategy appropriate?
2. Is our strategy superior to those of our competitors?
3. Do all of our members acknowledge and accept our strategy?
4. Are we trying hard enough to execute the strategy?
5. What are the risks associated with executing the strategy, and how will we deal with them?
6. Do we have strategic scenarios in executing the strategy?

Before the meeting, the LPL planning group selects the situation to be subjected to the war game. The situation might be entry into a new geographical market, dealing with direct competitors in existing markets, or introduction of a new strategy with a major existing or potential customer, such as to become the preferred supplier for a next-generation product. Background information is shared on competitors' strategies and capabilities, the region's principal customers, and external, macroeconomic, and market conditions.

The war game is conducted over three days; various teams go into depth on the LPL strategy and the likely actions and reactions by competitors and customers. From the various possibilities, LPL selects two or three likely scenarios; then it forecasts, for each one, the likely market share, income, and cash flow. At the conclusion, the LPL executive team selects a course of action in light of the market dynamics and likely outcomes simulated during the war game.

If strategy adjustments are deemed necessary, LPL revises its strategy and modifies action plans to carry out the new strategy. Afterward, the new strategic direction is discussed at the monthly strategy review meeting before a companywide announcement is made. Also, the strategic scenarios that were drawn up at the war game meeting act as strategy execution guidelines for the subsequent quarter.

The war game exercise generates active participation from all executive team members and engages them in formulating strategies using up-to-date external and internal information. It draws upon company experts in marketing, statistics, economics, and simulation. And, at completion, the executive team reaches a consensus on a specific course of action after consideration of extensive available information and likely responses of competitors and customers. LPL's execution premium is described in the insert below.

LG PHILIP LCD'S EXECUTION PREMIUM

- From 2001 to 2007, LPL's revenue increased from $1.8 billion to $15.5 billion, more than an eightfold increase.
- The company has ranked as either number 1 or 2 in the industry for the past five years.
- LPL is consistently the first in the display industry to mass produce for each generation in the LCD industry. It is currently building an eighth generation technology factory, which will start mass production in the first half of 2009.
- The company consistently receives customer satisfaction awards from industry research organizations.

EMERGENT STRATEGIES

Several strategy scholars, such as Mintzberg and Hamel, emphasize the limitations of top-down strategic direction.[16] They argue that some of the best ideas for new strategies come from employees within the organization. In their view, the role of senior management is to be ever alert to innovative ideas that employees, who are close to technologies, processes, and customers, can suggest, even when these suggestions originate outside the official strategy planning and review process. After all, these scholars argue, employee suggestions triggered Intel's switch from memory chips to microprocessors, Honda's shift in emphasis from motorcycles to automobiles, and 3M Corporation's marketing of Post-it notes.

The Balanced Scorecard strategy management system supports emergent strategies by creating a shared understanding among all employees about the organization's strategic objectives. Employees who understand the strategy—and are motivated to help the organization succeed with the strategy—are in an excellent position to see where gaps exist either in strategy implementation or in an underlying hypothesis. They may even identify where a new strategic approach might yield better performance.

In a previous book, we documented how a middle-level employee at Mobil US Marketing and Refining came up with the idea of a SpeedPass to make the purchase of gasoline, lubrication, and convenience store products faster and friendlier.[17] The employee had previously learned, through the excellent communication program of the company's new Balanced Scorecard, about its value proposition of fast, friendly service. Although the SpeedPass was not a major shift in the company's strategy, it represented a breakthrough in differentiating Mobil's value proposition from those of competitors with similar strategies. Mobil's executive team, recognizing the strategic significance of the SpeedPass innovation, modified its Balanced Scorecard in the middle of the year to add two new measures: the number of consumers acquiring a SpeedPass by end of year, and the percentage of Mobil retail outlets incorporating SpeedPass technology at every gasoline pump. The rapid implementation of the modified strategy contributed significantly to sustainable increases in market share, revenue growth, and margin.

At a routine quarterly meeting of the Operations Excellence Strategy Council at Canadian Blood Services (CBS), managers and employees discussed the behavior of blood donors. They were attempting to understand why certain locations had much higher levels of repeat donations, a key BSC customer metric. A meeting participant formulated the hypothesis that a friendly, personal approach by CBS personnel toward donors led to higher levels of donor retention. The meeting generated a special task force to analyze data from a cross section of donor locations. The statistical analysis validated the employee's hypothesis and also enabled the task force to identify the set of specific employee behaviors that generated higher donor retention rates. As with the SpeedPass innovation, CBS management updated its scorecard to incorporate the new behaviors. It then shared the modified scorecard with the entire organization, enabling the insight from a few successful locations to become the standard practice throughout the CBS system.

LINKING OPERATIONS TO STRATEGY

Strategy maps and Balanced Scorecards help organizations link strategy to operations. These tools help managers communicate the strategy in both visual and quantitative terms. They facilitate the cascading of strategy to business and functional units and the identification and rationalization of initiatives to execute the strategy. In addition, managers can link strategic priorities to process improvements and to decisions about resource capacity and operational and capital budgets.

Less well celebrated, however, is the link from operations back to strategy. Figure 9-13 summarizes the three types of management meetings presented in Chapters 8 and 9, which provide the feedback from operations to strategy. Operational review meetings use data from operational dashboards to monitor and improve operations and solve immediate problems that have arisen. Strategy review meetings monitor the execution of strategy during the year, fine-tuning strategies and initiatives to adjust to changing circumstances. These meetings enable organizations to make midcourse corrections in strategy execution continually during the year. Strategy testing and adapting meetings, described in this chapter, review the output of analytic studies, using tools such as activity-based costing and statistical analysis of operating data. At these meetings, managers learn how and whether the strategy is working. ABC models can identify defects in the strategy, such as inefficient processes, unprofitable products and customers, and significant quantities of unused capacity. Managers who have this information can correct the defects by making targeted process improvements, repricing, modifying customer relationships, or, in the final extreme, exiting unprofitable product lines and market segments.

Statistical estimation of the magnitude and time delays in a strategy map's causal linkages gives managers precise information about how to

FIGURE 9-13

Summary of three types of management review meetings

	Operational Review	Strategy Review	Strategy Testing and Adapting
Information requirements	Dashboards for key performance indicators; weekly and monthly financial summaries	Strategy map and Balanced Scorecard reports	Strategy map, Balanced Scorecard, ABC profitability reports, analytic studies of strategic hypotheses, external and competitive analyses, emergent strategies
Frequency	Daily, twice weekly, weekly, or monthly, depending on business cycle	Monthly	Annually (perhaps quarterly for fast-moving industries)
Attendees	Departmental and functional personnel; senior management for financial reviews	Senior management team, strategic theme owners, strategy management officer	Senior management team, strategic theme owners, functional and planning specialists, business unit heads
Focus	Identify and solve operational problems (sales declines, late deliveries, equipment downtime, supplier problems)	Issues in strategy implementation, progress of strategic initiatives	Test and adapt strategy based on causal analytics, product-line and channel profitability, changing external environment, emergent strategies, and new technology developments
Goal	Respond to short-term problems and promote continuous improvements	Fine-tune strategy; make midcourse adaptations	Incrementally improve or transform strategy; establish strategic and operational plans; set strategic targets; authorize spending for strategic initiatives and other major discretionary expenditures

manage strategy implementation. Managers also assess the proposals generated by employees, who can draw upon their firsthand knowledge of customer interactions, enhanced process capabilities, and ideas for new product development and customer services.

SUMMARY

Strategy testing and adapting should normally occur at the annual strategy development meeting first described in Chapter 2. It is part of the strategic analysis at that meeting, along with the updated PESTEL, industry, and competitor analysis. Occasionally, the meeting is triggered by a major discontinuity in the external environment or by a dramatic shortfall in performance that becomes apparent during the year. Or the meeting can be triggered—as in the money center bank and Store 24 examples in this chapter—when analytics conducted on Balanced Scorecard metrics reveal flaws in the company's existing strategy. In this case, the company modifies its strategy based on what it learned from careful analysis of operating data, along with any additional market and competitor research it conducts.

Companies can naturally find it difficult to orchestrate the complex set of processes that link strategy to operations and then operations back to strategy. We have found that no existing individual or department has sufficient oversight to coordinate and integrate all the diverse processes we have advocated in this book. In Chapter 10, we describe the role of a new office of strategy management (OSM), an extension of the strategic planning department. The OSM extends the traditional strategic planning department role, enabling the office to facilitate both the planning of strategy and its implementation.

NOTES

1. R. S. Kaplan and D. P. Norton, "Measuring the Strategic Readiness of Intangible Assets," *Harvard Business Review* (February 2004): 52–63.
2. Experience reported in T. LoFrumento, "Using Customer Profitability Analytics to Execute a Client-Centric Strategy," *Balanced Scorecard Report* (March–April 2007): 3–5.
3. R. S. Kaplan, "Kemps LLC: Introducing Time-Driven Activity-Based Costing," Case 106-001 (Boston: Harvard Business School, 2005).
4. The 20–80 rule is often referred to as Pareto's principle, named after the Italian economist who, two hundred years ago, observed that 20 percent of the Italian population had 80 percent of the income. This relationship subsequently has been observed in many diverse empirical data sets.
5. R. S. Kaplan and V. G. Narayanan, "Measuring and Managing Customer Profitability," *Journal of Cost Management* (September–October 2001): 5–15.
6. Kaplan, "Kemps LLC," 8–9.
7. J. Heskett, T. O. Jones, G. W. Loveman, W. E. Sasser, and L. A. Schlesinger, "Putting the Service Profit Chain to Work," *Harvard Business Review* (March–April 1994): 164–174, and J. L. Heskett, W. E. Sasser, and L. A. Schlesinger, *The Service Profit Chain: How Leading Companies Link Profit and Growth to Loyalty, Satisfaction, and Value* (New York: The Free Press, 1997).
8. A. J. Rucci, S. P. Kirn, and R. T. Quinn, "The Employee-Customer-Profit Chain at Sears," *Harvard Business Review* (January–February 1998): 83–97.
9. Ibid.
10. This finding replicates the independent work of F. Reichheld, "The One Number You Need to Grow," *Harvard Business Review* (December 2003), and F. Reichheld, *The Ultimate Question: Driving Good Profits and True Growth* (Boston: Harvard Business School Press, 2006).
11. Results reported by S. Kirn, "Statistically Validating the Cause-and-Effect Linkages in the Scorecard," Balanced Scorecard Collaborative Executive Conference, Boston, December 11–12, 2001.
12. The Store 24 experience is taken from D. Campbell, "Putting Strategic Hypotheses to the Test with Cause-and-Effect Analysis," *Balanced Scorecard Report* (September–

October 2002): 15–16; S. Kulp, V. G. Narayanan, and D. Campbell, "Store 24," Case 103-058 (Boston: Harvard Business School, 2003); and D. Campbell, S. Datar, S. Kulp, and V. G. Narayanan, "Testing Strategy with Multiple Performance Measures: Evidence from a Balanced Scorecard at Store 24," working paper 08-081, Harvard Business School, Boston, February 2008.

13. Kulp et al., "Store 24."

14. Ibid., 1.

15. Campbell et al., "Testing Strategy with Multiple Performance Measures."

16. H. Mintzberg and J. Waters, "Of Strategies, Deliberate and Emergent," *Strategic Management Journal* (1985): 257–272; H. Mintzberg, "Crafting Strategy," *Harvard Business Review* (July–August 1987): 66–74; G. Hamel, "Strategy as Revolution," *Harvard Business Review* (July–August 1996): 69–82.

17. R. S. Kaplan and D. P. Norton, *The Strategy-Focused Organization* (Boston: Harvard Business School Press, 2000), 52.

CHAPTER TEN

THE OFFICE OF STRATEGY MANAGEMENT

IN THIS BOOK, we have articulated a comprehensive and integrated system for linking strategy and operations. The system consists of multiple planning, control, and feedback processes (the central portion of Figure 10-1). It starts, in stage 1, with the executive leadership team reaffirming the entity's mission, values, and vision and then developing a strategy capable of closing a challenging value gap.

Once the strategy has been articulated and agreed upon, the executive leadership team, in stage 2, plans the strategy by translating it into a strategy map organized by several strategic themes. For each strategy map objective, the team selects measures and targets. Theme owners and theme teams then select a portfolio of initiatives and obtain approval for STRATEX, the financial resources required for the initiative portfolios.

In stage 3, the company aligns its organizational units by cascading strategy maps and scorecards to the units. These strategy maps and scorecards articulate the balance between achieving local objectives and integrating with corporate priorities and the strategies of other business units. It also communicates the strategy to all employees and aligns human resource processes so that employees' personal objectives, incentive programs, and competency development plans align with strategic objectives.

The link from strategy to operations starts in stage 4, as managers plan operations by highlighting where process improvements in efficiency and responsiveness are most needed for successful strategy execution. Managers also authorize the spending to supply the resource capacity

FIGURE 10-1

The typical management system is made up of many standalone subsystems that are not integrated or aligned with each other

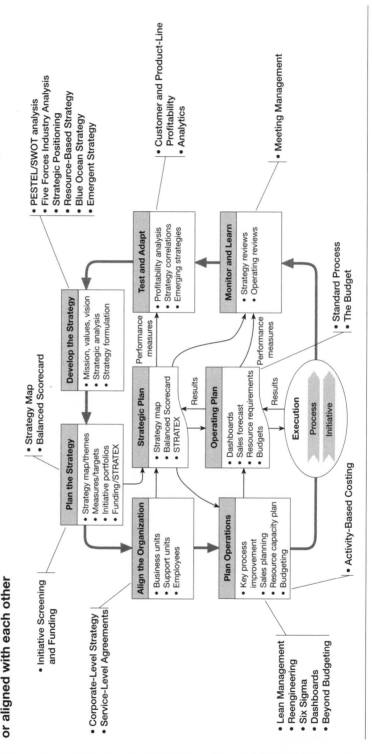

required to deliver on the sales and production forecasts embedded in the strategic plan.

Next, the company implements a new reporting system of operational dashboards and strategy scorecards to inform various management meetings: stage 5 operational review and strategy review meetings, which monitor and provide feedback on operations and strategy execution, and stage 6 strategy testing and adapting meetings, which allow learning and new information to feed back into the stage 1 strategy development process.

It would be easy for these various management processes to become fragmented and isolated from each other. Companies already use many of the individual management tools discussed in this book, as shown on the outer boundary of Figure 10-1. But they fail to integrate them effectively.

Several in our population of Balanced Scorecard Hall of Fame companies introduced a new office or function to help them better integrate their strategy management processes. They gave the head of this new office a variety of titles, such as vice president of organization transformation, vice president of performance management, and vice president of business excellence. We adopted the descriptive title *office of strategy management* (OSM) for this important function.

WHY COMPANIES NEED AN OSM

The OSM integrates and coordinates activities across functions and business units to align strategy with operations. The OSM can be viewed as the designer of an intricate watch, keeping all the various planning, execution, and control processes synchronized despite their running at various frequencies: daily and weekly for dashboards and operational control meetings; monthly for updates of strategy maps, scorecards, strategic initiatives, and strategy review meetings; and quarterly or annually for scanning the external environment and performing the analytic studies that inform strategy testing and adapting meetings.

The OSM can also be viewed as an orchestra leader. It is not the creator or the producer of the music being played. Instead, it keeps all the diverse organizational players—executive team, business units, regional units, support units (finance, human resources, information technology), theme teams, departments, and ultimately the employees—aligned so that they can create beautiful music together, executing the enterprise's strategy in unison, with each component playing its distinctive part.

Some people have challenged the need for a new staff position for strategy management. They point out that effective strategy execution should be the responsibility of CEOs and business unit heads. We concur. We don't advocate that the OSM either develop the strategy or have accountability for its execution. Instead, the OSM is analogous to a military general's chief of staff.

The general is responsible and accountable for developing the strategy to win wars and battles. But a general almost always has a chief of staff, often several ranks junior, who leverages the general's time and attention. The chief of staff does not create strategy or operational tactics and has no authority or accountability for execution. A chief of staff schedules the general's meetings, ensures that the appropriate people show up at the meetings, attends and takes notes at the meetings, and follows up after the meetings to ensure that the actions are carried out. The chief of staff leverages the general's time by making sure that all the information, people, and follow-up are in place for the general's strategy and tactics to be effectively executed.

Case Study on Defining Roles for an OSM: Canadian Blood Services

We recommend that a similar, but expanded, set of tasks be carried out by a small cadre of professionals to orchestrate the various strategy management processes for the executive team. Here we provide a case study in the words of one executive leader, Graham Sher, CEO of Canadian Blood Services, describing why he created an OSM right at the beginning of the Balanced Scorecard project.

As CEO, I face several major challenges in trying to implement my ambitious strategic agenda. First, I need to balance the time I spend dealing with external demands and constituents with the ability to focus and lead change internally. Like all CEOs, I report to a board of directors. However, as a publicly funded agency (funded by twelve provincial and territorial governments in Canada), I need to ensure that adequate attention is paid to the "corporate shareholders" of CBS: the ministers of health in each of these jurisdictions, and the government bureaucracies they lead. Furthermore, an agency with a high public profile such as ours, and one that is premised on retaining public trust, demands that I stay externally focused on stakeholder requirements, too.

Many people believe that CEOs wield direct and easy influence over their organizations. The reality is that any CEO has a difficult time directly influencing his organization. Attempting to command and control may only serve to undermine the authority of one's senior executives. To be most effective, I as CEO must exert my influence indirectly and in a way that empowers and creates an environment for my executives to lead and manage their parts of the organization. I should set the tone for the organization, define the strategic agenda, communicate it, and ensure that it gets undertaken, but not actually direct any parts of it.

A further challenge typical to most CEOs is that information, particularly bad news, tends to be filtered before it gets to me. I often do not see the most timely, valid information about the current performance of CBS, particularly when operating at a constant and unrelenting pace of change. Many of our early management meetings were spent debating the quality of the information, as opposed to the analysis and interpretation of it—obviously an unwieldy way of executing strategy and a very time-intensive way of conducting management meetings.

I came to believe that a management system based on the Balanced Scorecard, facilitated by an office of strategy management, could help me overcome these three challenges [limited time, inadequate management ownership and initiative, and filtered information]. The Balanced Scorecard empowers executives, as opposed to invading in their territory and undermining them. It gives me performance management information that is aligned at all executive levels and appropriately validated prior to coming to my attention. Much of management is a search for the truth. The Balanced Scorecard provides me with easy and direct access to timely, unfiltered information about the implementation of our new strategy.

Because of the urgency with which I want to accomplish change, I established an office of strategy management at the outset of our Balanced Scorecard project. The OSM is a critical resource to me and the executive team to ensure successful implementation of my change agenda across the organization. I also wanted the OSM to report directly to me—that was a way to highlight the importance of this office to my strategic agenda. But if it reported only to me, and didn't have any other clearly defined linkages or relationships, it wouldn't be quite as effective. I wanted change at CBS to come from within, not be imposed from above. I therefore created a dotted-line reporting relationship between the OSM and two other key executives at CBS—the CFO and the COO—who ultimately are going to help execute the change agenda.

We launched the OSM with three full-time individuals. The OSM leader is a vice president and a member of the executive management team, consistent with the importance we place on this function. She leads and facilitates the integration of strategy into all our core processes. In addition, we have two individuals reporting to the OSM leader to provide day-to-day management of the office, manage the multiple work streams and cross-functional teams, lead and facilitate meetings, educate others on Balanced Scorecard and strategy-focused organization practices and tools, and perform analysis of problems, performance, and metrics. This should be the right complement of individuals to help support the OSM leader and ultimately the rest of the executive team in undertaking our ambitious change agenda for the next few years.

At CBS, I believe that the Balanced Scorecard program is necessary to help us execute our strategy, but on its own, the Balanced Scorecard is not sufficient. The OSM provides the sufficiency. It is the critical, complementary piece in the chain to help us successfully execute our change agenda for the next few years. The OSM at CBS is not just a change in the organizational structure. I see it as a structure that helps us fundamentally change the way we think, change the way we plan, and change the way we do business and manage performance.[1]

The insert below itemizes some of the execution premium benefits that Canadian Blood Services has already enjoyed from its strategy implementation.

CANADIAN BLOOD SERVICES' EXECUTION PREMIUM

- Overall donor satisfaction with the experience of their last visit increased from 86 percent in August 2005 to 93 percent in December 2006.
- Donor "top box" satisfaction—those that rate their satisfaction as a 10 on a scale of one to ten—rose from 26 percent to 43 percent during the same time period.
- Overall hospital satisfaction with CBS's products and services rose from 94 percent in April 2005 to 98 percent in May 2007. Hospital "top box" satisfaction rose from 17 percent to 29 percent during the same period.
- The yield (percentage) of red blood cells preserved in the manufacturing process improved by over 20 percent from 2005 to 2007, a savings of more than $3 million.
- The national order fill rate increased from 80 percent to 98 percent from 2002 to 2006.

In the remainder of this chapter, we build upon the CBS experience to describe the various roles the OSM performs to keep the enterprise focused on effective strategy execution.

THE OSM: ARCHITECT, PROCESS OWNER, AND INTEGRATOR

The office of strategy management has multiple roles and responsibilities, as shown in Figure 10-2.[2] First, as an *architect*, the OSM uses the framework in this book to design and embed any missing strategy and operational management processes into the company's management system. The OSM ensures that all the planning, execution, and feedback processes are in place and that they are linked in a closed-loop system.

The OSM also serves as *process owner* of several strategy and operational management processes, such as those to develop the strategy, plan the strategy, and orchestrate the senior management strategy review meetings. Many of these processes are new to the organization. Because they cross existing business and functional organizational lines, it is natural for the OSM to be their owner. Assigning responsibilities for their execution to

FIGURE 10-2

The Office of Strategy Management (OSM): Roles and responsibilities

OSM Role	Strategy Management Process	OSM Responsibility
Architect	1. Define the strategy management framework and conventions	
	2. Design the strategy management process	
Process Owner	1. Develop the strategy	
	2. Plan the strategy	
	3. Align the organization	
	4. Review and adapt the strategy	
Integrator	1. Link to operational planning/budgeting	CFO
	2. Link to key operating processes	COO
	3. Link to HR, IT, and support functions	HRO, CIO
	4. Communicate strategy	CC
	5. Manage strategic initiatives	PMO
	6. Share best practices	CKO

Key:

▓ OSM Should run the process

[X] OSM links strategy to a process run by someone else (X)

CFO: Chief Financial Officer
HRO: Human Resource Officer
CIO: Chief Information Officer
CKO: Chief Knowledge Officer
CC: Corporate Communications
PMO: Program Management Office
COO: Chief Operating Officer

the OSM fills a gap in management practice without infringing on the current responsibilities of any existing department or function.

Finally, the OSM is the *integrator* of many existing activities. This aspect is challenging, because organizational and functional units already have primary responsibility for processes such as budgeting, communication, human resource planning and performance management, IT planning, initiative management, and best-practice sharing. The OSM must work with the existing owners of these processes to ensure that they become aligned with the strategy.

We elaborate further on the architect, process owner, and systems integrator roles for the OSM in the next sections.

The OSM as Architect

Many processes that are central for strategy execution, such as budgeting, employee performance management, and strategic planning, are run by separate parts of the organization, are executed at different times of the year, and use different frameworks, languages, and conventions. The isolation of these processes from each other is a major barrier to effective strategy execution. In addition, as noted earlier, some important strategy execution processes may not be implemented at all.

The OSM is the designer of the framework and processes for a single, integrated, closed-loop strategy planning and operational execution system; its tasks include introducing the missing strategy execution processes and bringing order to an otherwise incomplete and fragmented collection of management processes. This is the OSM's "watchmaker" role, designing missing components and embedding them in the management system while ensuring that all the components are in their proper place and work synchronously, without friction between them.

The OSM creates the design for the sequence and linkage of strategy execution processes shown in Figure 10-3. Typically, the strategy cycle is relaunched at the beginning of the second quarter, when the planning group begins its research and preparation for the annual strategy development meeting, at which the senior executive team updates the enterprise strategy, strategy map, and scorecard. After the enterprise strategy meeting, the OSM starts the process of aligning each business's or support unit's strategy with those of the enterprise and other units. It also ensures that process management priorities have been established to achieve targeted improvement in the Balanced Scorecard's process metrics.

FIGURE 10-3

Strategy management: An integrated closed-loop process

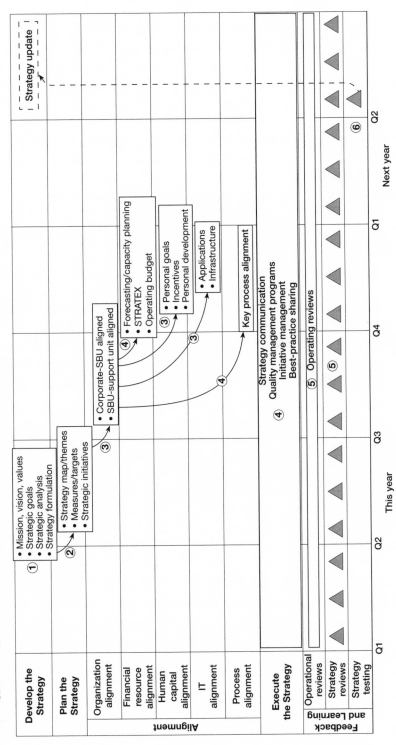

Note: Circled numbers represent stages of the Strategy Management System.

During the third quarter, the OSM ensures that the finance department's resource planning and budgeting process produces business and support unit plans and operating and capital budgets that can deliver the strategy and are consistent with forecast process improvements. In the fourth quarter, the OSM works with HR to help employees establish their personal objectives for the next year, to align employee competency development programs, and to review employee incentive plans.

In parallel with sequencing these annual processes, the OSM oversees several continual control and learning processes: communicating strategy, reviewing operations and strategy, managing strategic initiatives, and sharing best practices. The OSM monitors all these components to ensure that they are in place, introducing any missing ones and establishing the links that must exist between them.

Realistically, unlike the design of a new building by an architect, not all the structures in Figure 10-3 will be established before a company begins implementing the new management system. Typically, the processes and the new management calendar evolve over two to three years. Initially the OSM is the Balanced Scorecard project leader, with primary responsibility for helping the executive team develop the initial strategy map and scorecard and then facilitating its cascade and communication throughout the enterprise.

As managers become more familiar and comfortable with the use of maps and scorecards for describing and measuring the strategy, the OSM helps the organization migrate to the comprehensive strategy management system diagrammed in Figure 10-3. Having this structure in mind as the architecture for an evolutionary process will help the OSM implement the various components of the management system in a coherent way over time.

The OSM as Process Owner

On an ongoing basis, the OSM should have primary ownership of the following strategy execution processes.

Developing the Strategy. Typically, strategy development processes—such as preparing PESTEL, SWOT, market, and competitive analyses, along with planning and facilitating the annual strategy meeting—are the responsibilities of an existing strategic planning unit. But developing strategy should not be a one-time annual event. After all, performance measures, such as those supplied by the Balanced Scorecard, provide continual evidence about the validity of the assumptions underlying a company's strategy. The executive team, at its monthly strategy review meetings, discusses the assumptions and can fine-tune the strategy, strategic measures, or strategic initiatives as needed.

We've found that most planning units adapt fairly quickly to the cycle of monthly strategy review meetings we describe in Chapter 8. The additional processes represent a natural extension of, and complement to, their traditional work. Rather than put an artificial distinction or barrier between strategy development and strategy execution, we recommend that processes for developing strategy and executing strategy be performed within one group in the organization: the OSM. In effect, we encourage an expansion of the strategic planning department into a more comprehensive office of strategy management that has responsibility for facilitating both strategy development and its execution.

Planning the Strategy. By owning the scorecard process, the OSM ensures that any changes made at the annual strategy planning meeting are translated into the company's strategy map and Balanced Scorecard. Once the executive team has approved the objectives and measures for the subsequent year, the OSM coaches the team in selecting performance targets on the scorecard measures and identifying the strategic initiatives required to achieve them.

The OSM also standardizes the terminology and measurement definitions throughout the organization, selects and manages the scorecard reporting system, and monitors the integrity of the scorecard data. The OSM need not be the primary data collector for the scorecard, but it should oversee the processes by which the data are collected, reported, and validated. Finally, the OSM serves as the central scorecard resource, consulting with units on their scorecard development projects and conducting training and education on building strategy maps and scorecards.

Aligning the Organization. The OSM oversees the processes described in Chapter 5 to cascade strategies and scorecards vertically and horizontally throughout the organization. It validates whether the strategies and scorecards proposed by business and support units are linked to each other and to the corporate strategy. In this role, the OSM helps the enterprise realize the gains from corporate synergies.

Reviewing the Strategy. Chapter 8 describes the new strategy review meeting at which the executive team reviews strategic performance and adjusts the strategy and its execution. Managing this meeting is a core function of the OSM. It briefs the CEO in advance about the strategic issues identified in the most recent scorecard so that the agenda can focus on strategy review and learning, rather than on a short-term financial performance review and crisis management.

The OSM works with the strategic theme owners to get their assessments and their color-coding (green, yellow, or red) of the performance of the theme's objectives and portfolio of strategic initiatives. The OSM prepares the briefing booklet (paper-based, electronic, or both) for the executive team to review before the meeting.

The OSM, at the beginning of the meeting, provides a brief report on the progress of each action plan recommended at earlier meetings, records all new recommended action plans, and follows up with the assigned manager or department to ensure that the actions are carried out. This is the "chief of staff" function described earlier in our military analogy.

Adapting the Strategy. In Chapter 9, we describe the meeting at which the leadership team tests and adapts the strategy. This meeting requires a new input into the annual strategy meeting in addition to the traditional external and competitive analyses produced by the planning department. The company's internal competitive analysis should now include analytic studies of the existing strategy's performance. These studies use tools such as activity-based cost analyses of product-line, customer, channel, and regional profitability, and statistical analysis that estimates and tests a strategy map's causal linkages.

The calculation of detailed P&Ls for products, customers, and channels is a task that the finance department can reasonably be expected to perform. But the sophisticated analytics to statistically estimate and test strategic linkages may require a new capability for the company. The OSM is a natural home for building a corporate capability to analyze data coming from Balanced Scorecards throughout the organization. The OSM can present, at the annual strategy update meeting, the outputs from the detailed P&L calculations and the analytic studies conducted on the strategy's performance.

The OSM as Integrator

A variety of existing management processes must be informed by and aligned with the strategy. For most companies, strategic planning is conducted separately from budgeting and operational planning. The OSM ensures that near-term planning and budgeting—tasks typically performed by the finance department—are aligned with strategic priorities. Effective strategy execution requires active participation by all employees. The OSM must ensure that the strategy is communicated and internalized by the workforce.

Because strategy describes how to create value from intangible assets, the OSM must coordinate the linkage from strategy to planning for the acquisition and enhancement of human resources and information technology. It must ensure that the strategic initiatives are managed effectively. Finally, the OSM must verify that the knowledge management process focuses on best-practice sharing that enhances strategic processes.

Linking Strategy to Financial Resource Planning and Budgeting. The finance department oversees budgeting and the allocation of cash to organizational units. In addition to business and functional unit budgets, the corporate financial plan needs to incorporate the authorized spending (STRATEX) for cross-functional strategic initiatives.

Also, the business units' near-term targets for financial performance— including forecasts of revenues, capacity, spending, and profitability— should be consistent with achieving the corporate revenue growth and profitability targets and closing the value gap articulated at the start of strategy development. In addition, the OSM monitors whether the business unit plans provide adequate but not excessive spending to supply the resource capacity demanded by the strategic plan. In summary, the OSM integrates with finance to ensure that business unit profit plans, resource capacity planning, and performance targets are aligned with strategic objectives.

Aligning Plans and Resources of Important Functional Support Departments. In addition to coordinating the linkage between strategy planning and finance, the OSM ensures that the plans for other functional departments are consistent with executing the strategy. Particularly important are the human resource and information technology departments, but, in principle, all functional units—such as research and development, real estate, purchasing, logistics, environmental, marketing, and sales— contribute to successful strategy execution, and their plans must reflect their contributions. The OSM plays a consulting and integrating role with these functional departments to help them align their strategies and plans with enterprise and business unit strategy.

For example, consider the human resource department, which has primary responsibility for the motivation, training, and performance of employees. The HR department typically has the responsibility for the execution of annual employee performance reviews, personal goal setting, training, competency development, and the management of incentive and compensation programs. The OSM ensures that HR performs these activities in a manner consistent with corporate and business unit strategic objectives.

Communicating the Strategy. As discussed in Chapter 5, effective communication to employees about strategy, targets, and initiatives is vital if employees are to contribute to the strategy. Canon, a Balanced Scorecard user, describes its internal communication process as "democratizing strategy," and the Canon OSM actively promotes understanding of the company's strategy and the scorecard in all business units and support functions. If the strategy communication task is assigned to an existing internal communication department, the OSM plays an editorial role, reviewing the messages to see that they communicate the strategy correctly. If a corporate communication group does not exist or if the group has little knowledge of or focus on strategy, the OSM becomes the process owner for communicating both strategy and the scorecard to employees.

The OSM also helps craft the strategy messages delivered by the CEO, because one of the most effective communication channels is having each employee hear about strategy directly from the CEO. Finally, as part of its communication responsibilities, the OSM coordinates with the human resource department to ensure that education about the scorecard and about employees' role in delivering performance is included in employee training programs.

Managing Strategic Initiatives. In Chapter 4 we provide an extensive description of the process to select, rationalize, and manage strategic initiatives. When the organization uses theme owners and theme teams to manage selection and management of strategic initiatives, the OSM monitors the process, soliciting information about initiative status and performance and reporting this information to the executive team in advance of the strategy management review meeting.

For organizations that do not use theme owners and theme teams, the OSM is the default mechanism for running the team process to select and rationalize strategic initiatives. The OSM assigns responsibility to an appropriate unit or function for those initiatives that already have a natural home. The OSM manages initiatives that cross unit and functional lines, ensuring that they get the financial and human resources they need.

Linking Strategy to Key Operating Processes. Strategy is also executed through business processes. The strategy map identifies the processes that are most important to the strategy and that must be analyzed, redesigned, and managed. The OSM works with theme teams, local line management, and the quality management department to see that necessary resources and organizational support have been provided to improve the performance of the strategic processes.

Sharing Best Practices. The OSM needs to ensure that knowledge management focuses on sharing the best practices that will be most beneficial to the strategy. If managers use the wrong benchmarks, the company's strategy will fall short of its potential. At some companies, learning and knowledge sharing are already the responsibility of a chief knowledge or learning officer; in those cases, the OSM needs to coordinate with that person's office. But if such a function does not exist, the OSM must take the lead in transferring ideas and best practices throughout the organization.

POSITIONING AND STAFFING THE OSM

Executing strategy usually involves making changes that only a CEO can empower, and the OSM will be most effective when it has direct access to the CEO. Barbara Possin, director of strategic alignment at St. Mary's Duluth Clinic Health System, reported that she was able to overcome resistance to her initiatives because managers knew she had a direct reporting line to the company's COO and CEO. An OSM buried deep in the finance or planning department may find it difficult to command similar respect and attention from senior executives for strategy management priorities.

The simplest solution, therefore, is to have the OSM, like a general's chief of staff, report directly to the CEO. But if the OSM has originated within a powerful function, the OSM will usually report to the chief of that function—such as the CFO or vice president of strategic planning— but with occasional direct access to the CEO.

At Grupo National Provincial (GNP), a Mexican insurance company, the OSM reports both to the CEO and to the CFO. The OSM sets the agenda for a weekly meeting with the CEO and CFO and for a broader weekly meeting with the six top company executives. The office of strategy management at GNP also has a matrixed relationship with twenty Balanced Scorecard managers in the two major business units and nine support units, and with the owners of the major strategic initiatives. The relationship enables the OSM to coordinate the strategic planning that is done in the business and support units.

We have seen two models evolve for the structure of an OSM. In some companies, such as Mobil, Cigna Property and Casualty, Crown Castle, and Canon, the OSM is a centralized corporate office. In some of the more recent implementations, the OSM has been more of a network, with one or two persons serving at the corporate staff level, and one strategy management officer identified for each business and support unit. In this model, the OSM is more a networked organization than a centralized corporate staff department. The networked strategy management officers become strategy execution champions throughout the enterprise, helping customize the corporate strategic themes for local business and support units.

Even as a corporate office, the OSM doesn't have to be large; it is certainly not our goal to encourage companies to build a new bureaucracy. Companies with sales of $500 million to $5 billion and with one thousand to ten thousand employees have fewer than ten people in the OSM, which includes the employees already performing the existing strategic planning function at the corporate level.

Staffing the OSM

Establishing an OSM does not have to involve hiring expensive new talent. Typically, managers from planning and finance functions who have led Balanced Scorecard projects are the initial staff of the OSM. It can also include employees from other staff groups such as quality, human resources, and information technology.

More important than the departments they come from are the competencies they bring to the office. Among the most important competencies are having a good knowledge of the business, being capable of conceptual and strategic thinking, being a good communicator, having a background in project management, being a self-starter, being able to set priorities, working well in teams, and earning the respect of senior executives.

Perhaps the most important competency is being effective as a change agent. Leadership and strategy execution require change. For many companies, the shift from using the budget as the primary focus of the management system to using strategy maps and scorecards involves a transition from being financially driven to being driven by customers, processes, and employees. People who are familiar and comfortable with the previous culture may resist the change to the quite different one required for the new strategy to be successful. For the OSM to be an effective agent of the

CEO and leadership team, its members must recognize the barriers to change—the "silent killers."[3] They also must have the skills, respect, and influence to overcome them.

Companies report that having relatively junior managers serve for up to two years in an OSM position has been an excellent incubator of talent. They also report that the people assigned to their OSMs do not constitute a net increase in the organization's head count because of the associated streamlining and focusing of many planning and control processes and elimination of staff formerly engaged in data gathering and reporting. The value proposition for the OSM, however, is that it creates value from successful strategy execution, and not that it saves money by reducing the head count of planners and data gatherers.

Case Study on the OSM: Serono

Serono is the largest biotechnology company in Europe and third largest in the world.[4] It is the world leader in reproductive health, with strong market positions in neurology, metabolism and growth, and treatment of multiple sclerosis and psoriasis. Headquartered in Geneva, Switzerland, Serono employs more than five thousand people in forty-five countries around the world. In January 2007 it was acquired by Merck and reincorporated as Merck Serono, a division of Merck KGaA. Serono's office of strategy management played a significant role in Serono's successful strategy execution, leading up to its acquisition by Merck.

Key Roles of the Serono OSM. In 1991, long-time CEO Fabio Bertarelli introduced a small office, reporting directly to him, named the Office of MTH ("Make Things Happen"). He was searching for a way to make Serono a more nimble, less bureaucratic organization. The MTH office's primary responsibility was to track the execution of CEO-level decisions.

In 1995, new CEO Ernesto Bertarelli (Fabio's son) expanded the scope of the office. He wanted the MTH to take on responsibility for enhancing the strategic planning and performance management processes. He created a ten-member executive management board (EMB) consisting of the major corporate functions, such as research, product development, finance, and sales, and asked the MTH to support the EMB's centralized planning and cross-functional management processes.

Serono, like most pharmaceutical companies, implements its strategy through large, complex projects that bring new products to market over a five- to fifteen-year period. The projects require the coordination of the various functions. In 2000, Serono decided to extend the focus of its management system beyond central management of the cross-functional projects and the annual operating budget. It transformed the MTH into a new Office of Strategy Management—led by Roland Baumann, senior VP of corporate administration—to handle the management of centralized projects, formal strategic planning, Balanced Scorecards, and strategy maps.

The Serono OSM plays several roles (depicted in Figure 10-4) in managing strategy execution.

Strategist: The strategy delivers the vision and goals of the organization. The typical horizon for a strategy is about five years. Although the strategy and plans are reviewed annually, the vision and goals are updated only when the current vision has been accomplished. The strategy is captured in business plans (see Figure 10-5), one each for the four core business domains—multiple sclerosis, women's reproductive health, pediatric growth hormone, and psoriasis—which are updated annually. The business plan defines the approach to acquiring new medicines, molecules, and technologies, and includes plans for research (discovery), new product development, and business development. The

---

FIGURE 10-4

Serono OSM: Key roles and responsibilities

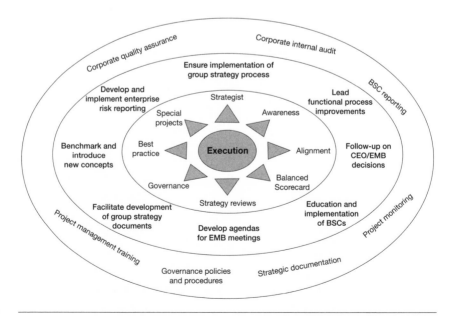

FIGURE 10-5

The Serono OSM manages a comprehensive annual cycle that translates strategy into action

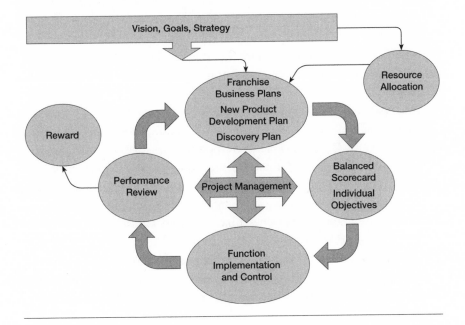

group plan integrates the four franchise business plans. The OSM does not write these plans. Instead, it oversees the process by which the individual businesses prepare the plans and submit them on schedule.

Balanced Scorecard (BSC): All strategies are translated into Balanced Scorecards. The OSM educates all managers about the BSC and helps implement the BSC worldwide. It ensures that each part of the organization uses the BSC, that the numbers are accurate, that the BSC is studied and acted upon, and that the spirit underlying the Balanced Scorecard is brought into the entire organization. As noted by Baumann, "We produce the Balanced Scorecard like the chief financial officer produces financial statements."[5]

Alignment: The OSM works with various functional departments to align their processes with strategy. For example, the BSC provides the high-level measures and targets in each functional department that link directly to employees' personal objectives. Five thousand employees have a variable pay scheme that is linked to the performance of their units as well as to their personal objectives.

Strategy reviews: The EMB meets monthly to review progress in implementing the strategy. The OSM develops the schedules, the agenda, and the content of these meetings. All EMB and CEO decisions are followed up by the OSM to ensure that they are implemented. If needed, the OSM organizes follow-up meetings and support.

Special projects: Managing key projects is the cornerstone of strategy management at Serono. Because cross-functional coordination is constantly required, the OSM has the responsibility, as Baumann describes it, to be "the guardians of the cross-functional project management process."[6] The OSM defines the rules for the strategy management process. It maintains the companywide database of all strategic initiatives, including checkpoints, milestones, objectives, and status. In a recent refinement of the OSM role, aimed at streamlining the process, the company grouped two to eight projects at a time into "clusters" called strategic initiatives; this practice allows the EMB to review fewer, larger initiatives rather than scores of seemingly unrelated individual projects.

Serono's OSM Structure. Serono's OSM consists of only four people. They are coordinators and facilitators who enhance the efforts of others. To achieve this leverage in a workforce of more than five thousand people, the OSM members require a blend of several competencies. As Baumann built the organization, he looked for several traits in the team:

- *A big picture mentality:* It prevents efforts from getting lost in the details.
- *Networking and influencing skills:* All work must be performed through others without resorting to hierarchical power.
- *Project management skills:* Most of the strategic work at Serono involves projects.
- *Cross-functional business skills:* Siloed functions need help to work together as a team.
- *Entrepreneurial attitudes:* Executing strategy requires the breaking of new ground.

Lawrence Ganti, director of office of strategy management, and Baumann identify the key competency for OSM membership as the ability to execute. Ganti observed, "We are a very pragmatic bunch. We focus on getting things done instead of simply just planning and analyzing."[7]

Some of Serono's execution premium results are summarized in the insert below:

SERONO'S EXECUTION PREMIUM

- Since 1999, Serono has had annual double-digit growth in revenues and income. Annual revenues are three times that of its European biotechnology peers.
- Rebif, Serono's flagship product for multiple sclerosis, reached blockbuster status in 2004, with $1.1 billion in sales.
- The company has increased its operational efficiency gross margin to 86% since introducing the BSC.
- In the last three years, Serono has doubled the "number of molecules" in pre-clinical development, a measure of its ability to bring new products to market that serve unmet medical needs.
- The company has revamped its organizational culture to be more performance driven.

Although it is difficult to attribute such performance to any one factor, such as the OSM, most executives agree that the EMB now devotes more of its time to strategy and performance reviews, that Serono has better alignment of priorities across the entire organization, and that strategy and direction are more transparent at all levels of the organization. Employees have been empowered to contribute to the strategy and are rewarded for it. Cross-functional management processes break down silos and increase efficiency. Baumann concluded,

> Three or four years ago, our executives spent lots of time in the operational details of the business. Today, our top management is absolutely capable of distinguishing strategy from operational management. There is no confusion anymore. We believe that our strategy is known by our five thousand employees and that, day in and day out, they execute according to the strategy.
>
> The building of the OSM must be based on the desire for change. The OSM is a change management project by itself. Long-term sustainability [of strategy execution] depends on support from the chief executive, but it's also important to have properly implemented processes.[8]

SUMMARY

Leadership and strategy formulation remain an art. Although we study and celebrate examples of great leadership and brilliant strategy, we don't yet have a systematic process to create them. But for enterprises that are fortunate to have excellent leadership and a moderately good, if not necessarily brilliant, strategy, we have identified an integrated set of best practices, proven in hundreds of enterprises around the world, that transforms the odds for successful strategy execution.

These best practices constitute a body of knowledge that now serves as the foundation for an emerging professional function focused on the management of strategy. We propose that an office of strategy management be assigned the responsibility and authority for managing and coordinating these strategy execution processes based on this body of knowledge.

The strategy execution processes are embedded in a six-stage closed-loop management system, extensively described in earlier chapters and summarized here:

1. Develop the strategy (Chapter 2).
2. Plan the strategy (Chapters 3 and 4).
3. Align organizational units and employees (Chapter 5).
4. Develop the operational plan (Chapters 6 and 7).
5. Monitor and learn through operational and strategy review meetings (Chapter 8).
6. Test and adapt the strategy (Chapter 9).

These processes are implemented at different times of the year, many by existing organizational units. The OSM, as architect, drives the organization forward to achieve the comprehensive management system in a synchronous fashion. As process owner, it takes primary responsibility for several of the newly introduced strategy execution processes, such as in stages 2, 3, 5, and 6, while incorporating the responsibilities of the strategic planning process of stage 1. As integrator, the OSM ensures that the remaining processes—performed by finance, human resources, information technology, quality management, communication, and knowledge management professionals—are aligned with strategic objectives.

The OSM, a previously missing link in strategy execution, runs several new management processes and connects and aligns existing but fragmented processes. It enables many companies to earn an execution premium from their strategies. CEOs have noted that they would rather have a good strategy that their enterprise can execute flawlessly than a brilliant strategy that their people do not understand and cannot deliver. Flawless execution requires an integrated management system that helps companies continually improve their strategy implementation. The office of strategy management leverages the time and attention of CEOs and executive team members to keep the multiple management processes described in this book synchronized for successful strategy execution.

Companies that follow the recommendations we have laid out in this book will have a complete management system that helps them set clear strategic goals, allocate resources consistent with those goals, set priorities for operational action, quickly recognize the operational and strategic impact of those decisions, and, if necessary, update their strategic goals. The closed-loop management system enables executives to manage both strategy and operations, and to balance the tensions between them.

NOTES

1. G. Sher, "How to Wield Influence and Stay Informed," *Harvard Business Review* (October 2005): 78.
2. The ideas in this section appeared originally in R. S. Kaplan and D. P. Norton, "The Office of Strategy Management," *Harvard Business Review* (October 2005) and have been extended through our work with OSM working groups of private, public, and nonprofit enterprises in North America and Europe.
3. M. Beer and R. Eisenstat, "The Silent Killers of Strategy Implementation and Learning," *Sloan Management Review* (Summer 2000): 29–40.
4. For more detail see A. Field, "Catalyst for Global Growth: The Strategy Management Office at Serono," *Balanced Scorecard Report* (January–February 2006): 10–12.
5. Roland Baumann, "Strategic Management: Turning Concept into Reality," Sustaining Winning Performance: Balanced Scorecard Leadership Conference, Boston, July 12–14, 2006.
6. Ibid.
7. Ibid.
8. Ibid.

INDEX

ABOUT THE AUTHORS

ROBERT S. KAPLAN is Baker Foundation Professor at Harvard Business School. He is the author or coauthor of seventeen *Harvard Business Review* articles, more than one hundred other papers, and fourteen books, including five with David Norton. His research, teaching, consulting, and speaking focus on linking strategy to performance and cost management systems, primarily the Balanced Scorecard and Activity-Based Costing. He has received numerous honors, including induction into the Accounting Hall of Fame, the American Accounting Association's Outstanding Educator Award and Seminal Contributions to Accounting Literature Award, and the Chartered Institute of Management Accountants (UK) Award for "Outstanding Contributions to the Accountancy Profession." He can be reached at rkaplan@hbs.edu.

DAVID P. NORTON is cofounder of Balanced Scorecard Collaborative and director of Palladium, a professional services firm that facilitates the worldwide use of the Balanced Scorecard approach to strategy execution. Previously he was the president of Renaissance Solutions, Inc., an international consulting firm he cofounded in 1992, and of Nolan, Norton & Company, where he spent seventeen years as president. Dr. Norton is a management consultant, researcher, and speaker in the field of strategic performance management. With Robert Kaplan, he is the cocreator of the Balanced Scorecard concept, coauthor of seven *Harvard Business Review* articles, and coauthor of four other books—*The Balanced Scorecard: Translating Strategy into Action, The Strategy-Focused Organization: How*

Balanced Scorecard Companies Thrive in the New Business Environment,
Strategy Maps: Converting Intangible Assets into Tangible Outcomes, and
Alignment: Using the Balanced Scorecard to Create Corporate Synergies. He
is a trustee of Worcester Polytechnic Institute and a former director of
ACME (the Association of Consulting and Management Engineers). He
can be reached at dnorton@thepalladiumgroup.com.